Programming
Joomla! Plugins
Written by Jisse Reitsma

 YIREO | EDUCATION

Colofon

Written by Jisse Reitsma
Edited by Yireo Education
Published by Academic Store

Content copyright © 2014 Jisse Reitsma - All rights reserved
Design copyright © 2014 Ruben Creemers - All rights reserved
Publishing rights © 2014 Yireo - All rights reserved

ISBN 978-90-822787-0-5

Edition 1 (October 2014)

Disclaimer

This book gives you insight into Joomla! plugins. Even though we have done our utmost to check and double check everything is correct, some of the facts stated in this book may still be wrong - due to mistakes of the author, or due to the fact that the Joomla! source code is changing constantly. The author and publisher disclaim any liability to any party for any loss, damage, or disruption caused by errors or omissions, whether such errors or omissions result from negligence, accident, or any other cause.

Copyright

Programming Joomla plugins

About this book

The Joomla CMS contains various types of extensions: Components, modules, plugins and templates. While most books only offer a small chapter on plugins, this book focuses on them entirely. Does the topic of plugins offer enough to fill an entire book? Yes! Plugins are vital to the workings of a Joomla site, and developing them correctly is a must. This book reveals everything that you need to know about programming plugins.

This book does not focus on the usage of plugins, but on the actual programming: It makes this book a must read for anybody who is involved in Joomla programming - both beginner and guru. Basic knowledge of PHP and XML is a requirement though.

First of all, this book gives you all the material to write your own plugins from scratch: It helps you deal with the basics of plugin classes and plugin methods, but also the XML code and framework calls. It does not stop there: Plugin development also deals with design patterns, autoloaders, parent classes, API hooks, backwards compatibility, and the list goes on. You may want to read the book from the start until the end, or just pick a specific subject that you really want to dive into.

About the author

Jisse Reitsma is the founder and lead-developer of Yireo. As a PHP developer he has developed over 300 extensions for Joomla and Magento, varying from a small plugin designed to do one specific thing to a full blown bridge between Joomla en Magento. He spends his days optimizing existing extensions and creating new extensions when there is a need for it. In 2008, Jisse wrote a book on Joomla template design, which appeared in Dutch and was written for Joomla 1.5.

Jisse is also a well known speaker at Joomla User Groups and Magento User Groups in the Netherlands, as well as at international conferences like Joomla World Conference and JAndBeyond.

About Yireo

Yireo is home for numerous extensions for both Joomla and Magento. Most extensions are free (as in free beer, not just free speech) while others are available with support subscriptions. Open source is at the heart of Yireo. It is more than just the licensing part – it also gives direction and shapes the vision of Yireo. More information on this vision is available online at the following link: **http://yireo.com/manifest**. Besides software, the Yireo site also offers hundreds of tutorials – both basic and advanced – on the usage and development of Joomla and Magento.

★ Benefits for you as reader

★ Know the basics of writing a Joomla plugin

★ Get the ins and outs of what is possible with Joomla plugins

★ Learn advanced tips and tricks

🏠 Book website

On the Yireo website you can find more information related to this book: code samples, errata, release information, future bonus content, etc. Registration is free.

```
http://yireo.com/jpb
```

git GitHub repository

All code of this book is available in the following GitHub repository:

```
https://github.com/yireo/JoomlaPluginsBook
```

₁₂₃ Chapters and sections

This book contains 15 chapters in total. Each **chapter** has various sub chapters, referred to as sections. Each section is numbered as part of a specific chapter. For instance, chapter 02 contains sections 2.1 and 2.2. Both chapters and sections have been added to the index at the beginning of the book, so you can easily lookup those parts that you find interesting.

The first chapter provides you with a basic introduction on the usage of plugins in Joomla and what kind of plugin types there are. Chapter 02 till 04 covers writing a basic plugin. It gives you a lot of input on what is possible in the code, without diving into too many details. This may make it a bit hard to read, but it will give you the necessary basics before diving into real-life examples.

Chapter 05 till 11 cover the various plugin types. They are filled with practical examples. Every plugin type is worked out in detail. Even if you have created a plugin before, these chapters will still hold enough information to teach you something new.

Last but not least, chapters 12 till 15 give background information and vital tips for creating plugins. They are set up to give you a complete overview of what is possible with plugin development.

📓 Copyright

Note that **Joomla!** is written as **Joomla** throughout this book - without the exclamation mark. This decision has been made to improve readability of the book.

💬 Acknowledgments

First of all, I would like to say thanks to my girlfriend **Tineke van Oosten**, who helped me with finding time and piece of mind to write this book. I also owe her a lot for correcting text. She is probably one of the first people to have read a programming book from A to Z without having any technical knowledge.

Also, many thanks to **Ruben Creemers** who created the design of this book. With his help, the book looks awesome.

Also, thanks to **Robert van Oosten** - with his input, we were able to publish this book under our own label.

In addition, I would like to thank the following people for their help with reviewing the various chapters. They were vital in the suggestions they made to improve the content. In alphabetical order:

- Babs Gösgens
- Brian Teeman
- Chad Windnagle
- Chris Davenport
- Hans Kuijpers
- Inge van Bremen-Valstar
- Johan Janssens
- Mark Dexter
- Peter Martin
- Roland Dalmulder
- Sander Potjer

</> About the code in this book

The intent was to write all code in this book following Joomla coding standards. However, to improve the readability of code in this book and to make sure code fits on a single line in the printed copy, sometimes the code syntax had to be modified into a less preferred alternative. But the good news is that all code in the GitHub repository is correct. The code in the book (which may or may not comply to the coding standard) should hence be seen as a reference to the GitHub repository (which complies to the coding standard). Use the code in the book to learn, but the GitHub code to base your own code on.

Also check chapter 14 on Joomla coding standards and code compliance for a better understanding of how proper code should be written.

Elaborate code versus readable code

Sometimes the PHP structure in this book is more elaborate than needed. For instance, the ternary operator frequently takes up a lot of space:

```
$a = ($b == $c) ? $d : $e;
```

This is sometimes rewritten to:

```
if ($b == $c)
{
    $a = $d;
}
else
{
    $a = $e;
}
```

As you can see, the ternary operator takes up only one line while the if-else structure takes up a whopping eight lines: The Joomla coding standards state that every opening and closing brace should have its own new line. The Joomla coding standards also state that the if-else structure is preferred over the ternary operator.

Still, in basic code structures like above, the ternary operator could be preferred in real-life. In this book, if the line is too long it would automatically be broken and therefore become less readable. If this is the case, the if-else structure is used to guarantee you can still read the code.

Single lines versus multiple lines

Another good example is a method definition like the following:

```
public function onContentBeforeDisplay($context, &$row, &$params, $page
= 0)
{
}
```

As you can see it the arguments do not fit on a single line. In this case, we have decided to split this out across multiple lines. This is definitely not following any coding standards, but again improves readability.

```
public function onContentBeforeDisplay(
    $context, &$row, &$params, $page = 0
)
{
}
```

Events versus event methods

You will find that event names in this book are sometimes written without parentheses like onAfterInitialise and sometimes with parentheses like onAfterInitialise(). In case the event name is written without parentheses, it refers to the **event** as it is triggered by the component.

```
onAfterInitialise
```

In the case, the event name is written with parentheses, it is referred to as **event method**, meaning the class function that is used to intercept an event within a plugin class.

```
onAfterInitialise()
```

✉ Contact the author

If you have any questions or remarks on the book, feel free to drop me a note via email (jisse@yireo.com) or twitter (@yireo or @jissereitsma).

Table of **contents**

Table of **contents**

Table of **contents**

Table of **contents**

1 Introducing Joomla plugins

Joomla plugins: You have probably already used them many times in Joomla. You most likely know how they can be configured in the Plugin Manager and what kind of plugins are useful for your site. While the difference between components and modules is easily explained, the concept of plugins is harder to bring across, because plugins cover so many different areas of Joomla. This chapter gives an overview of what plugins are and how they function within the Joomla CMS. It may be a bit basic. Yet, we need to get the basics straight first, before we can dive into the advanced programming.

1.1 What are plugins?

There are various extension types that can be used in combination with the Joomla core: components, modules, templates … and plugins. While components and modules are mostly used to deliver direct output, explaining the purpose of plugins requires a bit more effort. The main issue is that plugins are very diverse. Each plugin has its own purpose.

Let's organize plugins a bit. They are split up into **plugin groups**, also referred to as **plugin types**. Understanding the purpose of Joomla plugins is much easier when you explain each type on its own. This is also how this book is organized. For instance, there is one chapter on **Content Plugins** and another on **System Plugins**.

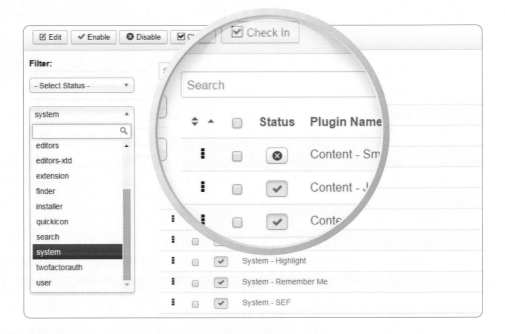

Luckily, it is not hard to write your first Joomla plugin (provided that you know how to code PHP). In chapter 2, you will see which PHP code is needed to write a basic plugin. In later chapters, we will add more and more features to that base plugin.

1.2 Plugin types in the Joomla core

The Joomla core comes with about 50 plugins spread out over 12 plugin types. These types (or groups) are the following:

- **Content Plugins**: When an article is displayed in the Joomla frontend, a Content Plugin can be used to modify the articles content just before it is being displayed. In addition to this, a Content Plugin can also modify content just before it is saved to the database, or do something completely different just after the article was saved to the database. In general, if you want to hook into the content handling of Joomla, this plugin type is the one to use. Content Plugins will be covered in chapter 5.

- **System Plugins**: These plugins can do many different things, so many that the only way to explain this in a good way is to get technical. A System Plugin is able to handle various tasks, depending on the system event that is generated. It sounds a bit vague. In chapter 6 you will learn what you can do with a System Plugin. To give you an idea of the diversity of these plugins: You can use System Plugins to add HTML code to the Joomla page after it has been generated; you can alter forms (`JForm`) before they are generated; you can add CSS or JavaScript; you can provide alternative error handling. And there are many more possibilities!

- **Authentication Plugins**: When somebody tries to login into Joomla, the Joomla application will need to authenticate this user. On most sites, authentication is performed against the Joomla database. This type of authentication is handled by the **Authenticate - Joomla** plugin. By using Authentication Plugins you can also use other external services to authenticate users: The core comes with plugins for GMail and LDAP (which can be used for Windows domains). In chapter 7 we will discuss authentication and Authentication Plugins.

- **Two Factor Authentication Plugins**: Besides regular authentication, there is also the option to add extra security by adding a second security authentication. These **Two Factor Authentication Plugins** (in short, TFA plugins) will be discussed in the same chapter as Authentication Plugins (chapter 7).

- **User Plugins**: Whenever something happens to a Joomla user, User Plugins can react to this. When a Joomla user record is saved or deleted; when a Joomla user logs in or out. Extensions that provide additional user information (Community Builder, JomSocial, VirtueMart, to name a few) hook into this. Chapter 8 will give you numerous examples of User Plugins.

- **Search Plugins**: When using the Joomla search component `com_search`, these plugins determine which content is searched. In the Joomla core, there are Search Plugins available for articles, article categories and more. For each type of content to be searched, a separate search plugin is required. These plugins are covered in chapter 9.

⊕ **Finder Plugins** (or **Smart Search Plugins**): Besides the regular Joomla search, there is also the Joomla `com_finder` component (dubbed as **Smart Search**). The main difference between the two is that `com_search` searches content real time (perhaps opening up many different database tables to make this happen), while `com_finder` creates index tables first and then only searches that index – which allows for more efficient (so it performs faster) full text searching. For each type of content, a separate Finder Plugin is required, just like with the regular search. Finder Plugins are also discussed in chapter 9.

The remaining plugin types will be covered in chapters 10 and 11:

⊕ **Editor Plugins**: When a textarea is transformed into a full blown JavaScript based editor, this plugin type is used. Familiar plugins in this group are the TinyMCE editor and the JCE editor. Actually if no WYSIWYG editor is used, the basic textarea is still shown through a plugin called `none`.

⊕ **Editors-xtd Plugins** (or **Button Plugins**) At the bottom of an editor field, extra buttons may appear - for instance a button to add a **Read More** link or a button to add a page break. These buttons are generated by plugins of type `editors-xtd`.

⊕ **Captcha Plugins**: Plugins of this type allow you to extend forms with a Captcha check (Completely Automated Public Turing test to tell Computers and Humans Apart). The Joomla core comes with a plugin for Google reCaptcha. Other Captcha methods can easily be added.

⊕ **Extension Plugins**: While there are not so many plugins yet of this group, it is an interesting group nonetheless. Whenever a Joomla extension is installed or removed (component, module, plugin, template, library, package), plugins of this group can hook into this event and do something. The core Joomla plugin is used to cleanup update sites (used for updating extensions in the **Extension Manager**). Since Joomla 3.2, it is also possible for commercial extensions to use this plugin group to allow private downloads through a subscription key.

⊕ **Quick icon Plugins**: To place a quickicon on the dashboard of the Joomla Administrator, you can use a plugin of this type.

There are even more plugin types in the core. They will be discussed briefly in chapter 11.

1.3 Plugins & events

You already may have noticed that different plugins can perform different tasks while still belonging to the same plugin group. For instance, Joomla comes with a **Content - Email Cloaking** plugin (folder `plugins/content/emailcloak`) - of type `content` - which

tries to hide email addresses from spammers. It does this when the c
displayed. The **Content - Smart Search** plugin (folder `plugins/con`
again of type content - fulfills a completely different purpose: It make
content in the **Smart Search** index is updated, after saving the article

Displaying content and saving content are two very different things, but are still both
part of the Content Plugins group. The reason for this diversity is that a plugin type (like
`content` or `authentication`) is just a way to group plugins – an artificial way of
organizing plugins. The actual thing that drives plugins are events.

On the webpage **http://yireo.com/matrix** you will find a listing of all plugin groups with all
their events. If you have a certain task you need to complete, you can use this listing as a
quick reference.

Dispatching events

Events are points in the Joomla code where the code states "Hey plugins, you have to do
something here!". For instance, the user component (`com_user`) uses the JForm library
to print a form with all the user fields available. Just before the form is generated, the
component allows plugins to modify that form. To make this possible, it calls upon a class
called `JDispatcher` that then triggers an event `onContentPrepareForm`. Plugins
listening to the event `onContentPrepareForm` can then modify the `$form` object.

The code used by the user component looks more or less like this:

```
JPluginHelper::importPlugin('user');
$dispatcher = JDispatcher::getInstance();
$results = $dispatcher->trigger(
    'onContentPrepareForm', array($form, $data)
);
```

We will not discuss this code yet - it is covered in chapter 11. However, you can see that the
component code is referring to the plugin event. It is responsible for defining the action,
that plugins then hook into. Without this action, plugins will never be called. Learning how
to write plugins, boils down to learning about these plugin events.

Extra plugin types

Plugin events offer a clean way of modifying existing functionality, without the need to
modify the original code. This is true for the Joomla core and for third party extensions.
A good third party component allows other developers to hook into the component by
strategically adding events (and actually provide API documentation on how to use these

events). In chapter 11, we will explain how to add your own events to your own extension (most likely a component). Throughout the book, we will also discuss various events of third party extensions.

1.4   Some words on using plugins

Using plugins is peanuts. You install the plugin using the Joomla **Extension Manager**, then you enable the plugin within the **Plugin Manager**, and you are done. There is no actual configuration of a plugin, except for enabling it or disabling it.

Possibly, a plugin may include a couple of parameters. Because it really depends on the plugins functionality whether parameters are available and, if they exist, whether they should be modified or not, it is best to check the plugins documentation.

Importance of ordering

When using plugins it is important to inspect the ordering of these plugins. This determines which plugin is executed first and which plugin is executed last. Plugins with a low ordering number (for instance, 0 or -999) will be loaded and executed earlier then plugins with a high ordering number. New plugins are installed with a default ordering of 0.

It may be necessary to reconfigure the ordering. Let's say you are using a plugin that provides page caching and there is another plugin that modifies the HTML source to add Google Analytics code. The first plugin is configured with ordering 22 and the second plugin is configured with ordering 38. Both plugins respond to the event `onAfterRender`.

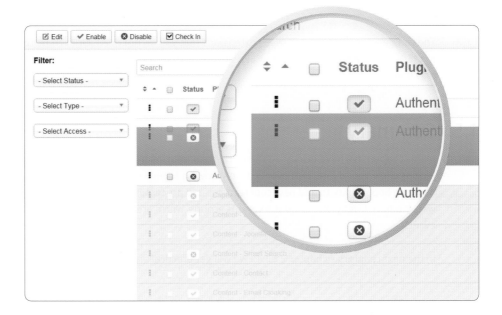

This will have the result that Google Analytics is never loaded, because the page is always cached or served from cache before the Google Analytics plugin is able to do anything. To make this work, the Google Analytics plugin needs to be loaded before the page caching plugin. In order for this to happen, its ordering number needs to be lower than the ordering number of the page caching plugin.

Be aware that the ordering of plugins is not always efficient. Plugins can be ordered. However, events cannot. This may sound confusing. Just realize that a single plugin can be used to react on two events. Reordering the plugin for the sake of the first event, may also change the ordering of the second event for the worse.

Not too many plugins!

When building a Joomla site, it may be tempting to install many extensions quickly through the Joomla **Installation Manager**. In the end, you may find yourself faced with dozens of plugins installed within Joomla. However, be careful here! Too many plugins will probably slow down your frontend and clutter your backend, making it harder to administer your site.

For instance, if you tried to implement some kind of Lightbox (modal popup) effect to create your own image gallery, there are numerous plugins to choose from. One way to find the best plugin for your site is to quickly install them, test them and disable them again if they do not fit the job. Just disabling them may still leave you with numerous Lightbox plugins showing up in your **Plugin Manager**. Worse, if this keeps on going for a long time, you may be left with a lot of plugins, of which you do not know the purpose anymore.

The simple advice is: Uninstall these extensions that you do not need. Or even better: Do not test out new extensions on your live site. Instead, setup a testing copy of your site and play there.

1.5 Summary

In this chapter, we have discussed the workings of plugins from a technical point of view: Plugins allow you to intercept events, thrown by the Joomla system. Thanks to this, you have the opportunity to add new cool features and processes to Joomla in a non-obtrusive way. We have briefly discussed the various groups, which are used to categorize different events.

In the next chapters – chapter 2 till 4 - we will get practical and start writing our own plugin.

Ingredients of a basic plugin

2

Writing a basic plugin involves PHP code that is often the same for other plugins. In this chapter we will discuss the ingredients of a basic content plugin that modifies the text of an article before it is shown.

you begin

ou have setup your favorite IDE for Joomla development first. Which Joomla
use to develop your plugin, depends a bit on the target platform. You can
ither the latest stable release – Joomla 3.4 for instance - or the latest GitHub
However, perhaps you also want your plugin to work in Joomla 2.5, so having this
version installed also makes sense. Ideally, your plugin will work on all these versions. Make
sure to test it on the various versions after finishing development.

2.2 Start of a Joomla plugin

We will start off with an example of a Content Plugin called **Chapter 02 Test 01** (with a
technical name `ch02test01`). We do not know what the functionality will be. However,
we will setup the skeleton first. Instead of creating a package first and then installing it into
Joomla, we will add the files directly to Joomla and install them afterwards (through the
Discover feature of the **Installation Manager**). First, create a folder `plugins/content/`
`ch02test01` and add two files to this folder: `ch02test01.php` and `ch02test01.`
`xml`. Open the file `ch02test01.php` so we can start creating the PHP code inside it.

Choosing the right name

When defining a name for your plugin, you should not be using spaces or other weird
characters. This is not only a convention, it is a necessity as well. The plugin name is used
to construct filenames. It is also used to determine the class name of your plugin (which we
will see later in this chapter):

Package name	Name	Class name
`plg_content_ch02test01`	`ch02test01`	`PlgContentCh02test01`
`plg_system_debug`	`debug`	`PlgSystemDebug`
`plg_authentication_ldap`	`ldap`	`PlgAuthenticationLdap`

Stick to the standards and use only lowercase characters in your name.

 You do not need to retype any of the code in this book. The code for this test plugin is
available in the GitHub repository **https://github.com/yireo/JoomlaPluginsBook** in the
subfolder **chapter02/plg_content_ch02test01**.

2.3 PHP opening with _JEXEC()

Of course, the code needs to start with a PHP opening tag - it is not a mixed HTML/PHP file, it only contains PHP. Do not use the short opening tag (<?), because that will not work on all systems (PHP configuration `short_open_tag = 0`). Use the full opening tag (<?php) instead:

```php
<?php
```

For security reasons, any PHP script that is called by Joomla should have a check to prevent direct calling of the script:

```php
<?php
defined('_JEXEC') or die;
```

When somebody tries to run your PHP script directly, only a blank page will be shown. Optionally you can add a pointless message:

```php
<?php
defined('_JEXEC') or die('Direct access not allowed.');
```

Or even more pointless:

```php
<?php
defined('_JEXEC') or die('So long and thanks for all the fish.');
```

Remember that none of your users will see this message. Only people who are looking for security openings (call them hackers or enthusiasts) will see this message. The `_JEXEC` check should be present in all your PHP files.

Instead of a check for the `_JEXEC` constant, you may also encounter a check for the `JPATH_BASE` constant. Using either constant is fine. In this book, we will prefer the `_JEXEC` constant, simply because it is being used the most.

After this check, you can start defining your plugin class, which contains the actual logic of your plugin.

2.4 A plugin class and its methods

Creating a plugin involves little more than declaring a single class. This class gets instantiated into an object, at the time when a certain event needs to be intercepted by this plugin. For instance, if you have written a Content Plugin, nothing happens with it when Joomla throws a system event. However, when Joomla throws a content event instead, the plugin class gets instantiated into an object and Joomla will check whether the event method exists within that object. Later we will describe this process in more detail, covering the JPlugin class itself, its JPluginHelper class and the JEventDispatcher class, which implements the **Observer-Observable** pattern.

The name of the class follows a strict naming standard: a prefix Plg followed by the name of the plugin group (for instance Content) followed by the name of your plugin (for instance Ch02test01 without any spaces). Previously, the plugin class started with a lowercase character instead of a capital – so plgContentCh02test01 instead of PlgContentCh02test01. PHP as a language does not distinguish the case when it comes to class names, so you can use both. Currently the uppercase variation seems to be the new standard, so stick to that. Note that standards can change though.

Extend JPlugin

The class should also extend the JPlugin class, which extends again the class JEvent. Theoretically, you can skip the JPlugin class and extend JEvent directly, because JEvent actually contains the required functionality. Because JPlugin also contains useful tools (like initializing the plugin parameters), it is best to stick to the standard and extend JPlugin.

```
class PlgContentCh02test01 extends JPlugin
{
}
```

jimport()

Because the file containing this parent class JPlugin may not yet be included in the Joomla core, the jimport() function needs to be used first to autoload that class. Some plugins skip this part – for instance, with Content Plugins it is pretty obvious that System Plugins have already been fired, which in turn have included the JPlugin class already.

Things changed also a little bit with Joomla 3. With Joomla 2.5, the usage of jimport() was needed to load classes explicitly. With Joomla 3, classes are autoloaded by the JLoader class (which is discussed in chapter 13). To be on the safe side (and to be compatible with Joomla 2.5), it is best to use jimport() anyway.

```
jimport('joomla.plugin.plugin');

class PlgContentCh02test01 extends JPlugin
{
}
```

2.5   Adding an event method to the class

When an event is thrown by Joomla, the event always specifies the plugin group (content, system, etc) and the event method. If the event method exists as a class method within your plugin, that method is called automatically. Depending on the event method, extra method arguments may be available. You will see this when we are discussing all events of the Joomla core one by one. As an example, we will add the event method to add extra data to an articles text before it is being displayed:

```
jimport('joomla.plugin.plugin');

class PlgContentCh02test01 extends JPlugin
{
    public function onContentBeforeDisplay(
        $context, &$row, &$params, $page = 0
    )
    {
    }
}
```

Note that the method name and the arguments are divided across multiple lines for readability in this book only. In your own code make sure to put everything on a single line. Use the GitHub sources of this book as reference.

Arguments of onContentBeforeDisplay

You can see that the method onContentBeforeDisplay contains four arguments: an array, $context, containing meta data on the type of content being handled (for instance com_content.article); an object $row, which is a reference to the actual content item being displayed; the used parameters (for instance, the article parameters); and the current $page that is being displayed (in case a list of articles is being displayed).

The variable $row is a reference to the original content. It means that we can modify the content directly through the $row variable. However, it allows modifying not only the article text, but also the article title, the article author and other attributes of the content. If you want to modify the original text only (so not other parts of the text), it is best to use the event method onContentPrepare instead.

Finding out plugin parameters

Note that with every event method (and the Joomla CMS offers dozens of them), there will be different event parameters as well as a different purpose for the return value. To find out how to use the parameters and return value, you need to look it up. Either using the **Joomla Documentation Project** site (**docs.joomla.org**), books like this or the actual Joomla code.

I recommend the last option (the code). By reading the source code in full or finding the place in the source code where the event is being fired, you will get a better understanding of how plugins work, plus you will always have a cross reference when the documentation is insufficient.

2.6 Dummy code

The code we have so far does not contain any real functionality yet. Let's add some dummy code. We will just modify the articles text and title a bit:

```php
public function onContentBeforeDisplay(
    $context, &$row, &$params, $page = 0
)
{

    $row->title = $row->title.' [test01]';
    $row->text = $row->text.'<p>[test01]</p>';
}
```

This code will work fine. Of course it is nothing fancy. There is no check whether the text is empty, the code is applied to all articles, there are no parameters. In the upcoming chapters, we will see how to create more advanced and useful code with a couple of examples.

Public, private and protected

With PHP, you have the ability to specify the visibility of class members (class methods and class variables). They can be set to either public, private or protected. Public access means that PHP code outside of the plugin class can directly call upon the plugin class methods or variables. Private access means that only PHP code from within the plugin class has access to it. Protected access means that PHP code from within the plugin classes, plus the parent class plus any child classes has access to it.

The class itself is always public, otherwise no other code would have access to it. In the case of Joomla plugins, the event method (`onContentBeforeDisplay`) also needs to be public, because Joomla (or the `com_content` component and optionally other components) will call upon that method to do its stuff.

A class method that is missing a visibility indication, automatically has the visibility public. Often you will see plugins that have functions that are missing the `public` indicator. In the

Joomla coding standards it is defined that a plugin method should have a visibility indicator at all times. It is best to stick to these standards and always explicitly declare your methods as either `public` or something else:

```php
class PlgContentCh02test01 extends JPlugin
{
    public function onContentBeforeDisplay(
        $context, &$row, &$params, $page=0
    )
    {
    }

    protected function doSomethingWithinThisPlugin()
    {
    }
}
```

Adding your own task methods

In addition to the event method, you can add extra methods to keep your code clean. I will refer to these kind of methods as **task methods**: Each method is meant for a certain task. It is up to you to use them. In most cases, a task method will be private. Later on, when we will discuss using custom parent classes and cross linking plugins, we will also discuss the option to define your methods as protected instead.

It is best to define all internal variables as either private or protected. If some PHP code outside of the plugin class needs to access it, use a getter method (a method that gets a value from a class variable) or setter method (a method that adds value to a class variable) instead. If some PHP code inside of your plugin class needs to access it, access it directly. Still, task methods can be useful for simple tasks that may otherwise clutter your code. Tasks, that are meant only for usage within this class, can be kept private. In the code below for instance, the `resetNumber()` method is private.

```php
class PlgContentCh02test01 extends JPlugin
{
    /*
     * Internal variable
     */
    private $number = array();

    /*
     * Getter method
     */
```

```php
    public function getNumber()
    {
        return $this->number;
    }

    /*
     * Setter method
     */
    public function setNumber($number)
    {
        $this->number = (int)$number;
    }

    /*
     * Reset method
     */
    private function resetNumber()
    {
        $this->number = 0;
    }
}
```

Traditionally, variable declarations are put at the top of the class. It is best to define your event methods directly after that, so that everybody can easily see what your plugin is doing. Your task methods would therefore go at the bottom of the class.

PHP 5.4 and E_STRICT

Note that all code in this book is compatible with PHP 5.4, which requires that all code is written with the error reporting level set to E_STRICT. This makes sure that your code does not contain any PHP Notices and PHP Warnings.

You can either enable this kind of reporting by setting the parameter **Error Reporting** within the Joomla **Global Configuration** to **Development**. As an alternative, you can also set this value to **Server Default** and define the error reporting value on the PHP level. Within a php.ini file you would use the following configuration line:

```
error_reporting = E_ALL | E_STRICT
```

Or you can add this to your htaccess file (when using PHP as an Apache module):

```
php_value error_reporting 8191
```

2.7   Reserved variables and methods

Note that the following variables are already defined by the `JPlugin` class (or its parents):

o   `$params` = Containing the plugin parameters
o   `$_name` = Containing the name of your plugin (`test01`)
o   `$_type` = Containing the name of the plugin group (`content`)
o   `$_subject` = Containing the name of the event object
o   `$_errors` = Containing a list of error messages (empty by default)

The following methods are already defined by the `JPlugin` class (or its parents):

o   `loadLanguage()`
o   `update()`
o   `def()`
o   `get()`
o   `getProperties()`
o   `getError()`
o   `getErrors()`
o   `set()`
o   `setProperties()`
o   `setError()`

Note that you also need to be careful not to override the default constructor. This will be discussed in chapter 13 thoroughly.

GNU General Public License

The Joomla core is released under the GPL, and this requires Joomla plugins to be released under the GPL as well. As simple as that. There are however a couple of more things to add. Because a plugin becomes automatically open sourced, another question you should ask yourself is: Do you want to distribute the plugin or not?

If not, the whole GPL thing is irrelevant. It only sets up rules when the code (written by you, the author, so the copyright holder) is distributed to others. If you keep the code to yourself, then the GPL does not come into effect. However, if you decide to distribute the plugin to others, not only the GPL becomes important, but the proper way of distribution as well: code standards, comments, documentation.

As part of making your plugin GPL compliant, the PHP code needs to refer to the GPL by using a `phpdoc` style comment at the top of your code. Code commenting using the `phpdoc` standard is a good idea anyway.

Let's go back to the beginning of the class file and add some PHP comments:

```php
<?php
/**
 * Content Plugin for Joomla - Test 01
 *
 * @author Jisse Reitsma (jisse@yireo.com)
 * @copyright Copyright 2014 Jisse Reitsma
 * @license GNU Public License version 3 or later
 * @link http://www.yireo.com/books/
 */

defined('_JEXEC') or die;
```

It is good practice to write all code in English. If you plan to share code with other developers, make sure your comments as well as the naming of your methods and variables are in English.

2.8 Basic XML manifest

In the next chapter, we are going to see how to write a full blown XML manifest, which is needed to install any Joomla extension. For now we will just create a minimum XML file – called ch02test01.xml – that allows us to install the plugin using the **Discover** button of the **Installation Manager**. This assumes that the two files, ch02test01. php and ch02test01.xml are both in place inside the folder /plugins/content/ch02test01/. The XML file looks like this:

```xml
<extension type="plugin" group="content">
    <name>plg_content_ch02test01</name>
</extension>
```

What? Yes, this is all the XML code needed to get started with your first plugin.

Note that this is definitely not the recommended way to setup a real life plugin. It serves the purpose of quickly installing an extension. Some of the XML values that are skipped in this example cannot easily be added afterwards. For a good example of the XML file, refer to chapter 3.

2.9 Empty index.html file

Finally, create an empty file called index.html in the same folder. Why this file needs to exist, is explained in the next chapter as well.

2.10 Discover using the Installation Manager

When you have all the files in place, you can simply navigate to the Joomla **Extension Manager** and hit the **Discover** button. Joomla should detect your new plugin and install it.

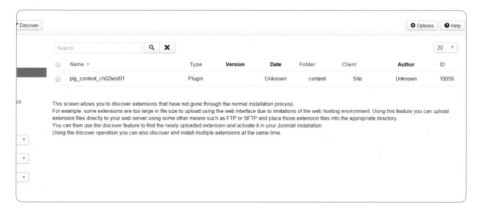

After installation, the plugin should be available in the **Plugin Manager**.

2.11 Result on the frontend

After enabling the plugin in the **Plugin Manager**, the frontend should give results right away. The plugin should modify the title of every Joomla article, appending the keyword [test01] to it. And it should also do the same with the article text.

Note that the article text is only modified on a full article page, not in the blog layout.

2.12 Summary

In this chapter, we have put together a plugin with basic functionality. It will serve as a skeleton for all examples that follow in this book. Each plugin folder contains a PHP file and an XML file. We have discussed the logic of the plugin class with event methods and task methods. Notes were also made on error reporting, reserved variables and visibility.

The next chapter focuses on what you can put in the XML file, which is quite a lot.

(3) XML and related stuff

In the previous chapter we have seen a very basic XML file (the XML manifest) to install our plugin, which does not comply to the standards. In this chapter, I will show you how to write an XML file that includes all the recommended tags. This includes SQL statements, language files and extension updates.

In this chapter we will extend the Content Plugin used in chapter 2. The code of this test plugin is available in the GitHub repository **https://github.com/yireo/JoomlaPluginsBook** in the subfolder **chapter03/plg_content_test01**.

3.1 Extension tag

The XML manifest of a plugin starts with the `<extension>` tag, making clear to Joomla that this package is actually an extension. There are many different kind of extensions in Joomla (components, modules, plugins, templates). Therefore, it is needed to define which extension type we are dealing with. For example, an XML file for a component would look like this:

```
<extension type="component">
```

For a plugin, it is also important to define the plugins `group`, because this defines which subfolder of the `/plugins/` directory the files should be copied to. In our example, we are still busy writing a Content Plugin so the `content` group is used:

```
<extension type="plugin" group="content">
```

Commonly, you will also see a `version` argument. In the example below, this refers to the Joomla core version 3.4. The argument is not required and is not used by Joomla at all, but it may well be in the future. Consider it good practice to enter the Joomla version that you were using when developing the plugin. The complete `<extension>` tag would look like this:

```
<extension version="3.4" type="plugin" group="content">
```

The `<extension>` tag serves as the body for all other tags. At the end of the XML manifest, the tag therefore needs to be closed as well:

```
</extension>
```

Opening and closing tags counts for all other XML tags as well.

3.2 XML header or not

Often the `<extension>` tag is preceded by an XML header. It defines the current file as an XML file, which is actually obvious when inspecting the rest of the file. More importantly it defines the character set to be used. Most commonly, this character set is `utf-8`, which for example allows author names to be written in non western languages as well.

```
<?xml version="1.0" encoding="utf-8" ?>
<extension ...>
...
</extension>
```

Actually, this definition of UTF-8 is not really needed. For parsing XML files, Joomla makes use of the **SimpleXML** library and that library will use UTF-8 as default. If your XML file is already UTF-8, you can skip the tag. If you are not using UTF-8 but some other character set, defining this character set using the encoding argument is mandatory. My advice would therefore be to only use UTF-8 anyway. It even supports Klingon, so what else would you need?

3.3   Basic tags

Within the `<extension>` tag, we will define a set of subtags that add meta information regarding the plugin. First of all, the name of the plugin needs to be defined. This is following Joomla standards, starting with a `plg` prefix followed by an underscore, followed by the name of your plugin group, followed by another underscore, followed by the name of your plugin (lowercase, no spaces).

```
plg_content_ch03test01
```

This `<name>` tag does not contain the technical name as for your plugin on the filesystem. Instead, this is a label that can be translated using a language file, which we will discuss later. After installation, administrators can change this label using the **Plugin Manager**. While the technical name is in lowercase, all language strings should be in uppercase:

```
<name>PLG_CONTENT_CH03TEST01</name>
```

Optionally, you can also add a small description for your plugin. Again, this is only a language string, for which we will add a proper translation later on in this chapter. In some plugins this description ends with `_XML_DESCRIPTION`. However, it can be any string that you like, as long as it is properly translated.

```
<description>PLG_CONTENT_CH03TEST01_DESCRIPTION</description>
```

Next, a version for your plugin is needed. This can be in any format that you like:

```
<version>1A</version>
<version>24 beta</version>
<version>my first attempt</version>
```

Best practice is to use a format following the `x.y.z` standard, where `x` refers to a major version, `y` refers to a minor version and `z` refers to a patch version. If your code is far from finished, you can set both major and minor to zero. Version 0.0.1 would be seen as the first version ever. Version 1.0.0 would be seen as your first stable version. In chapter 15 you can find a section on semantic versioning, which covers this type of versioning.

```
<version>0.0.1</version>
```

We add a date when this plugin was created. It is up to you, whether you modify this date each time you increase the version. Also, you can decide yourself which date format you want to use (August 2014, 08-2014, 08/2014).

```
<creationDate>August 2014</creationDate>
```

Now we add some author information:

```
<author>Jisse Reitsma</author>
<authorEmail>jisse@yireo.com</authorEmail>
<authorUrl>http://joomla-plugins-book.yireo.com/</authorUrl>
```

License and copyright

Last but not least, the plugin requires some legal information. The license should be the GNU/GPL (either version 2 or version 3). Because the Joomla **Extension Directory** requires you to add a `LICENSE.txt` with a copy of your license to the package archive (ZIP or tar file), you can refer to this file here. In the final chapter of this book we will discuss packaging your plugin and including this `LICENSE.txt` file in your package.

```
<license>GNU/GPL version 3 or later; see LICENSE.txt</license>
<copyright>Copyright of Jisse Reitsma (2012)</copyright>
```

The XML file also includes a copyright statement. While open source is often called copyleft, it does not mean that regular copyright laws do not apply. Open source still means that as an author, you can claim the ownership of the source code. Open source also guarantees that the source code can be used and improved by other developers. A copyright statement should contain the keyword `copyright`, the name of the copyright holder (in this case me myself) and the date for which the copyright is valid. The period for which a copyright remains valid varies per country (from 1 year to various decades), so you can also add a period instead:

```
<copyright>Copyright of Jisse Reitsma (2014-2019)</copyright>
```

3.4 Files & folders & media

The <files> tag is important when Joomla installs the plugin. Using this tag, it knows which files to copy from the source folder (a temporary folder where the package archive is extracted to) to the destination folder (a subfolder of /plugins/, for instance /plugins/content/). The <files> tag should always have the main PHP file and the XML file included:

```
<files>
    <filename plugin="ch03test01">ch03test01.php</filename>
    <filename>index.html</filename>
</files>
```

You can see that the <filename> tag identifying the main PHP file also includes an extra argument plugin. This is needed to inform Joomla which PHP file to call upon when calling your plugin. If you would want your main PHP file to be /plugins/content/ch03test01/main.php, you can use this plugin indicator to accomplish this. I recommend you stick to the standards instead and use a main PHP file that is named after the name of the plugin.

Skipping the XML file

Note that the ch03test01.xml is not mentioned in the <files> section. However, it is still being copied from the installation folder to the plugin folder.

index.html files

The <files> section also includes an index.html file with hardly any content:

```
<html><body></body></html>
```

This file allows for a small trick that prevents outsiders from seeing the contents of your plugin folders. Files like these can be found in all the Joomla directories. While it can be argued that this kind of security should actually be dealt with on a different level (for instance, the .htaccess file could be used to block these requests), the **Joomla Extension Directory** has a requirement for these files. Instead of arguing, just include these files anyway.

Note that we do not really care what is inside that HTML file. It can be totally empty and have a text Hello World in it. Another alternative is entering the code:

```
<!DOCTYPE html><title></title>
```

Either way there is no purpose for its content except blocking directory views.

Extra files and subfolders

When your plugin has a lot of logic, it is better to spread that logic out over multiple PHP files. You can use a `helper.php` file containing a class with useful methods that just do not fit in the main plugin class. If you need numerous extra PHP files, it can even be better to include an entire subfolder. When you are adding your own field types - let's say a custom dropdown box in the plugin parameters - then it is best to add a folder `fields` (with an absolute path `/plugins/content/ch03test01/fields/`). Do not forget to add an `index.html` file in this subfolder as well.

```
<files>
    <filename plugin="ch03test01">ch03test01.php</filename>
    <filename>index.html</filename>
    <filename>helper.php</filename>
    <folder>fields</folder>
</files>
```

LICENSE.txt

Note that you do not need to include the `LICENSE.txt` file (which was discussed earlier) in the `<files>` section. This file is for reference and is only seen when people extract the package archive manually and inspect the license of your code. It is not used by Joomla.

3.5   Media

If you want to add static files (images, CSS files, JavaScript files, or other files that are to be called directly by the browser), do not add them to your plugin folder but add them to the `/media/` folder instead. It is common practice to create subfolders like the example below:

```
<media destination="plg_content_ch03test01">
    <folder>images</folder>
    <folder>css</folder>
    <folder>js</folder>
</media>
```

The argument destination refers to the folder `/media/plg_content_ch03test01/` in this case. If we package our plugin in a ZIP file, this ZIP file will contain the subfolders `images`, `css` and `js`, and it will be copied to this folder `/media/plg_content_ch03test01/`.

Alternatively, you can create a ZIP file with a subfolder `plg_content_test01` (and within it again the three subfolders `images`, `css` and `js`) and omit the destination argument:

```
<media>
    <folder>plg_content_ch03test01</folder>
</media>
```

3.6   Using language files

Defining language files within the XML file is similar to the `<files>` section and `<media>` section. Each language file (defined with a `<language>` tag) needs a tag argument, which refers to the language the file is serving. The Joomla core always comes with the English language (`en-GB`), so make sure to include that language as a minimum.

```
<languages>
    <language tag="en-GB">
        en-GB.plg_content_ch03test01.ini
    </language>
    <language tag="en-GB">
        en-GB.plg_content_ch03test01.sys.ini
    </language>
</languages>
```

Both these files will be copied to the `/administrator/language/en-GB/` folder. Something that may confuse you is that the `en-GB.plg_content_ch03test01.ini` file is used for both the frontend and the backend, while the `en-GB.plg_content_ch03test01.sys.ini` file is only used for the backend. If your plugin does not add things for the frontend, you may want to skip the frontend file.

In the backend, the translations of `en-GB.plg_content_ch03test01.sys.ini` are used within the **Plugin Manager**. The values of the `<name>` tag and the `<description>` tag are translated here into human readable strings by using the language file `en-GB.plg_content_ch03test01.sys.ini`:

```
; Language file for our test plugin 01
PLG_CONTENT_CH03TEST01="Content - Chapter 03 / Test 01"
PLG_CONTENT_CH03TEST01_DESCRIPTION="This is an example plugin"
```

The convention is to define a source string with `PLG_CONTENT_CHTEST01` (the technical name of your plugin) followed by the substring you want to translate. We will see more of this when creating plugin parameters in the next chapter.

When creating the package archive, make sure to include these two files within the root of the archive, on the same folder level as the main PHP file (`ch03test01.php`) and XML file (`ch03test01.xml`).

Translating strings in the frontend

We can also apply translation on the frontend. While Joomla in the backend magically translates XML strings, in the frontend we need to tell Joomla what to translate. For this translation the call `JText::_($string)` is used - `JText` is the object and the underscore (`_`) is the method. We modify the `onContentBeforeDisplay()` method a bit to make the test string translatable:

```
public function onContentBeforeDisplay(
    $context, &$row, &$params, $page = 0
)
{
    $test = JText::_('PLG_CONTENT_CH03TEST01_TEST');
    $row->title = $row->title.' ['.$test.']';
    $row->text = $row->text.'<p>['.$test.']</p>';
}
```

Loading the language file

Before the language file `en-GB.plg_content_ch03test01.ini` is used, we need to modify our PHP code first. By default, when the plugin is loaded, it does not load its language file `en-GB.plg_content_ch03test01.ini`. To make sure it does, we have to manually load the language file depending on the Joomla version. With Joomla 3 we can simply add a flag `$autoloadLanguage` to the class definition:

```
class PlgContentCh03test01 extends JPlugin
{
    protected $autoloadLanguage = true;
```

With older Joomla versions we add the PHP code `$this->loadLanguage()` to the constructor:

```
class PlgContentCh03test01 extends JPlugin
{
    public function __construct(&$subject, $config)
    {
        parent::__construct($subject, $config);

        $this->loadLanguage();
    }
```

Without this extra code the **Plugin Manager** will still load the language file `en-GB.plg_content_ch03test01.sys.ini` automatically. If you have no frontend translations, you can choose to put all your translations in that file instead, which will save resources.

Using HTML within the description

One trick is to use the translation strings as a way of formatting the description, using basic HTML code. The various HTML entities need to be encoded to display properly. So < becomes `&lt;` and > becomes `&gt;`.

```
PLG_CONTENT_CH03TEST01_DESCRIPTION="This is an example
&lt;strong&gt;Content Plugin&lt;/strong&gt;"
```

While this is a cool trick, try to keep this HTML formatting to a minimum. It is best to show Joomla administrators the same interface all over the backend. Highlighting specific words using `<strong>` and `<em>` is fine. Just do not go crazy on background styling and `div` structures. It will annoy your users.

3.7 Installation parts and real time information

Some XML tags will be used by Joomla to install the plugin properly (for instance, the `<files>` tag). However, once the install procedure has been completed, this information is not needed anymore. Other tags are read from the XML manifest when you access a certain page – for instance the **Extension Manager** shows the author, version and date. If you modify these values in the XML manifest, you only need to hit the **Refresh Cache** button to make sure that Joomla parses the XML manifest again.

This will not work with the `<name>` tag. This field is copied to the database once the plugin is installed. And because the name can be edited through the **Plugin Manager**, changing the `<name>` tag afterwards has no effect. If you have used a name like `plg_content_ch03test01`, you can instead modify the language file `en-GB.plg_content_ch03test01.sys.ini` at any time.

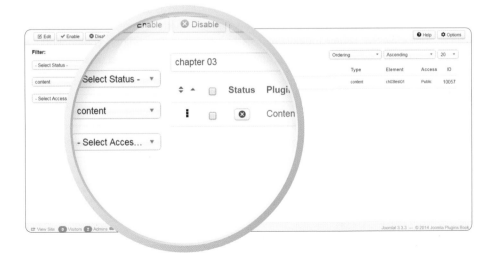

3.8 Packaging plugins with other extensions

When you want to bundle various plugins into a single package, you can simply create a ZIP file that contains these plugin packages plus an additional manifest file with type `package`. This XML manifest can have any name - for instance `package.xml` - and allows you to offer your users one single installable Joomla package that installs multiple plugins.

```xml
<?xml version="1.0" encoding="UTF-8" ?>
<extension type="package" version="2.5">
    <name>Test</name>
    <packagename>test</packagename>
    <author>Yireo</author>
    <authoremail>support@yireo.com</authoremail>
    <authorurl>http://www.yireo.com</authorurl>
    <creationDate>July 2012</creationDate>
    <copyright>Copyright 2012 Yireo.com</copyright>
    <license>http://www.gnu.org/licenses/gpl-3.0.html</license>
    <version>0.0.1</version>
    <url>http://www.yireo.com</url>
    <packager>Yireo</packager>
    <packagerurl>http://www.yireo.com</packagerurl>
    <files>
        <file type="plugin" id="ch03test01" group="content">
            plg_content_ch03test01.zip
        </file>
        <file type="plugin" id="ch03test02" group="content">
            plg_content_ch03test02.zip
        </file>
    </files>
</extension>
```

All files defined in the `<files>` section will be treated as separate extension files and will be installed by Joomla when uploading this extension archive using the **Extension Manager**. This allows for adding multiple plugins, multiple modules, multiple components – the only thing to be aware of are hosting limits, like execution timeout and maximum upload sizes.

The sample XML code of this package can be found in the GitHub repository **https://github.com/yireo/JoomlaPluginsBook** in the subfolder **chapter03**. The file is called `package.xml`.

3.9 Adding SQL statements to your plugins

As with components and modules, it is possible to add XML code to your manifest file that is executed once your plugin is installed (`<install>` section), removed (`<uninstall>` section) or updated (`<update>` section). The procedure here is to add SQL files to your plugin folder and call upon these SQL files using the following code:

```
<install>
    <sql>
        <file driver="mysql" charset="utf8">
            install.mysql.utf8.sql
        </file>
    </sql>
</install>
<uninstall>
    <sql>
        <file driver="mysql" charset="utf8">
            uninstall.mysql.utf8.sql
        </file>
    </sql>
</uninstall>
<update>
    <schemas>
        <schemapath type="mysql">
            sql/updates/mysql
        </schemapath>
    </schemas>
</update>
```

Updates using schemas

Working with updates is a little bit more complex. The folder `sql/updates/mysql` should contain a file for every version of your plugin - so with version 0.0.1 you should have a file in place called `0.0.1.sql`; with version 0.0.2 you should have a file in place called `0.0.2.sql`. You must place a file there for each version, even if it means having an empty file.

When installing version 0.0.1 for the first time, obviously only the install procedure is run. Joomla also adds a record to the database table `#__schemas` containing the ID of your extension (referring to the database table `#__extensions`) and the version of your plugin (`0.0.1`).
This step is omitted if your XML file does not include a `<update>` tag.

Here is a problem: When your first version 0.0.1 did not include the `<update>` section, the `#__schemas` table will not have an entry yet for your version 0.0.1. If you then upgrade to version 0.0.2, which has a valid `<update>` section, your plugin will be added to the `#__`

schemas table with that version 0.0.2. However, the SQL update in your `sql` folder (`sql/updates/mysql/0.0.2.sql`) will not be executed, because Joomla does not mark this as an actual schema update. Reinstalling version 0.0.2 again and again will not have any effect either. This is the reason why it is best to have schema files ready from the beginning unless you know your plugin is definitely not going to require its own SQL install queries.

Manually downgrading

To manually downgrade your plugin (for instance, when trying to test upgrades locally), modify the XML file of your plugin. Also make sure to modify the plugin entry in the database table `#__schemas`.

3.10 Executing custom scripts

You can also add a script that is executed every time this plugin is installed, uninstalled or upgraded. This script is simply added by using a `<scriptfile>` tag to the XML manifest, which refers to a PHP script:

```
<scriptfile>ch03test01.script.php</scriptfile>
```

The PHP script in turn needs to define a predefined class plus some methods. The classname should be `Plg` + group + name + `InstallerScript`, so in our case `PlgContentCh03test01InstallerScript`. There are five methods that can be used:

- `install(JAdapterInstance $adapter)`
- `update(JAdapterInstance $adapter)`
- `uninstall(JAdapterInstance $adapter)`
- `preflight(string $route, JAdapterInstance $adapter)`
- `postflight(string $route, JAdapterInstance $adapter)`

The methods `install()`, `update()` and `uninstall()` are executed during the actual install, update or uninstall of the plugin. When these methods fail, Joomla will perform a rollback of the action at hand. For instance, you can undo the installation of the plugin when some kind of system requirement is missing.

Instead of using `install()`, you can use the `preflight()` method. The main difference is that with `preflight()` the plugin files are not yet copied, while with `install()` the plugin files are already copied. So, use `preflight()` when there is a condition that has to be met, before your plugin can be installed. And use `install()` when you have some additional tasks to perform, while your plugin is being installed.

$adapter and $route arguments

Following the Joomla documentation the argument `$adapter` refers to the class
`JAdapterInstance`. As we are dealing with plugins here, it always refers to the class
`JInstallerPlugin`, which is a subclass of `JAdapterInstance`. The `$route`
argument contains the action being performed - either `install`, `uninstall` or
`discover_install`. As it only runs either before the installation of a plugin, or after the
installation of a plugin, it has no knowledge of whether a specific installation is an upgrade
or not. There is no `$route` with value `update`.

Overwriting changes

Be very careful with using `postflight()`. In general, it is not a good idea to return
`false` using this method, because it does not allow for a rollback of the extension install.
Worst case scenario, you are stuck with a plugin that did not install. Joomla does not allow
removing the plugin either, because the XML manifest cannot be found at this point.

To solve this, edit the XML code of your plugin code to include the argument
`method="upgrade"` in the `<extension>` tag. This instructs Joomla to override files if
they already exist and allows you to forcibly install the plugin.

```
<extension version="3.4" type="plugin"
    group="content" method="upgrade">
```

Example with plugin dependency

As an example, we take a new plugin `ch03test02` that uses the `preflight()` method
to check for the plugin `ch03test01`. If `ch03test01` is not available, the method returns
`false` and Joomla will not install anything.

```
class Plgcontentch03test02InstallerScript
{
    public function preflight($route, JAdapterInstance $adapter)
    {
        $folder = JPATH_SITE.'/plugins/content/ch03test01/';
        $file = $folder.'ch03test01.php';

        if (file_exists($file) == true)
        {
            return true;
        }
        JError::raiseNotice('warning', 'Install "Test 01" first');
        return false;
    }
}
```

3.11 **Dealing with updates**

Joomla offers a way to upgrade extensions from within the backend using the **Extension Manager**. When a new extension like a plugin is installed, it is able to add an update server, which is then inserted by Joomla into the Joomla database. This update server is queried by the **Extension Manager** to see if there are any updates for the extension. Enabling this feature requires various steps, which are explained here.

Step 1 – Making the package upgradable

First of all, we go back to the beginning. The `<extension>` tag that we started off with also has an extra attribute `method`, which defaults to the value `new` and which is better set to the value `upgrade` to allow Joomla to use this package for upgrades as well.

```
<extension version="3.4" type="plugin"
    group="content" method="upgrade">
```

This marks the package as an upgrade package and adds a flag to the Joomla installer saying that this package is allowed to override existing files. To be honest, using the value `new` does not prevent us from using the package as upgrade package. However, let's stick to conventions. Use `upgrade` to make your extension upgradable.

Hidden in the Joomla source, there is also another argument `overwrite` that can be set to `true` (`overwrite="true"`). However, that is not the recommended way for creating upgradable packages either.

Currently, there is no major difference between upgrading plugins or installing plugins, except that upgrading also allows for overwriting existing files. However, the Joomla architecture also allows for plugins to listen to installer events (discussed in chapter 11). There could be a plugin that does something different on an upgrade than on an install.

Step 2 – Defining the update server

The first step is to define the update server itself within the XML file of the plugin. Just add the following section to the bottom of your XML file, but still within the `<extension>` section.

```
<updateservers>
    <server type="extension" priority="1" name="Test 01">
        http://example.com/ch03test01_update.xml
    </server>
</updateservers>
```

Joomla needs to be able to contact the URL that you define to download the XML file. Other than that, the URL can be anything you want. It can be a static XML file. It can be a PHP script that is generating the required XML structure. However, it cannot be a redirect to another page.

Step 2 – The update server XML

The update server URL needs to return an XML structure defining the most recent version of your plugin and the location of the new download. Let's create the entire code for our XML file test01_update.xml first:

```xml
<?xml version="1.0" ?>
<updates>
    <update>
        <name>Chapter 03 / Test 01</name>
        <description>Example plugin</description>
        <element>ch03test01</element>
        <type>plugin</type>
        <folder>content</folder>
        <version>0.0.1</version>
        <infourl title="URL">
            http://example.com/plg_content_ch03test01
        </infourl>
        <downloads>
            <downloadurl type="full" format="zip">
                http://example.com/plg_content_ch03test01.zip
            </downloadurl>
        </downloads>
        <maintainer>Yireo</maintainer>
        <maintainerurl>http://www.yireo.com</maintainerurl>
        <tags>
            <tag>test01</tag>
        </tags>
        <targetplatform name="joomla" version="3.4" />
    </update>
</updates>
```

When comparing this ch03test01_update.xml to our original XML manifest ch03test01.xml, you can see that instead of the <extension> tag the <updates> tag is used. Various other tags can simply be copied, assuming that the writer of the plugin is the same person as the maintainer of the plugin:

ch03test01.xml	ch03test03_update.xml
`<version>`	`<version>`
`<author>`	`<maintainer>`
`<authorUrl>`	`<maintainerurl>`

For plugins, the `<element>` tag refers to the technical name again, while `<folder>` equals the group name (`system`, `authentication`, `content`, etc). It is important to take note of the tag `<targetplatform>`. The entire `<update>` section needs to specify one target platform. In the example above that is any Joomla 3.4 site.

There are multiple Joomla core versions available (2.5, 3.x). When your plugin works the same across all these versions, you still need to copy the entire `<update>` section and use different `<targetplatform>` tags in each section. The XML file becomes quite lengthy because of this. It will look a bit like the following. Note that I left out the main part of the `<update>` section:

```xml
<?xml version="1.0" ?>
<updates>
    <update>
        ...
        <targetplatform name="joomla" version="2.5" />
    </update>
    <update>
        ...
        <targetplatform name="joomla" version="3.0" />
    </update>
    <update>
        ...
        <targetplatform name="joomla" version="3.1" />
    </update>
    <update>
        ...
        <targetplatform name="joomla" version="3.2" />
    </update>
</updates>
```

There is a shortcut though: You can match multiple versions by using basic regular expressions. The following will match all Joomla 3 versions:

```xml
<targetplatform name="joomla" version="3.[0123456789]" />
```

Another note concerns the `<downloads>` section. Currently only the first `<downloadurl>` will be used by Joomla. It is best to use the format `zip`, because this is the most common archive type, but you can also use the format `tar`.

```
<downloadurl ... format="zip">
```

Support for multiple `<downloadurl>` types may be added to the Joomla core in the near future. The type can be `full` or `upgrade`. Currently, plugin packages are always full packages, you will set the type always to `full`. The value `upgrade` is only used for packages that contain only these files that are upgraded, and not all files.

```
<downloadurl type="full" ...>
```

Step 3 – Offering your users the download file

The last step is to offer the actual download file on your website. By making your plugin archive downloadable through the URL mentioned above, Joomla will be able to download and install this plugin once a new update is released and once the **Update** button is pushed within the **Extensions Manager**. Note that in order for this to work, Joomla needs to be running on a hosting environment with the PHP value `allow_url_fopen` enabled. The setting should be enabled with all hosters that have optimized their environment for Joomla.

Protecting your XML files from unwanted access

One last thing that does not necessarily belong in this book, but is an important tip anyway: The XML file contains important information on your plugin, such as the version. While this information is needed by Joomla, normally people can also use their browser to open up the file directly

```
http://example.com/plugins/content/ch03test01.xml
```

To prevent this unwanted access from happening, it is good practice to have a valid `.htaccess` file in place in the root of your Joomla site and the following section to it, if it is not already there:

```
# Do not allow access to XML files
<Files ~ "\.xml$">
    Order allow,deny
    Deny from all
    Satisfy all
</Files>
```

Any user agent that tries to inspect XML files (files ending with `.xml`) directly will be denied access through this rule.

This is a good security measure. However, it can also block access to some XML files that you actually want to be accessible. If you have for instance a `sitemap.xml` file that needs to be accessible by search robots, you can first block access to all XML files and then allow access again to this specific file using an additional rule:

```
# Do not allow access to XML files
<Files ~ "\.xml$">
    Order allow,deny
    Deny from all
    Satisfy all
</Files>

# Allow access to sitemap.xml
<Files ~ "sitemap\.xml$">
    Order allow,deny
    Allow from all
</Files>
```

3.12 Summary

This chapter was all about XML. We have seen how XML can be used to define the basic workings of a plugin. XML is also used to install all files and folders in the correct places, including media and language files. We did not stop there: We discussed how SQL statements can be added to your plugin installation and we have also seen how to implement an update server.

Additionally, within the XML manifest, you can define parameters. Chapter 4 will focus on the usage of those parameters, including the definition of new field types.

Plugin parameters

Within the XML manifest of a plugin, you can define parameters that can be modified by Joomla administrators via the Plugin Manager. This way you can offer administrators more control over the behavior of your plugin. This chapter covers the ins and outs of working with parameters.

4.1   Using parameters

Joomla offers a backend with many different configuration options in many different place. This allows for managers and administrators to easily configure things. It makes Joomla flexible. Each extension - component, module or plugin - can add additional **parameters** or **options**.

Parameters allow for basic configuration options of your plugin. For instance, in case your plugin relies on API credentials to be configured by the administrator, you can add input fields to the plugin's XML manifest. These input fields are then shown on the plugin's form in the Plugin Manager. Another example: If your plugin automatically corrects the article when it is being saved, you may want to add some plugin parameters, that allow the administrator to configure how the corrections should be made: Should the plugin automatically uppercase the first letter of the title, or not? Should the plugin trim whitespaces from the beginning and ending of the article text? By adding plugin parameters, you can allow the administrator to make these choices himself.

4.2   Defining parameters in XML

Within the XML manifest, parameters are added by using the `<config>` tag. Defining parameters for plugins is not very different from defining parameters in components or modules. If you are already familiar with that, plugin parameters will hold little surprise.

The example below shows a single fieldset named `basic` and an input field named `test`. The input field allows an administrator to save a value, which can later be reused within the PHP code of the plugin.

```
<extension>
    ...
   <config>
      <fields>
          <fieldset name="basic">
              <field
                  name="test"
                  type="text"
                  default="Hello World"
                  label="PLG_CONTENT_CH04TEST01_FIELD_TEST_LABEL"
                  description="PLG_CONTENT_CH04TEST01_FIELD_TEST_DESC"
              />
          </fieldset>
      </fields>
   </config>
</extension>
```

When an administrator uses the **Plugin Manager** to open up your plugin, the **Plugin Manager** will take this XML code and translate it automatically to a working HTML form in the parameters section of the editing screen.

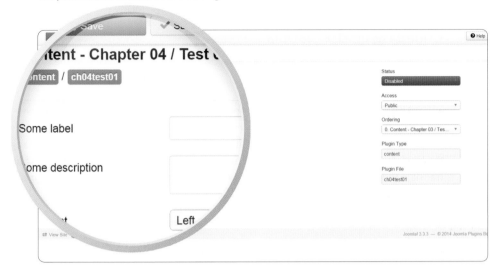

Our example has one fieldset with one input field inside that fieldset. Joomla allows you to add numerous fieldsets and numerous fields to forms. It even allows you to create your own field types. For instance, you can create a custom dropdown with custom values or some fancy JavaScript driven input method. We will deal with these field types later on in this chapter.

Translating XML strings

When translating strings like `PLG_CONTENT_CH04TEST01_FIELD_TEST_LABEL`, you can use both the file `en-GB.plg_content_ch04test01.sys.ini` (in short: the plugin's system file) and the file `en-GB.plg_content_ch04test01.ini` (in short: the plugin's frontend file). Which file to use depends on your strategy. As the frontend file is used for frontend translations of your plugin, you may be tempted to put all the XML strings in the system file instead, to prevent your form strings from being loaded in the frontend.

However, putting them in the system file will also load all of your XML strings on pages other than the plugin form, for instance the **Plugin Manager** overview. Both files will add strings to places where they are not needed. Which file to choose depends on how many XML strings you need to translate. Best advice is to just add the strings to the frontend file and use comments (lines starting with a semicolon) to bring structure.

```
; Strings for the plugins frontend behavior
...
; Strings for the plugins backend form
...
```

Changing fieldset labels

If you want to translate the label of the fieldset `basic`, you may notice that the example above is missing a `label` attribute:

```
<fieldset name="basic">
```

In this case, the fieldset is labeled automatically by the Joomla core. If you want to change the label value, the best way is to add a `label` attribute with your own `label` string and translate that string, as opposed to overriding the original `label` in your own plugin's frontend language file.

```
<fieldset name="basic"
    label="PLG_CONTENT_CH04TEST01_FIELDSET_BASIC_LABEL">
```

Plugins commonly have only two fieldsets (`basic` and `advanced`), which are labeled automatically by Joomla. You can also add your own fieldset, in which case the `label` is best set manually:

```
<fieldset name="customx"
    label="PLG_CONTENT_CH04TEST01_FIELDSET_CUSTOMX_LABEL">
```

If the label is omitted, the label will automatically be filled with the following value:

```
COM_PLUGINS_CUSTOMX_FIELDSET_LABEL
```

This language string actually belongs to the `com_plugins` component. You can still translate the string though in your own plugin's language file, but it simply looks less preferred because it does not include your own plugin prefix `PLG_CONTENT_CH04TEST01`.

Where and how is it stored?

When you save the plugin parameters within the **Plugin Manager**, the values are stored in the database table `#__extensions`. The database row of your plugin contains a field `params`, which contains the parameters stored in JSON format. Whenever the plugin is loaded from the database, its parameters are decoded from JSON into a `JRegistry` object and attached to the plugin object. This is all done automatically. You do not need to worry about it.

4.3 More field types

Just like within an HTML form, you can specify various field types. The most common field types are:

- Generic textfield (type `text`)
- Textbox (type `textarea`)
- Dropdown (type `list`)
- Radio boxes (type `radio`).

There are also more advanced field types like `calendar` (JavaScript driven popup), `combo` (an input field and dropdown at the same time), `color` (a popup color chooser), some alternatives to the normal input box but including extra validation (`email`, `password`) and much much more.

The example code of the `plg_content_ch04test01` plugin contains various examples of these form fields, including the type `sql` that performs a custom query. The code is available on GitHub. Go to **https://github.com/yireo/JoomlaPluginsBook**. The XML file can be located in **chapter04 > plg_content_ch04test01 > plugins > content > ch04test01 > ch04test01.xml**.

A simple dropdown

A dropdown is created using a field of type `list`. Just as in HTML code, you can add `<option>` tags as child elements to create values in the dropdown.

```
<field
    name="apply_color"
    type="list"
    default="1"
    label="PLG_CONTENT_CH04TEST01_FIELD_APPLYCOLOR_LABEL"
    description="PLG_CONTENT_CH04TEST01_FIELD_APPLYCOLOR_DESC"
>
    <option value="0">JNO</option>
    <option value="1">JYES</option>
</field>
```

If you create a dropdown, you can translate the options again by using your own language strings. In the case of a yes/no dropdown, use the Joomla core language strings `JNO` and `JYES`.

A color selector

Joomla also comes with a simple color selector. Use `color` as type and you are done.

```
<field
    name="color"
    type="color"
    default="#ffffff"
    label="PLG_CONTENT_CH04TEST01_FIELD_COLOR_LABEL"
    description="PLG_CONTENT_CH04TEST01_FIELD_COLOR_DESC"
/>
```

 Documentation on which field types are available can be found online:
http://docs.joomla.org/Standard_form_field_types

4.4 Using plugin parameters in PHP

 In this chapter, we use a clone of the `plg_content_ch03test01` which was used in chapter 3. The plugin is now named `plg_content_ch04test01`.

Once the parameter value is saved in the plugin's settings, it is time to make use of this parameter value in our code. In our plugin `plg_content_ch03test01`, the **Content Plugin** contained a function `onContentBeforeDisplay()` that was modifying articles by adding a variable `$test` to it. This `$test` value was translated using the language file. We will rewrite this plugin and now use the value of a plugin parameter instead.

Within the plugin class `PlgContentCh04test01`, we can use the `$this->params` object to reference the plugin parameters. This object is of type `JRegistry` and it contains a simple `get()` method with the name of the parameter as first argument.

```
public function onContentBeforeDisplay(
    $context, &$row, &$params, $page = 0
)
{
    $test = $this->params->get('test');
    $row->title = $row->title . ' [' . $test . ']';
    $row->text = $row->text . '<p>[' . $test . ']</p>';
}
```

Setting a default value

The get() method also has an optional second argument, which sets the default value for the parameter. Let's say that we never want the parameter value to be empty, because that would break our logic. One approach is to configure the parameter to be a required parameter, by adding the required argument to the XML manifest. However, when a Joomla Super User installs and enables the plugin, there is no guarantee yet that he actually opened up the plugin form and stored the parameters using that form. The parameter can still be empty.

If you want the parameter to have a default value, give the get() method a second argument as follows:

```
$message = $this->params->get('message', 'Hello World');
```

A quick word on JParameter and JRegistry

In previous versions of Joomla, plugin parameters and other parameters were handled through the class JParameter. However, JParameter has become deprecated and should no longer be used. It will be removed from the Joomla core in the future. Instead, the $this->params variable is now an instance of the class JRegistry, which makes it possible to store the parameter values as JSON data in the database.

The difference between $params and $this->params

This specific event method onContentBeforeDisplay() has four arguments – these arguments have been discussed briefly in chapter 1. The third argument is $params, which behaves in a similar way as $this->params: Both are JRegistry objects. However, the $this->params object contains the plugin parameters as managed through the **Plugin Manager**, whereas the $params object contains content parameters that belong to that content type. For instance, article parameters as managed through the **Article Manager**.

Security checks for parameters

Parameter values are stored in the Joomla database. Perhaps, you think the Joomla database can be considered secure enough to read values from, however opinions differ. With some security guidelines, everything that is not generated by the PHP code itself, should be considered external and therefore insecure. This includes input from a POST request (a form submission) or GET request (URL parameters), but also sources like the session and the database.

Imagine you have a plugin parameter that is expected to be an integer:

```
$integer = $this->params->get('integer');
```

Now imagine the database has been hijacked by some evil person through an SQL injection attack. The value stored for this parameter may not be an integer at all. To make sure your plugin behaves exactly like it should be, you can add a simple integer conversion to bypass this:

```
$integer = (int) $this->params->get('integer');
```

Similarly, if you have a parameter value that is stored through a dropdown box, you can check again to make sure that the value is part of the actual list. In the example below, the color can never be **green**:

```
$value = $this->params->get('color');

if (in_array($value, array('yellow', 'red', 'blue')) == FALSE)
{
    $value = 'yellow';
}
```

Once you are coding, make sure you code with maximum security in mind. When a hacker has found an exploit through SQL injection, there is a chance this hacker has also gained access to the file level somehow. This would mean any PHP code is compromised. Even though this may not be the case, you do not want to run the risk that one security breach leads to another.

Comma separated or newline separated values

The **Plugin Manager** only allows you to save one value per parameter. It takes a workaround to save multiple values for one parameter. For instance, what if you ask the admin to enter a list of colors, allowing for any value. A common approach is to create a textbox (type `textarea`) in which the colors can then be inserted as a CSV list, each color being separated by commas:

```
green,yellow, #ffcc00, #000,
```

The saved parameter can then be turned into an array using the `explode()` function:

```
$list = $this->params->get('list_from_textarea');
$list = explode(',', $list);
```

Never trust the user input completely though. If an admin creates a CSV list with values, that list can easily contain white spaces and newlines that should be filtered out. Also empty values should be removed. A little bit of extra code will fix this:

```
foreach ($list as $index => $value)
{
    $value = trim($value);

    if (empty($value))
    {
        unset($list[$index]);
        continue;
    }

    $list[$index] = $value;
}
```

Multiple select

If the input values are preset and not custom defined, it is easier to create a dropdown that allows for selecting multiple values instead of creating a textarea. This can easily be accomplished by adding a `multiple` argument to a field of type `list`:

```
<field
    name="letters"
    type="list"
    size="7"
    multiple="true"
    default=""
    label="PLG_CONTENT_CH04TEST01_FIELD_LETTERS_LABEL"
    description="PLG_CONTENT_CH04TEST01_FIELD_LETTERS_DESC"
>
    <option value="a">a</option>
    <option value="b">b</option>
    <option value="c">c</option>
</field>
```

The example above requires you to manually define all 26 characters of the alphabet (if you are using the western alphabet that is), which is a one-time job only. Creating all `<option>` elements by hand is not a large job.

If the option list needs to be created dynamically, you may want to opt for creating your own field type. This way you can make it easy for your users to configure the field properly, while still making sure no errors are made.

4.5 Defining new field types

Parameters in Joomla are based on the `JForm` library, which contains a set of classes, that offer an object oriented approach for creating and validating forms. The library allows you to add an HTML form quickly without worrying about its appearance: The `JForm` class will render the XML code automatically to Joomla compliant HTML and it also takes care of form validation (based upon validation rules).

In the case of the `Plugin Manager`, you do not need to worry about either the rendering part or the validation part. The only thing you do is add XML code and the **Plugin Manager** takes care of the rest.

In addition to existing field types, you can add new field types to your plugin by writing your own `JForm` based classes and adding them to your form. When, for instance, you want a dropdown list with custom options but the static `<option>` fields are too limiting.

For this example of creating new field types, we will create a plugin `plg_content_ch04test02` of which the source can be viewed in the folder **chapter04** through the repository URL **https://github.com/yireo/JoomlaPluginsBook**.

XML options

To show you how this works, we are going to create a new field type called `testselect` (a name which is not conflicting with other field type names). For this new field type, we will need to create a corresponding class `JFormFieldTestselect` that will sit inside the folder `fields` in the plugin folder.

When we are done, we will be able to invoke our new field type like this:

```
<field type="testselect" ... />
```

First, the folder containing your field classes should be added to the XML manifest `ch05test02.xml` like this:

```
<config>
    <fields name="params">
        <fieldset
```

```
            name="basic"
            addfieldpath="plugins/content/ch05test02/fields">
        ...
        </fieldset>
    </fields>
</config>
```

The addfieldpath argument ensures that the JForm library will search your folder fields for field types when constructing the form. We will discuss this addfieldpath argument later in this chapter.

Dropdown with automatic options

Let's define our field type testselect. Our objective is to create a select field. However, without the <option> tags: We want to add them programmatically. We define the field as we would with a field of type text, but now using the type testselect:

```
<field
    name="test"
    type="testselect"
    default="1"
    label="PLG_CONTENT_CH04TEST02_FIELD_TEST_LABEL"
    description="PLG_CONTENT_CH04TEST02_FIELD_TEST_DESC"
/>
```

Within the folder plugins/content/ch04test02/fields, we will create a file testselect.php and add thecode below to it.

```
<?php
defined('_JEXEC') or die();

jimport('joomla.form.formfield');

class JFormFieldTestselect extends JFormField
{
    protected $type = 'Testselect';

    protected function getInput()
    {
        return '';
    }
}
```

The `jimport()` function is used to load the parent class `JFormField`. With later Joomla versions, `jimport()` is not even needed. See chapter 13 for an explanation.

Next, we create a new class `JFormFieldTestselect` that extends this parent class. Within our new field class, a `$type` variable contains the name of the field class (in this case`JFormFieldTestselect`) minus the `JFormField` part: `Testselect`. The real magic lies within the `getInput()` method: The `getInput()` method returns the proper HTML code for the form.

To create a dropdown list, we can add the following code to the `getInput()` method:

```php
protected function getInput()
{
    $options = array();
    $options[] = JHtml::_('select.option', 'sample01',
        JText::_('JFORM_FIELDTYPE_TESTSELECT_SAMPLE01'),
        'value', 'text'
    );
    $options[] = JHtml::_('select.option', 'sample02',
        JText::_('JFORM_FIELDTYPE_TESTSELECT_SAMPLE02'),
        'value', 'text'
    );


    return JHtml::_('select.genericlist', $options,
        $this->name, 'class="inputbox"', 'value', 'text',
        $this->value, $this->name
    );
}
```

We could have directly outputted HTML code, but instead, we use the `JHtml` class to generate the `<option>` tags and the `<select>` tags that contains them. The variables `$this->name` and `$this->value` are used to add the correct attributes to the form element.

The language strings are added to the plugin's frontend language file.

```
JFORM_FIELDTYPE_TESTSELECT_SAMPLE01="Sample 01"
JFORM_FIELDTYPE_TESTSELECT_SAMPLE02="Sample 02"
```

Fetching the values from the database

Instead of using a static list in PHP, we can take this a step further by performing a database query to get these values from a specific database table. We are using the

JFactory::getDbo() method to fetch the database instance that connects to the actual database. To maintain compatibility with different databases (MySQL, PostgreSQL, Microsoft SQL), we do not write direct queries but use an object oriented approach instead.

```
protected function getInput()
{
    $db = JFactory::getDbo();

    $query = $db->getQuery(true);
    $query->select($db->quoteName(array('w.url', 'w.title')));
    $query->from($db->quoteName('#__weblinks', 'w'));
    $query->where($db->quoteName('w.approved').' = 1');
    $query->order($db->quoteName('w.title'));

    $db->setQuery($query);

    $options = array();
    $rows = $db->loadObjectList();

    if (!empty($rows))
    {
        foreach ($rows as $row)
        {
            $options[] = JHtml::_('select.option', $row->url,
                $row->title, 'value', 'text'
            );
        }
    }

    $attribs = 'class="inputbox"';

    return JHtml::_('select.genericlist', $options,
        $this->name, $attribs, 'value', 'text',
        $this->value, $this->name
    );
}
```

The example creates a select box from the #__weblinks table, allowing you to choose a weblinks URL by selecting its title.

Reading XML field arguments

To make your field type more useful to third party developers, you may want to support additional XML arguments that can be set in the form XML. For instance, you may want to make it possible to switch your select from a single select to a multiselect. To do this we add some arguments to the XML:

```
<input type="testselect" multiple="1" size="10" />
```

The `multiple` argument defaults to 0 (`false`), however by changing it to 1 (`true`) we can enable the multiselect behavior which follows below.

The argument `size` does nothing by default. When `multiple` is `true` however, the `size` argument is used to determine the size of the multiselect box. If the size is smaller than 3, it will be ignored and the size will be set to 3. If the size is larger than or equal to 3, the size will be equal to the amount of options available.

```
$multiple = 0;
$size = 3;

if (isset($this->element['multiple'])
{
    $multiple = (bool) $this->element['multiple'];
}

if (isset($this->element['size']))
{
    $size = (int) $this->element['size'];
    if ($size < 3) $size = 3;
}
```

Now that the variables are prepared, we can add them to the dropdown attributes. We do this by adding a fourth argument to the `JHtml::_('select.genericlist')` call, which allows us to add additional HTML attributes to the `select` element. We now dynamically construct these attributes as a variable `$attribs`, in order forthe HTML attributes to change depending on the given XML arguments.

```
$attribs = 'class="inputbox"';

if ($multiple == true)
{
    $attribs .= ' multiple="multiple"';
}

if ($size > 0)
{
    $attribs .= ' size="' . $size . '"';
}
```

```
return JHtml::_('select.genericlist', $options,
    $this->name, $attribs, 'value', 'text',
    $this->value, $this->name
;
```

Using multiple fieldpaths in one XML manifest

In the earlier example the `addfieldpath` attribute is added to the `<fieldset>` tag. This makes our custom field type `testselect` accessible to `JForm` and usable in our form definition. However, it does not mean that this field type is only limited to that fieldset. The field type can be reused again in the `advanced` fieldset as well. The `addfieldpath` attribute is just a way of instructing the `JForm` library to look into your folder when searching for field types. However, because the entire `JForm` class is used to render the entire form, that instruction is valid throughout the form. This is shown in the following example:

```
<fieldset name="basic"
    addfieldpath="plugins/content/ch04test01/fields">
</fieldset>
<fieldset name="advanced">
    <field type="testselect" ... />
</fieldset>
```

You cannot apply more than one `addfieldpath` attribute to one single tag. That is not how XML works. The following will only add the first and not the second path:

```
<fieldset addfieldpath="path1" addfieldpath="path2" ...
```

To add multiple paths anyway, you can add one path to the `<fields>` tag and a second path to the `<fieldset>`. You can even add the required path to the `<field>` tag that actually needs it:

```
<config>
    <fields addfieldpath="path1" ...
        <fieldset addfieldpath="path2" ...
            <field addfieldpath="path3" ...
```

When the `addfieldpath` argument is applied to add a new path to the `JForm` library, the new path will be added at the end of the path listing. When you try to override a field type that already exists in the core, it is best to introduce your own path as early as possible in the Joomla boot procedure - for instance through a System Plugin with the event `onAfterInitalise`:

```
JFormHelper::addFieldPath($path);
```

The usage of System Plugins and the event method `onAfterInitalise()` is explained in chapter 6. See chapter 12 for an explanation of the Joomla boot procedure.

What if the field type cannot be located?

If the Joomla XML field type cannot be located by the `JForm` library and is therefore unknown, the type will default to the type `text`:

```
<field type="unknown" ... />
```

The field XML above would translate into HTML like below:

```
<input type="text" ... />
```

4.6 Summary

In this chapter, we have discussed plugin parameters: How to define them in the XML manifest and how to use them in your plugin logic. We have also seen how you can add new field types using the `JForm` library. Using the knowledge of these first four chapters, you can now write a plugin, complete with installation steps, update procedure and custom forms. It does not focus on a specific scenario though.

Now, it is time to dive into the specifics by discussing the various plugin types. We will start with Content Plugins in the next chapter.

5

Content Plugins

In the previous chapters we created the basic code for a Content Plugin. But what is a Content Plugin exactly and how can we write a real life Content Plugin? That is the topic of this chapter. We will discuss the common use of Content Plugins, as well as all the available events.

5.1   Introducing content plugins

The Joomla CMS is all about content. When dealing with content there are various tasks that can be performed using Content Plugins. When an article is being created, a Content Plugin allows you to modify that article just before its values are stored in the Joomla database. Similarly, when an article is loaded from the database to be shown in either the backend or the frontend, a Content Plugin can be used to alter that article in various ways. A Content Plugin can even be used to modify the editing form of the article!

When you speak of Joomla content, the first thing that comes to mind are Joomla articles. However, there is much more content that can be dealt with: weblinks, contacts and content from third party extensions (**K2**, **ZOO** and others) – the list goes on and on. Joomla itself aims to make the plugin events of Content Plugins work on the various core components - the articles component being the main focus. For third party extensions things become a bit more complicated. This will be discussed at the end of this chapter. Let's start with the basics first.

5.2   Plugin events

The following events are available in the Joomla core (in alphabetical order):

```
onContentAfterDelete
onContentAfterDisplay
onContentAfterSave
onContentAfterTitle
onContentBeforeDelete
onContentBeforeDisplay
onContentBeforeSave
onContentChangeState
onContentPrepare
onContentPrepareForm
```

5.3   When are these content events thrown?

When writing a plugin to react on a certain event, it is vital to know when this event is thrown. Unfortunately there is no solid standard to find out when an event is generated. Some of these events are available on the frontend, some are available on the backend. It is the component code that decides if and when events are used. The main component com_ content offers a lot of these event handles, but many other components do not.

One of the concepts the Joomla project is working on is a generic way for extensions to handle content. For instance, the title of a weblink should be handled in the same way a title of an article is being handled. The working name of this concept is **Unified Content**

Model (UCM). While it can be debated whether UCM will ever be fully implemented in the Joomla core, parts of it have made their way into the Joomla core already. It can have a great impact as well on the usage of Content Plugins. We will discuss UCM in more detail at the end of this chapter.

Scanning the code

There is no standardization yet. The best way to find out whether a specific component is throwing a specific event is to read the component code. The code will make use of the `JDispatcher` class to trigger a specific event - the details of this will be explained in chapter 11. Another method is to search for the name of the event itself - for instance `onContentAfterTitle`. Chapter 13 will give you more tips on how to scan the code.

The com_content component code

As an example, let's scan the code of the `com_content` component. By searching for the word `trigger` you can find a lot of instances of the `JDispatcher` class triggering events. In the case of the `com_content` frontend (folder `components/com_content`), you will find that the events are thrown in the `view.html.php` files of each view (`featured`, `article`, `category`).

For example, take a look at the file `components/com_content/views/article/view.html.php` to view the definition of these four events:

```
onContentPrepare($context, &$row, &$params, $page = 0)
onContentAfterTitle($context, &$row, &$params, $page = 0)
onContentBeforeDisplay($context, &$row, &$params, $page = 0)
onContentAfterDisplay($context, &$row, &$params, $page = 0)
```

Strangely enough, the parameters of these four events are exactly the same. Moreover, the events are thrown right after each other, line after line. In other words, when you want to modify the article title (part of `$row`), any of these four events will allow you to accomplish this.

The following is an example, which works fine, however it violates standards:

```
public function onContentAfterDisplay(
    $context, &$row, &$params, $page = 0
)
{
    // Bad example
    $row->title = $row->title . ' [test]';
}
```

Obviously, this is a bad example: This is not how this event was intended to work. Only the onContentPrepare event is supposed to modify the $row object. The other three methods (onContentAfterTitle, onContentBeforeDisplay, onContentAfterDisplay) are supposed to return a specific value (HTML code) that is appended to the $row object. For instance, the output of onContentAfterTitle is added to a property $item->event->afterDisplayTitle. This $item->event->afterDisplayTitle property is then used in the template file default.php for output.

It is all about sticking to the standards. Even though these standards may not always be documented, common sense still shows which event should be used for which purpose. Definitely, the event onContentAfterDisplay() is not supposed to be modifying the original content. Content cannot be modified after it is being displayed (in theory). The event onContentPrepare should be used instead.

Template overrides can stop these events from functioning

The onContentPrepare() method will always have the desired effect. The $row object is directly modified. However, the other three methods only append their additional properties to the object $row and they require the template file (tmpl/default.php) to display these additional properties.

In the template file, the $row is referred to as $this->item and after running the event onContentAfterDisplay it now has a property event->afterDisplayTitle:

```php
<?php  if (!$params->get('show_intro')) :
    echo $this->item->event->afterDisplayTitle;
endif; ?>
```

If the template file default.php is overridden by a Joomla template with an override folder html/com_content/article/default.php, then it may result in the $item->event->afterDisplayTitle property not being used in this override.

Make sure to check your template periodically, to ensure the overrides still live up to the latest standards and contain all required code.

Backend components based on JModelAdmin

When creating your own component, the common standard is to use the MVC architecture. It gives your component a lot of features simply by implementing it (like sublinks based on each view, template overrides, etc). Under Joomla 1.5, you would create a model class that extended JModel, a view class that extended JView and a controller class that extended JController.

With later Joomla versions, new subclasses were added to Joomla, allowing you to automate more things - for instance, your model can extend `JModelAdmin` - automating the various batch methods in your overviews; applying ACL rules; saving data.

Extending from the `JModelAdmin` class gives you the benefit of applying the following events automatically:

```
onContentAfterDelete
onContentAfterSave
onContentBeforeDelete
onContentBeforeSave
onContentChangeState
```

With Joomla 3, the usage of both `JModel` and `JModelAdmin` changed. The class `JModel` is an interface, which allows you to implement its behavior but not extend from it. The class `JModelAdmin` is an abstract class and is now placed in the `/libraries/legacy` folder, suggesting that its usage is again deprecated. The `JModelLegacy` class is now a copy of the original (non-interface) version of `JModel`. It is only meant as an intermediate solution.

The `Legacy` suffix indicates that the class may be removed from the core one day. At the time of writing it is uncertain how future Joomla versions will deal with these parent classes. Therefore, it is also uncertain how plugin events will apply to components that use these parent classes in the future.

Framework on Framework (FoF) events

With Joomla 3.2, the **Framework-on-Framework** (or **FoF**) library written by Nikolas Dionysopoulos has been added to the core. FoF is, as the name itself suggests, an extended version of the Joomla framework itself. It allows developers to quickly setup an MVC component with lots of functionality but a minimum of code.

This is accomplished by offering a set of parent classes from which your own classes can extend, similar to the original `JModel` classes. The model parent `FOFModel` for instance contains most of the functionality you need, when writing a standard model class in a standard MVC component. There is no need to write your own **CRUD** methods (Create, Read, Update, Delete). If you stick to the correct database structure, the generic `FOFModel` methods will do all the work for you.

This includes event handling. For example, the method `FOFModel::delete()` triggers the events `onBeforeDelete()` and `onAfterDelete()` automatically. In other words, any component that is based upon FoF, automatically supports content events without requiring any additional code. This is why FoF is referred to as a **Rapid Application Development** (RAD) framework. It allows you to build Joomla applications quickly, because the generic methods of the various FoF classes do all the heavy lifting.

FoF events are beyond the scope of this book.

What is included in those plugin event parameters?

Looking at the Joomla content events, you can see that most content events take the same parameters: a variable $context, then a variable $row, then a variable $params. Optionally, a variable $page.

```
onContentPrepare($context, &$row, &$params, $page = 0)
```

The first variable $context indicates in which part of the Joomla application the event is triggered. For instance, when an article form is being handled, the context may be set to com_content.form. Checking for the correct $context may be vital to your plugin. If your plugin should only work for article forms and not weblink forms, you can add an if-else statement in your plugin to make sure that the $context is set to com_content.form and otherwise just return true. Later in this chapter I will give you some examples, that show you how to do this.

Some $context values found in the core are:

```
com_content.article
com_content.category
com_content.form
com_categories.category
com_finder.indexer
```

The list of $context values is much larger. Instead of listing everything, it is much more worthwhile to scan the Joomla source code for the event you want to implement, and see what $context is being used for that event.

The second argument – often named $row or $item – contains the content that is handled. Often, this object equals an article. However, it may be a different content type as well: category, weblink, etc. The $row or $item is a simple object with basic properties and in most cases it is derived from the database using methods like $db->loadObject() and $db->loadObjectList().

A quick way to check what properties belong to the content object is to browse the database table. In some cases, like with articles, the content object also has a getProperties() method (inherited from JObject), but this is not always the case. To guarantee that all content plugins can handle all content types in a generic way, an object is expected to have a title, an alias and a text. These fields are not required though. When you inspect the #__content table you will learn that an article does not have a text field, it has an introtext field and a fulltext field. Within the com_ `content` component this difference is overcome by copying either the `introtext` or the `fulltext` or the concatenation of the two to a new property `text`. Note that the events still allow for handling the `introtext` and `fulltext` properties. However, to make your plugin compatible with all types of content, it is best to use a `text` property as the primary text field.

The `$params` argument contains the parameters belonging to the content: an object of type `JRegistry` with a `get()` method, just like we have seen in the previous chapter on plugin parameters. To learn which parameters are contained in a `$params` object, you can create a plugin, add an event method to it and debug the `$params` object on screen:

```
public function onContentBeforeDisplay(
    $context, &$row, &$params, $page = 0
)
{
    echo '<pre>';
    echo __FILE__ . ' [' . __LINE__ . '] ';
    print_r($params->toArray());
    echo '</pre>';
}
```

The `JRegistry::toArray()` method gives you a clean array containing all parameter fields. If the parameters contain a field `show_title`, you can use this field within the plugin as follows:

```
$show_title = $params->get('show_title');
```

5.4 Adding your own fields to com_content

Let's say we want to add some custom fields to articles. We could create a separate component for managing these fields, but instead, we will create a plugin that will add our fields to the existing article form in the Joomla backend.

Ingredients

For this to work, we will need to write a plugin that catches the event `onContentPrepareForm`, in order for us to extend the `JForm` object that generates the article form. With the correct code to extend this form, our input fields will be added to some fieldset and will show up on the **Article Edit** page.

But, when the `com_content` component saves this form, it will not know to do anything with our field input. The posted values will simply be disregarded. To fix this, we can make our extra fields part of the fieldset `params`, so that our values are automatically stored in the `params` field of the `#__content` table.

```
params[extra1]
params[extra2]
```

For the purpose of exercise, we are going to make it a bit more challenging though. There is yet another way in which we can intercept the values of our new fields: We can use the `onContentAfterSave` event to extract the new field values from the POST data and store it in our own separate database table. This gives us more flexibility when deciding what should be stored where. So, the event method `onContentAfterSave()` will also be implemented in our plugin.

Whenever an article is being saved, there should be also be the option to delete it. When the article is removed, we also have to clean up our additional fields in these tables. For this, we will use the `onContentAfterDelete` event.

Last but not least, we want to display our own stored field values on each article page in the Joomla frontend. This is where the event `onContentBeforeDisplay` comes to the rescue.

In total we will need a Content Plugin with four events:

```
onContentPrepareForm
onContentAfterSave
onContentAfterDelete
onContentBeforeDisplay
```

Starting with a new plugin

Following the steps explained in chapter 2, you can now create a new plugin together with its own folder, basic PHP class and XML file. Next, in your PHP class, create the four event methods in your plugin class:

```php
public function onContentPrepareForm(
    $form, $data
)
{
}

public function onContentAfterSave(
    $context, $article, $isNew
)
{
}
```

```
public function onContentAfterDelete(
    $context, $article
)
{
}

public function onContentBeforeDisplay(
    $context, &$row, &$params, $page = 0
)
{
}
```

 The source code of this example can be found online in the GitHub repository **https://github.com/yireo/JoomlaPluginsBook** in the subfolder **chapter05/plg_content_ch05test01**.

Adding form data using onContentPrepareForm()

First, we will add our fields to the article form using the method onContentPrepareForm(). The method has two arguments. The first argument $form contains an instance of the JForm class, offering an object oriented way of modifying forms before they are being displayed.
The second argument $data contains the form data - we will deal with this later.

It is a good idea to make sure that the $form argument is indeed a JForm object. If the $form variable is an array for some reason, we will not be able to modify it. The onContentPrepareForm() method should return true, if the form is to be rendered properly. In the case that $form is not a JForm object, continuing to render that form does not make sense. So when $form is not a JForm, we make sure to return false.

```
public function onContentPrepareForm($form, $data)
{
    if (!($form instanceof JForm))
    {
        $this->_subject->setError('JERROR_NOT_A_FORM');
        return false;
    }
    ...
}
```

The Joomla application contains many forms that are based on JForm and all of these can be modified through this method. You can imagine how powerful this really is. In our case, we only want to modify the article edit form, so we need to check for the name of the article form first. This is similar to checking for the correct `$context` with other event methods. However, the `onContentPrepareForm` event does not have such a `$context` argument:

```
$name = $form->getName();

if (!in_array($name, array('com_content.article')))
{
    return true;
}
```

Next, we are going to add our own fields. While the `JForm` API has some ways to do this entirely through PHP code, it is easier to simply define your own form in a separate XML form and merge this XML form with the existing `JForm` object. Let's create a simple `form.xml` file:

```xml
<?xml version="1.0" encoding="utf-8"?>
<form>
    <fields>
        <fieldset name="jmetadata">
            <field
                name="test"
                type="text"
                label="PLG_CONTENT_CH05TEST01_FIELD_TEST_LABEL"
                description="PLG_CONTENT_CH05TEST01_FIELD_TEST_DESC"
            />
        </fieldset>
    </fields>
</form>
```

This XML file defines a single field `test` within a fieldset `jmetadata`. You may be tempted

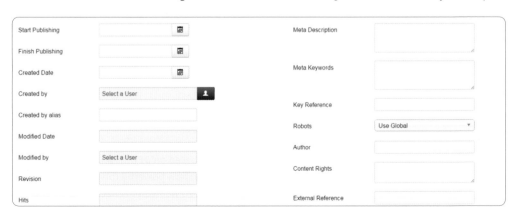

to place this `form.xml` file directly within your plugins folder. Do not do that. If you do, the Joomla **Extension Manager** will mistake this XML file for a manifest file for a new extension, even though the manifest is incomplete. A warning in the backend is the result. Instead, create a subfolder `form` within your plugin folder and create the `form.xml` in that folder.

Now that the XML file is in place (`form/form.xml` within the plugin's folder), we can add a `JForm` call to load that XML file and add its contents to the current form:

```
JForm::addFormPath(__DIR__ . '/form');
$form->loadFile('form');
return true;
```

The `$form->loadFile()` call has an interesting parameter `$reset`. This defaults to `true` and indicates whether a newly imported form field can overwrite an already existing form field or not. In our case, the metadata fieldset of the article form already contains a field **Meta Description (meta_description)**. If we would add the same field `meta_description` to our own `form.xml` and for instance change the type from `textarea` to `text`, then the `$reset` flag can be used to determine whether this is allowed or not.

```
$reset = true;
$form->loadFile('form', $reset);
```

If our plugin is installed and enabled using the **Extension Manager**, you should be able to see a change in the article form. When you open an article, the **Publishing** tab should now list our field as part of the **Meta Data** fieldset.

Adding a field to different fieldsets

What about adding our field to other fieldsets? We can change the XML to move the new field to the **Options** tab as well:

```xml
<?xml version="1.0" encoding="utf-8"?>
<form>
    <fields>
        <fieldset name="basic">
            <field
                name="test"
                type="text"
                label="PLG_CONTENT_CH01TEST01_FIELD_TEST_LABEL"
                description="PLG_CONTENT_CH01TEST01_FIELD_TEST_DESC"
            />
        </fieldset>
    </fields>
</form>
```

Which fieldset should be used depends on how the form is rendered by the layout. If the layout file is automatically generating each field for each fieldset, then adding new fields will work just fine. However, if the layout file adds each field manually, our new field will not be added. For instance, if we set the fieldset to advanced, our field will never be shown, because the core's layout file for the article form manually adds each field.

Adding a field to different field groups

There are some interesting things to be said on the `<fields>` tag. A `name` attribute can be added to this tag to indicate a group of fields:

```
<fields name="example">
    <fieldset>
        <field ...
```

If our test field is placed within a fieldset within this fields group, the POST name of this field is no longer `test`, but `example[test]`. The HTML element will look like this:

```
<input name="example[test]" ...
```

This already happens with all of the fields under the tab **Options**. The article component loads these fields as part of the field group `attribs`, and because of this, all values are posted back to the `com_content` controller in an array `attribs[]`. This array is again saved as JSON-encoded string in the `attribs` field of #___content table.

As mentioned earlier, if we would add our value to this array `attribs[test]`, it will be saved automatically to the database without any additional steps:

```
<?xml version="1.0" encoding="utf-8"?>
<form>
    <fields name="attribs">
        <fieldset name="basic">
            <field
                name="test"
                type="text"
                label="PLG_CONTENT_TEST05_FIELD_TEST_LABEL"
                description="PLG_CONTENT_TEST05_FIELD_TEST_DESC"
            />
        </fieldset>
    </fields>
</form>
```

If you only have a few fields to add, this is definitely the easiest way to add things. In our example, we will be adding values to our own table instead.

Saving the data

If our field is added to a new fieldset `example`, in order for our field to become `example[test]`, we can submit the form and the POST will include the value of this new field. However, if we do not do anything with the new value, it is useless. A new plugin method is needed to pickup this value and deal with it:

```
public function onContentAfterSave($context, $article, $isNew)
{
    if ($context != 'com_content.article')
    {
        return true;
    }
    ...
    return true;
}
```

The `$context` argument gives a clue on where we are in the Joomla application. We want to make sure this event is only being loaded when the article is being saved, so the `$context` is checked to be `com_content.article`. If this is not the case, we return true.

We always return `true` in this method. It seems logical to do this. Whatever happens, the article is always still saved. If we would return `false`, it will not change anything in the saving process of the article, because the event `onContentAfterSave` is generated after the article has been saved.

Now that we are able to hook into the event of an article being saved to the database, we are going to inspect the POST request and get our own value from it. For this we use the `JFactory::getApplication()->input` call, which gives us a reference to `JInput`. With this class, we first extract the `jform` array from the POST, and within that array we try to find our `test` field value. If the `jform` value is not an array, or if our `test` field value is not set, there is no need to continue, so we return `true`. If the `test` field value is set but empty, we still use it – it is only that no value was entered by the user or the previous value was emptied.

```
$jinput = JFactory::getApplication()->input;
$form = $jinput->post->get('jform', null, 'array');

if (is_array($form) && isset($form['test']))
{
    $test = $form['test'];
}
else
{
```

```
        return true;
}
```

To save the data, we are going to use a very simple database table #__test, which consists only of three columns: a content ID (an article ID), the $context string and the value of our test field. If you implement this plugin for articles only, the context column is not needed. However, it seems like a good idea to create this plugin in such a way that it will also work for other content types.

The CREATE statement looks as follows:

```
CREATE TABLE `#__test` (
    `content_id` int(11) NOT NULL,
    `context` varchar(50) NOT NULL,
    `test` varchar(255) NOT NULL
)
```

For every article, we insert a new row into our new table with the ID of the article and the posted value. When we run this plugin, we do not know whether a row for the current article already exists. Our logic will be to first perform a tiny SELECT query to see whether the row exists. If it does exist, an UPDATE query will follow. If it does not exist, an INSERT query will follow.

More and more code is being added at this point, and to keep things readable, we are going to introduce a new method saveTest() into our plugin class. This way our main event method stays clean:

```
$content_id = $article->id;
$this->saveTest($content_id, $context, $test);
return true;
```

Within this new method, we are going to determine whether an INSERT or an UPDATE needs to be used. The event method now only needs to call upon this method to get the hard work done. As arguments, the saveTest() method receives the content ID and the value of our test field:

```
protected function saveTest($content_id, $test)
{
}
```

The SELECT statement is constructed using the JDatabaseQuery class. We first fetch an empty instance of that class. The argument of getQuery() is set to true to make sure the new query object is indeed empty and not reused from some previous query. We use the select() method to initialize the $query object as a SELECT statement and use the from() and where() methods to define which data we exactly need.

Finally, the $query is handed over to the $db object and executed. We use the getNumRows() method to get the number of rows. The result is cast to a boolean. We only want to know whether there are rows (true) or not (false).

```
protected function saveTest($content_id, $context, $test)
{
    $db = JFactory::getDbo();

    $query = $db->getQuery(true);
    $query->select($db->quoteName('content_id'))
        ->from($db->quoteName('#__test'))
        ->where($db->quoteName('content_id') . ' = ' . $content_id);

    $db->setQuery($query);
    $db->execute();
    $exists = (bool) $db->getNumRows();
    ...
}
```

After determining the flag $exists, we can perform an UPDATE if the flag $exists is true and an INSERT if the flag $exists is false. While we can use the $query object again to construct the actual query for us, we are using the updateObject() and insertObject() methods instead – just to show you the various possibilities of the database layer:

```
$data = new stdClass();
$data->content_id = $content_id;
$data->context = $context;
$data->test = $test;

if ($exists)
{
    $result = $db->updateObject('#__test', $data, 'content_id');
}
else
{
    $result = $db->insertObject('#__test', $data);
}
```

This should now all work: When the article is saved, our plugin should be able to capture the POST request, fetch the test value out of it, and store that in our new table.

If you have a component to manage these entries from the backend, you probably have models, views and controllers ready in that component. In this case, it makes more sense to replace the manual database queries with the usage of your model or table class.

Loading the data in the form again

Now, let's get back to the event methods. We have now stored information in the database table. However, once the article is saved, the saved value of the field `test` does not appear in the input field `test`. We have not loaded the saved data into our form yet. For this, we go back to the `onContentPrepareForm()` method. Just after we load our custom XML form, we are also going to add the right data:

```
public function onContentPrepareForm($form, $data)
{
    ...
    JForm::addFormPath(__DIR__ . '/form');
    $form->loadFile('form', false);

    if (!empty($data->id))
    {
        $data = $this->loadTest($data);
    }

    return true;
}
```

To insert the `test` field value back into the form, we first need to fetch it from the database. This logic has been moved to a separate method `loadTest()`. Again a `$query` object is used for this. It only makes sense to load data if the data (the article) actually has an ID. If it is a new article, there is no need to to attempt to fetch data from our own table.

```
protected function loadTest($data)
{
    if (empty($data->id))
    {
        return $data;
    }

    $db = JFactory::getDbo();

    $query = $db->getQuery(true);
    $query->select('*')
        ->from($db->quoteName('#__test'))
```

```
        ->where($db->quoteName('content_id') . ' = '.$data->id);

    $db->setQuery($query);

    $testData = $db->loadAssoc();
    $data->test = $testData['test'];

    return $data;
}
```

Our own values are simply added to the `$data` object. The modified object is then inserted into the article form and therefore our custom field is now filled with the stored `test` value. You should be able to use the field in the backend now.

Displaying data on the frontend

Now that we have our backend working properly, let's move our attention to the frontend. Our newly added field can be managed in the backend. However, it does not display on the frontend yet.

The event `onContentBeforeDisplay` allows us to modify the contents before they are displayed. Let's assume here that we only want to display our own `test` value when the entire article is being shown, not in a blog layout. Because of this, we are going to add the `test` value to the `$row->text` property (which is used in the full article layout) and not to the `$row->introtext` property (which is used in the blog layout).

The `loadTest()` method, which we created earlier, is useful now, allowing us to add the data loading quickly to this event method:

```
public function onContentBeforeDisplay(
    $context, &$row, &$params, $page = 0
)
{
    if (!empty($row->id))
    {
        $row = $this->loadTest($row);
    }

    if (!empty($row->test))
    {
        $row->text .= '<p>TEST: ' . $row->test . '<p>';
    }
}
```

5.5 Changing forms conditionally

An interesting aspect of the earlier examples, in which we modified forms, is that you can add fields by using either the `JForm` PHP API or XML files. With this, we can change the workflow of creating content. You can add a new field `test` that is required when creating a certain article. An author can be required to enter a `title`, a `body`, a publication date, but also a value for this field.

It becomes even more interesting when these modifications are depending on other conditions. We will first show an example that adds to our existing `test` value, only on the condition that the article is part of a certain category. We will create an extra parameter **Select Categories** in our plugin to select a category.

This code is based upon the code of a new plugin plg_content_ch05test02, which is a direct copy of the plugin plg_content_ch05test01 we have used so far.

For demonstration purpose, our site has two categories **News** and **About**. We will configure the plugin to have the parameter **Select Categories** set to **News**. The workings should be that the plugin is loading our extra fields when the article is part of the category **News**, but not when the article is part of other categories.

Adding the plugin parameter

To add an extra parameter, we are going to open up the plugins XML manifest file (in this case `plugins/content/ch05test02/ch05test02.xml`) and add a `<config>` section containing an `include_categories` parameter.

Joomla already has a form field type `category` that shows an autocomplete box for selecting the right category. We only need to add an `extension` attribute to define which type of categories we want to to be able to select. In our case we are referring to regular articles, so the `extension` is set to `com_content`.

```
<config>
    <fields name="params">
        <fieldset name="basic">
            <field
                type="category"
                name="include_categories"
                multiple="true"
                extension="com_content"
                label="PLG_CONTENT_CH05TEST02_FIELD_INCL_CATEGORIES"
            />
        </fieldset>
```

```
        </fields>
</config>
```

The `multiple` argument is added as well. This allows us to select more than one category.

We also need to update our language file `en-GB.plg_content_ch05test02.ini` to include our new parameter:

```
PLG_CONTENT_CH05TEST02_FIELD_INCL_CATEGORIES="Select Categories"
```

Now, we can browse to the **Plugin Manager** and change our new plugins parameter **Select Categories** value to include the category **News**.

Checking for the right category

With our new parameter in place, we are going back to the original `onContentPrepareForm()` method, which looked a bit like this:

```
public function onContentPrepareForm($form, $data)
{
    ...
    JForm::addFormPath(__DIR__ . '/form');
    $form->loadFile('form', false);
    ...
    return true;
}
```

Right before the XML was loaded into the `$form` object, there were some checks already in place. To make sure `$form` was an instance of the class `JForm`; to make sure we were in the correct context. Now we are going to add some extra checks to make sure the form is only being modified when the current category is part of the categories as configured in the plugin parameter `$include_categories`:

```
$include_categories = $this->params->get('include_categories');

if (empty($include_categories))
{
    return true;
}


if (empty($data->catid))
{
    return true;
}
```

```
if (!in_array($data->catid, $include_categories))
{
    return true;
}
```

When $include_categories is empty, there is no need to modify the form. When the category ID of the article is not set (for instance when the article is still new), there is no point in modifying the form either. And when the category ID is not part of the $include_categories selection, again it is not needed to the form. If these checks do not result in an exit, the code will continue to modify the form.

Note that when fetching the parameters value, we will receive an array. This is because the XML definition has the multiple attribute set. If the multiple attribute is removed, we will receive an integer.

```
$include_categories = $this->params->get('include_categories');
```

This already works great. Whenever the article is being loaded with the category being set to **News**, the XML file is loading and our test field is being added to the form.

Validating the field when switching categories

There is one flaw in our plugin design: When a new article is being created, the form is being loaded without any category (catid) being set. Therefore, the form will not include our test field. When the test field is not required this is no problem. However, when it is a required field and it should never have an empty value, the flaw becomes apparent: A new article will be saved with the required field having an empty value, which is wrong. The same is true when the article was first in the category **About** and is now moved to the category **News**.

The onContentPrepareForm event allows us to change the form when the article is being loaded. However, the flaw that we discuss here is occurring when the article is being saved to the database, not when the article is being loaded. The shortcoming can be fixed by hooking into the event onContentBeforeSave and checking for the required value there.

```
public function onContentBeforeSave($context, $table, $isNew)
{
    if (!in_array($context, array('com_content.article')))
    {
        return true;
    }

    $include_categories = $this->params->get('include_categories');
```

```
    if (empty($include_categories))
    {
        return true;
    }

    if (!in_array($table->catid, $include_categories))
    {
        return true;
    }

    $input = JFactory::getApplication()->input;
    $form = $input->post->get('jform', null, 'array');

    $test = null;
    if (is_array($form) && isset($form['test']))
    {
        $test = $form['test'];
    }

    if (empty($test))
    {
        $table->setError('PLG_CONTENT_CH05TEST02_ERROR_TEST_EMPTY');
        return false;
    }

    return true;
}
```

Within the `onContentBeforeSave()` method, we first repeat some of the checks that were in the `onContentPrepareForm()` method as well – whether the context is correct, whether the **Select Categories** parameter was set and whether the current category is included by that parameter. If this is all true, we also want to make sure our `test` value is filled in as well.

Unfortunately, the `test` value is not part of the `$table` object (which is actually the `JTable` instance that will save our data), because it is not saved in the usual way by the `JTableContent` class. We need to do something hackish. We need to extract the value from the `$_POST` array. Because the context is checked upon, we can be pretty sure that this event is only called with this POST being in place. If the value does not exist in the `$_POST` array we are returning an error.

It is still hackish though, because theoretically there can be cases where the article is saved (so the event is being thrown) without a POST being involved. Instead of fetching the form data from the POST variable, you could also fetch it from any request variable:

```
$form = $input->get('jform', null, 'array');
```

Fix with wrong $data in onContentPrepareForm()

There is one more flaw in the code. When you save the article, the method `onContentPrepareForm()` behaves a little bit weird. After a POST request, it may happen that the `$data` is no longer set. Also the data is sometimes an array and sometimes an object. Checking the Joomla source itself, confirms this: The `$data` variable is of type `mixed` - meaning it can be an array, an object or even `null`.

The following code is being added to the `onContentPrepareForm()` method right before we need to check the contents of the `$data` variable:

```
if (empty($data))
{
    $input = JFactory::getApplication()->input;
    $data  = (object)$input->post->get('jform', array(), 'array');
}
```

This fixes things when the `$data` is not properly set in the event dispatcher. If there is no data, we are simply going to extract the data from the POST.

```
if (is_array($data))
{
    jimport('joomla.utilities.arrayhelper');
    $data = JArrayHelper::toObject($data);
}
```

This makes sure that the `$data` is always an object, so we can use it in our code properly.

Working with batches

Still, using this Content Plugin to add a new required field, does not guarantee that this required field is always set in articles. When the article is moved from the category **About** to the category **News** by using the batch form in the articles overview, the `JTableContent` class is called upon, without any plugin event being triggered. To make sure this field has a value in all records, the existing articles need to be checked periodically, either through a cronjob or through some kind of backend page.

Adding fields based upon an access level

Based on the previous Content Plugin of using an **Select Categories** parameter, we can also check for further conditions to apply our own changes. We can check for a user's group:

```
$user = JFactory::getUser();
$groups = $user->get('groups');
```

You can also check for certain access levels, as configured within the ACLs of Joomla:

```
if ($user->authorise('core.edit.own', 'com_content'))
{
}
```

If you take this all into account when developing a plugin, you can easily imagine yourself building complete new workflows based on the user's privileges and roles. Plugins really allow you to reshape Joomla.

5.6 Removing and modifying fields

Removing fields

Just as we can use the onContentPrepareForm() method to add new fields, we can also use it to remove existing fields. Instead of using some kind of XML file for this, we need to use the JForm class. It has a removeField() method, that allows us to remove a field by its name:

```
public function onContentPrepareForm($form, $data)
{
    ...
    $form->removeField('metakey');
}
```

To see which fields and groups are available in the article form, it is best to inspect the articles default form file components/com_content/models/forms/article.xml. Here, you can see that there is a field metakey, which we removed using the code sample above.

Removing entire groups of fields is also possible. For instance, the following code sample removes all fields in the group metadata and therefore the group metadata itself.

```
$form->removeGroup('metadata');
```

It can be a little bit difficult to find out which fields belong to which group, at least in the case of articles. While the file article.xml is the base of the article form, the form is being processed in multiple steps. With every step, the form is modified and extended. Not knowing how the form is generated and through which steps it is generated, might introduce strange issues.

For instance, when implementing the removeGroup('metadata') call above, you can use the article.xml file for reference to see which fields are removed. In the XML file you will find that the field group `metadata` includes fields like `robots` and `author`. However, the group does not include the field `metakey`. This field `metakey` is defined in the same XML file, however in a different field group (without a `name`) instead. Still, removing the group `metadata` removes the field `metakey`. The reason for this can be found in the logic of the template file `layouts/joomla/edit/metadata.php`. There you will find that if the `jmetadata` fieldset (which belongs to the field group `metadata`) is removed, the output of `metakey` will not appear either.

There are many more situations that might seem weird. You either need to remove fields and groups with some trial and error or you need to study the Joomla source code thoroughly.

Removing required fields

Of course you need to beware of removing fields that are defined as a required field. A good example is to have a plugin hide the category field, when an author is adding or modifying an article in the Joomla frontend. The article is normally placed in the **Uncategorized** category, which has an ID greater than 0. However, when the category field is removed entirely, the ID will be 0. This is not allowed by the article component and an error is given. It is possible though to set default values for specific usergroups through various plugin methods.

Modifying fields

One way to modify a specific field is through the `setFieldAttribute()` method of `JForm`. Its arguments specify the fields `name` and the `group` in which the field is located. For instance, to set the field `metakey` as required, we can use the following call:

```
$form->setFieldAttribute('metakey', 'metadata', 'required', true);
```

In some cases, it is better to remove fields and add replacements. For instance, we can remove the field `metakey` using the `removeField()` call and then add an extra XML file that adds the field again, now with the `required` flag set:

```
$form->removeField('metakey');
$form->loadFile('override', false);
```

A new XML file `override.xml` is now added to the plugins `form` folder:

```
<?xml version="1.0" encoding="utf-8"?>
<form>
    <fields>
        <field
            id="metakey"
```

```
            name="metakey"
            type="textarea"
            required="true"
            label="JFIELD_META_KEYWORDS_LABEL"
            description="JFIELD_META_KEYWORDS_DESC"
            class="inputbox"
            rows="5"
            cols="50" />
    </fields>
</form>
```

You can also simply override fields – meaning that you redefine a field in your own XML and merge your XML with the existing `JForm` object, without removing the original field first (so without the `removeField()` call). This sort of works. However, some settings might not be applied properly like validation rules. I highly recommend removing the field first and then redefining it as you wish.

5.7   onContentChangeState

The event `onContentChangeState` allows you to hook into content that has changed state (being enabled or disabled). The `$context` parameter is the same as with the other content events. The `$pks` variable contains an array with the primary key used to identify the database rows that have changed state. For most Joomla core tables, the primary key is simply `id`. Other components might use different standards like `item_id`. The `$pks` variable allows for different field names for the primary key. The third parameter `$value` of the event method refers to the actual `state` value: 1 being published, 0 being unpublished.

```
public function onContentChangeState($context, $pks, $value)
{
    // Do something
}
```

The event `onContentChangeState` can be used to automatically publish other content that this content item is based on. A good example is the **Content – Finder** plugin that uses this event to update its own indices. Content can be indexed by the Finder mechanism to make searching content more efficient and increase performance. Of course, indexed content that is unpublished should not appear in the search results. Therefore, the Finder indexes are automatically updated, whenever the original content changes state.

Other extensions might use the same state value for more states than just **Published** and **Unpublished**. For instance, a status **Pending** might be assigned to the value 2. It is the task of that extension to see whether content plugins are able to pick up on such a new value or not.

5.8   Adding CSS and JavaScript

In chapter 3 we learned that the proper location to store static files like stylesheets and scripts, is the /media folder. Let's take the following location of a CSS stylesheet, which we want to add to the plugin:

```
/media/plg_content_example/css/style.css
```

To add this stylesheet to the plugin, we can use the following code:

```
$stylesheet = 'media/plg_content_example/css/style.css';
$document = JFactory::getDocument();
$document->addStyleSheet($stylesheet);
```

We can also choose to add a CSS string inline to the HTML document:

```
$css = 'p.introduction {font-weight:bold;}';
$document->addStyleDeclaration($css);
```

And similarly, we can also add JavaScript:

```
$script = 'media/plg_content_example/js/script.js';
$document->addScript($script);
```

```
$js = 'jQuery.noConflict()';
$document->addScriptDeclaration($js);
```

There are also ways to add stylesheets and scripts using the JHtml class. However, this only gives you the ability to add complete files. There is no equivalent of the addScriptDeclaration and addStyleDeclaration methods in the JHtml class.

In which part of the plugin?

Where to add these stylesheets and scripts? In this chapter, we have introduced various methods to our example plugin. The logical place to add stylesheets or scripts is at the top of an event method. If there are multiple event methods, the CSS and JavaScript should only be added once in the event method that is called first.

```
public function onContentPrepare(
    $context, &$article, &$params, $page = 0
)
{
    $stylesheet = 'media/plg_content_test05/css/style.css';
    $document = JFactory::getDocument();
    $document->addStyleSheet($stylesheet);
```

```
...
}
```

Another option is it to add the code to the constructor. If your plugin uses various event methods, you only need to add the stylesheet once:

```
public function __construct(&$subject, $config)
{
    parent::__construct($subject, $config);

    $this->loadLanguage();

    $stylesheet = 'media/plg_content_test05/css/style.css';
    $document = JFactory::getDocument();
    $document->addStyleSheet($stylesheet);
}
```

 When listening to multiple events with one single plugin, Joomla will only create one single plugin instance, even when the events are thrown in completely different parts of Joomla. The JDispatcher class makes up a listing of all plugins, creates an instance of them if needed, and reuses that instance across multiple event calls. In chapter 11 the workings of this are explained.

Allowing overrides of CSS

When you are offering your plugin to other developers, they might want to change the CSS code you have included in your plugin. Of course, your CSS rules can be overruled with template CSS. However, this also causes extra CSS to be loaded (by your plugin), which is unnecessary.

You can also load the CSS conditionally. By adding a parameter `enable_css` to the XML manifest, you can use the `$this->params->get('enable_css')` statement to check whether to include the CSS or not.

```
if ($this->params->get('enable_css', 1) == 1)
{
    $stylesheet = 'media/plg_content_example/css/style.css';
    $document = JFactory::getDocument();
    $document->addStyleSheet($stylesheet);
}
```

Another approach is to allow for a template override of the CSS file itself. Our plugin will check whether its CSS file is present in the current Joomla template and use that when available. When no template override is available, the original file in the /media folder is used instead. This requires a little bit more code, so we will add a task method within our plugin class to allow for this type of template override:

```php
public function __construct(& $subject, $config)
{
    parent::__construct($subject, $config);

    $this->loadLanguage();

    $stylesheet = 'style.css';
    $this->addStyleSheet($stylesheet);
}

protected function addStyleSheet($stylesheet)
{
    $tmpl = JFactory::getApplication()->getTemplate();
    $document = JFactory::getDocument();

    $original_path = 'media/plg_content_ch05test02/css/';
    $tmpl_path = 'templates/' . $tmpl . '/css/plg_content_ch05test02/';

    if (file_exists(JPATH_SITE . '/' . $tmpl_path . $stylesheet))
    {
        $document->addStyleSheet($tmpl_path . $stylesheet);
    }
    else
    {
        $document->addStyleSheet($original_path . $stylesheet);
    }
}
```

Naturally, the same thing can be applied to JavaScript files.

5.9 Changes when looking back at Joomla 1.5

Joomla has had various major rewrites. The migration from Mambo to Joomla 1.0 was a basic rewrite. However, stepping from Joomla 1.0 to Joomla 1.5 was major, because the entire core was rewritten. With Joomla 1.5 to Joomla 1.6, again a lot of things changed, while Joomla 1.6, Joomla 1.7, Joomla 2.5 and Joomla 3.0 more or less use the same architecture (though version numbering suggests otherwise).

In Joomla 1.6 all of the content events of Joomla 1.5 have been renamed. Instead of having an event `onPrepareContent`, the event is now `onContentPrepare`. Also, the following events were added:

```
onContentBeforeDelete
onContentAfterDelete
onContentChangeState
onContentPrepare
onContentPrepareData
onContentPrepareForm
```

5.10 The onContent prefix

The events `onContentSearch` and `onContentSearchAreas` might appear to be part of the group `content`, however they are part of the group `search`. They will be discussed in chapter 9. You can argue the method prefix `onContent` is wrong. You can also say the prefix is `onContentSearch`. Either way, it might be confusing.

The events `onContentPrepareData` and `onContentPrepareForm` are used in various places in various groups. For instance, the `onContentPrepareForm` event allows you to modify a form before it is being outputted - provided that the component is throwing this `onContentPrepareForm` and provided that the form is based on `JForm`.

The `onContentPrepareForm` event is used by all components that have a model class that extends the class `JModelForm` class. It is not only used by `com_content` but also by `com_contact` and by `com_login`. When looking for methods on how to apply events to a specific component, the best way to get started is to read the source code of that component to see where each event occurs where.

5.11 Shortcuts

JHtml::_('content.prepare')

The call `JHtml::_('content.prepare', $text, $params, $context)` can be used for content that does not stick to the standards of the Joomla framework. The standards are that the `$row` object, which is handed to the event `onContentPrepare`, has an attribute `text`. If your object has no attribute `text`, but for instance an attribute `description` instead, you will not be able to use the event `onContentPrepare` directly.

Instead, your extension should transform things in such a way that there is an object with a `text` attribute. You can do this yourself with a few lines of code:

```
$item = (object)null; // or: $item = new stdClass;
$item->text = $description;
$dispatcher->trigger('onContentPrepare', array('com_example', $item));
$description = $item->text;
```

Alternatively, you can let Joomla do this work for you. This is what the call `JHtml::_` (`'content.prepare'`) is meant for. Under the hood, the value of `$description` is used to initialize an empty object with a `text` attribute. This object is used as an argument for firing plugin events. You can add the following one-liner to your code:

```
$description = JHtml::_('content.prepare', $description);
```

The `JHtml::_('content.prepare')` method is a magic method that takes the first argument `content.prepare` and splits it using the dot as separator. It uses the first part of that argument as a class identifier (`content`) and the second part as a method of that class (`prepare`). In the case of `content.prepare`, the call is made to the `JHtmlContent` class (`libraries/cms/html/content.php`) and its method `prepare()`.

5.12 Plugin events in third party CCKs

While the Joomla article component `com_content` offers a solid interface for constructing basic content that can easily be extended using plugins, there is also a fair amount of CCK (**Content Construction Kit**) extensions that allow you to define your own type of content.

While plugins (combined with the power of `JForm`) allow you to build most - if not all - of the functionality of a full blown CCK, with a CCK most of the work has already been done for you. A CCK gives you a great kickstart, when you need to define your own fields on top of basic content. However, it also adds a new layer of complexity. Plugins on the contrary, allow you to extend Joomla in exactly the way you need, without all the bloating and cluttering that a CCK might add.

Most CCKs offer a way to extend their forms with additional form fields using plugins. This is where third party developers like you can start coding. The form field is defined through a plugin in some way or another, and the CCK takes care of storing and retrieving the values.

Usually, other plugin types are also available within the CCK suite. Like a Content Plugin allowing for including the CCK content within normal articles using tags (`{pointless example}`) or Search Plugins.

We are not going to dive into a deep discussion which way is best. Using your own custom built plugins or using an existing CCK. There is a need for both. Also, we are not going to discuss which CCK is the best. Instead we are just going to focus on plugin events that can be used within Joomla plugins to extend the CCK.

Plugins for K2

One of the most popular CCKs with Joomla is **K2**. K2 uses its own system of content items and categories and offers its own content events to manipulate these items. The K2 website lists an example plugin, which contains all of the plugin events. The plugin events start with an onK2 prefix to easily distinguish the events with others.

```
class PlgK2Example extends K2Plugin
    public function onK2PrepareContent(
        &$item, &$params, $limitstart
    ) {}

    public function onK2AfterDisplay(
        &$item, &$params, $limitstart
    ) {}

    public function onK2BeforeDisplay(
        &$item, &$params, $limitstart
    ) {}

    public function onK2AfterDisplayTitle(
        &$item, &$params, $limitstart
    ) {}

    public function onK2BeforeDisplayContent(
        &$item, &$params, $limitstart
    ) {}

    public function onK2AfterDisplayContent(
        &$item, &$params, $limitstart
    ) {}

    public function onK2CategoryDisplay(
        &$category, &$params, $limitstart
    ) {}

    public function onK2UserDisplay(
        &$user, &$params, $limitstart
    ) {}
}
```

New fields can be defined with XML tags similar to `JForm` that are added to the XML manifest. The field values are filled in through a form in the Joomla backend, automatically stored by K2 into the database and rendered using the K2 event system in the frontend.

A common use case for creating a K2 plugin is to add a new form field and display it within a K2 item in the frontend. Other use cases are possible too. For instance, you can modify the way that another field (or element) is rendered. There is only one plugin group named `k2`. So one K2 plugin can be used to catch all events.

Plugins for ZOO

ZOO, created by **YOOtheme**, has various ways to extend its behavior. However, it does not use the Joomla plugin architecture for this. **Apps** can be installed through the ZOO backend, and **elements** (defining form fields and their visibility on the frontend) are copied usually by file. While ZOO does not support regular Joomla extensions (plugins, modules, components) to extend its core, elements are also frequently offered as installable Joomla extensions, using the extension type `file`. Sometimes, these packages are even referred to as plugins, however they really are not Joomla plugins. What can be said about plugins for ZOO can be short: There are none.

YOOtheme is also working on its own CMS called **PageKit**. With PageKit, there is only one extension type – components – which can hook into the application (and other components) using events. Joomla extensions will not be compatible with PageKit.

Plugins for FLEXIcontent

FLEXIcontent differs in its approach from ZOO and K2. It reuses the core `#__content` table for storing its content. Because of this, FLEXIcontent can be seen as Joomla articles with extended features: additional fields, multiple categories, etc.

A plugin of type `flexicontent_fields` allows you to define new field types. The plugin class allows for four event methods that enables you to change the field behavior. Within the `onDisplayField()` method you can define what kind of input your field will show - an input box, textarea, radio. You can make many combinations of form elements through a single plugin. The `onBeforeSaveField()` method allows you to extract the right data from the POST, so in the case of multiple form elements you are just handling multiple POST values.

```
class PlgFlexicontent_fieldsExample extends JPlugin
{
    public function onDisplayField(
        &$field, $item
    ) {}
```

```
    public function onBeforeSaveField(
        $field, &$post, &$file
    ) {}

    public function onAfterSaveField(
        &$field, &$post, &$file, &$item
    ) {}

    public function onDisplayFieldValue(
        &$field, $item, $values = null, $prop = 'display'
    ) {}

    public function onDisplayFilter(
        &$filter, $value = ''
    ) {}
}
```

Plugins for Fabrik

The wiki of the Fabrik site defines the functioning of **Fabrik** by stating it is a way to collect information from users through various forms, store this information in a database table and display that stored information yet again in a different place. It is a definition that would fit any modern web application of course. However, by defining it as such, Fabrik makes clear that its architecture is setup to be very flexible. Forms can be custom made from within the admin interface, data can be stored in custom database tables and views can be easily created as well.

You can create various plugins to extend Fabrik in its behavior. At the time of writing there was not a whole lot of documentation available for developers. However, because the Fabrik extensions are freely available - and there are quite a lot of core plugins available - you can simply learn from the examples available.

The primary goal of Fabrik is to create forms, not by using JForm but by using its own dynamic form API. Plugins can extend from the parent class PlgFabrik_Element and in general need to implement the render() method to show the actual HTML form element and optionally a validate() method to validate input received from the user. Fabrik uses these methods to display the form, validate the form and store the form data in the correct database. Just like JForm forms can be extended using JFormField classes, Fabrik forms can be extended using PlgFabrik_Element plugins. The layout of such a plugin can look like this:

```
class PlgFabrik_ElementExample extends PlgFabrik_Element
{
    public function render(
        $data, $repeatCounter = 0
    ) {}
```

```
    public function validate(
        $data, $repeatCounter = 0
    ) {}
}
```

Similarly, a form can also be handled once it has been submitted and validated. For instance, once a form is submitted in the frontend or backend, you can send an email to notify an administrator or you can set a flag in some other database tables.

To handle a form, a plugin can extend the **PlgFabrik_Form** parent class and implement the **onAfterProcess()** method:

```
class PlgFabrik_FormExample extends PlgFabrik_Form
{
    public function onAfterProcess() {}
}
```

There is a lot more to discover with Fabrik. There are visualization plugins (which for instance allow you to use a certain longitude and latitude as saved through Fabrik to display a certain location in Google Maps, or display content in a slideshow), there are validation rule plugins (allowing you to add new validation rules like postcode checks or certain database lookups) and listing plugins (which enable you to influence how content is shown in listings).

Plugins for Seblod

Just like Fabrik, **Seblod** takes the concept of a CCK to higher levels. Instead of just defining custom fields, storing them and displaying them, Seblod differentiates between preparing a field before displaying and rendering it to display. Preparing for displaying means modifying the $field object (which is an argument of most Seblod event methods), which can mean setting a default value or doing some filtering of the current value. Rendering it, means spitting out HTML code that is inserted into the form layout.

It is interesting that Seblod plugins also allow you to implement a fields behavior on search. When you have a new content item with a new field, a search query will include that field as well.

Seblod extends the normal article behavior of com_content, allowing backwards compatibility similarly to FLEXIcontent. It also allows for modifying other parts of Joomla like categories, users and usergroups.

Below is an overview of the most important event methods. The plugin is part of the plugin group cck_field and the methods have a prefix onCCK_Field:

```
class PlgCCK_FieldExample extends PlgCCK_FieldGeneric
{
    public function onCCK_FieldPrepareContent(
        &$field, $value, &$config
    ) {}

    public function onCCK_FieldPrepareForm(
        &$field, $value, &$config, $inherit, $return
    ) {}

    public function onCCK_FieldPrepareSearch(
        &$field, $value, &$config, $inherit, $return
    ) {}

    public function onCCK_FieldPrepareStore(
        &$field, $value, &$config, $inherit, $return
    ) {}

    public static function onCCK_FieldRenderContent(
        $field, &$config
    ) {}

    public static function onCCK_FieldRenderForm(
        $field, &$config
    ) {}

    public static function onCCK_FieldBeforeStore(
        $process, &$fields, &$storages, &$config
    ) {}

    public static function onCCK_FieldAfterStore(
        $process, &$fields, &$storages, &$config
    ) {}
}
```

More CCKs

There are many more CCK extensions for Joomla: SobiPro, Cobalt, OneContent, ContentBuilder. Many of them offer even more plugin events that allow you to extend the normal behavior. It is simply too much to cover in one book.

5.13 **UCM (Unified Content Model)**

There are many possibilities when using a CCK. However, many of the CCK extensions perform the same tricks - creating new form fields, storing the field values of these new fields and displaying these values again in the frontend. Tricks that the Joomla core allows for as well, as explained in this book with various examples.

The CCK world has become a bit of a mess. While the user interface is perhaps unique to each CCK, the tricks they apply to implement flexible forms and extendable content types is not new. However each CCK introduces its own namespace and its own plugin types. Plugins for one CCK do not work for another CCK. The same ideas are written all over again for each CCK.

For sure, each CCK was built for a specific purpose. However, the underlying architecture for generating fields is so identical, that the question arises why there has not been a common standard, a kind of API, for plugins to create new field forms in all CCKs at once.

What if ...?

This is where UCM comes into the picture - **Unified Content Model**, a term which is used to describe a common content structuring, designed for both Joomla core components (articles, weblinks, contacts) and third party extensions. Do not think of it as a solid solution. Think of it as a concept, as a movement in the Joomla community to create more flexibility in a more generic way.

If all content types would use the same types of database fields (`state` instead of `published`, etc) or if they would perhaps all use the same database table `#__content`, life would be much easier when building new content features. The current consensus is to allow content to be stored in any database table, but with naming conventions to define specific fields in such a way that content features are easily implemented.

There is more than one road to get to something like a UCM. If all components are based on the same MVC parent classes, new features can also be implemented quicker. Perhaps the features should not even be included in the parent class. Perhaps they should be inserted dynamically into the model by other extensions (like plugins?) through design patterns like **Dependency Injection**. The discussion which architecture should be preferred has led to offspring like Nooku and FOF.

Current state of UCM

This is all work in progress and UCM should be seen more as a general concept - a perfect goal to be working to - instead of a golden solution that is suddenly presenting itself. However, UCM is already more than just a concept: tagging, content versioning, plugin events - they are already implemented for various core components and they can be implemented in custom components as well.

UCM classes can be found in the `/library/cms/ucm` folder. On the database level, the tables `#__ucm_content`, `#__ucm_base` and `#__ucm_history` are used when implementing tags and content versioning. It is expected that other features of the core components will slowly migrate to these tables as well.

To some, a migration to UCM is in full progress. To others, UCM leads to too much discussion and should be considered obsolete. How and whether it will get implemented is more of a discussion between core developers, than it is a discussion between plugin developers. Of course, the outcome of that discussion might have its impact on plugins. Perhaps new events are added, existing events will be renamed. Let's hope these changes will simply make plugins more powerful.

5.14 A word on content versioning

Starting with Joomla 3.2, content versioning - a long requested feature - has been added to the Joomla core. It allows you to view and restore from previous content versions. Content versioning can also be added to other components programmatically. This requires changes in the component options (`config.xml`), the component's `JTable` classes, the toolbar and various other parts of the component. However, content versioning does not require the installation of additional plugins and it does not touch the area of plugin events.

The **Joomla Documentation Project** has an excellent guide on how to implement content history for your own component. While mentioning the changes you have to make, the guide also mentions the usage of the `JObserverMapper` class, to allow your component to notify the core behavior of content history. This class is part of the **Observer/ Observable** pattern that will be discussed in the final chapters of this book.

 Link: **http://docs.joomla.org/Using_Content_History_in_your_Component**

5.15 Summary

In this chapter, you have learned what you can do with Content Plugins. It covers much more than just modifying content. This does not only include Joomla articles, but other types of content as well. We also discussed the content of third party extensions and the concept of UCM. You have learned how to extend any Joomla form using the `JForm` library. Moreover, we have covered more generic plugin practices, like adding CSS and JavaScript.

The next chapter will focus on the next plugin group: System Plugins.

6

System Plugins

In the previous chapters, you have learned about Content Plugins. System Plugins take events to the next level. While Content Plugins are limited to content, System Plugins are not: They allow for changing system-wide behavior. This chapter gives you an overview of the possibilities that system events offer and how to implement them in your own own plugin.

6.1 Introducing System Plugins

While Content Plugins deal with Joomla content specifically, System Plugins allow you to hook into the behavior of the Joomla core application. A very common use case for a System Plugin is to modify the HTML code, before it is being sent to the browser - this is done by implementing the event method `onAfterRender()`. System Plugins also allow you to re-route URLs to another component, modify the HTML header before it is being inserted into the Joomla template, and change the way that Joomla handles errors.

6.2 Plugin events

The following system events are available in the Joomla core (in alphabetical order):

```
onAfterCompress
onAfterDispatch
onAfterInitialise
onAfterRender
onAfterRespond
onAfterRoute
onBeforeCompileHead
onBeforeRender
```

Instead of listing the events in alphabetical order, a more common way is to list the available events in order of occurrence, the first event being the event that is fired first by the Joomla core (which is `onAfterInitialise()`):

```
onAfterInitialise
onAfterRoute
onAfterDispatch
onBeforeRender
onBeforeCompileHead
onAfterRender
onAfterCompress
onAfterRespond
```

Non CMS events

There are some more events that belong to System Plugins. For instance, there are a couple of events when Joomla is run as daemon, and not as CMS. The usage of this is explained in the final chapter of this book – as a dessert - like pudding:

```
onBeforeExecute
onAfterExecute
onReceiveSignal
onFork
```

6.3 Example: Add HTML tag to body

Let's start with a simple example of a System Plugin. We are going to add a dummy HTML tag `<foobar>` at the end of the HTML document, right before the `</body>` tag. When creating a System Plugin, the first question you will need to ask yourself is which system event to use for this. To answer this question, we need to understand a little bit more about how Joomla comes to the point of generating an HTML document - how the Joomla boot procedure works.

First, the Joomla core is started. Next, the component is called for output, with or without styling of the Joomla template. When the template is used and the template defines module positions, the modules on these positions are called upon as well. HTML code is being generated and stored in temporary buffers. When all HTML code has been gathered, the HTML code is combined into one big chunk (which resembles an HTML document) and this chunk is then sent to the browser.

The complete boot procedure of Joomla is explained more thoroughly in chapter 12. At the end of this book, you will also find a workflow diagram of all System Events.

At the point when the plugin event `onBeforeRender` is fired, the component has not been asked yet to render its HTML output. So this would be too early to modify HTML code. At the event `onAfterRespond`, the HTML code (the response) has already been sent to the browser, so this event would come too late. The event `onAfterCompress` allows for content to be dealt with after that content is compressed, using the PHP function `gzencode()` and this does not allow for modifying HTML either.

The correct event for modifying the existing HTML is `onAfterRender` - right before the response is compressed and sent back, but after the HTML has been rendered. In our System Plugin we will therefore implement the event method `onAfterRender()`.

New plugin code

So far, we have worked on Content Plugins. The code for System Plugins (and actually all plugins) is very similar to that of Content Plugins. Instead of having a class with a prefix `PlgContent`, our class now has a prefix `PlgSystem`. The basic skeleton of our plugin looks like this:

```
jimport('joomla.plugin.plugin');
class PlgSystemCh06test01 extends JPlugin
{
    public function onAfterRender()
    {
    }
}
```

Modifying HTML

As you can see, the event `onAfterRender()` does not include any parameters. This shows you that the event is generic. It requires calls to the Joomla framework to do something useful.

To modify the HTML, we need to fetch this HTML first. This can be done through the call `JApplication::getBody()`. Because we need to call upon the correct application (which has already been initialized by Joomla and should not be started twice), we should never access the `JApplication` class directly. Instead we should always use the `JFactory::getApplication()` call, which returns us the appropriate `JApplication` object. The application will be used a couple of times in our plugin, so it is better to put it into a variable first:

```
$app = JFactory::getApplication();
$body = $app->getBody();
```

Since Joomla 3.1, every instance of `JPlugin` also has a `$this->app` variable available, pointing to the Joomla application. If your plugin only needs to work under Joomla 3.1 or later, you can use this internal variable instead – it requires less code:

```
$body = $this->app->getBody();
```

Please that this still requires you to initialize `$app` as a class variable in your plugin:

```
protected $app;
```

Do not get confused by the naming body. While the method is named `getBody()`, it returns our entire HTML document, not just the HTML body (the stuff contained between <body> and </body>). It therefore also contains the HTML head (the stuff contained between <head> and </head>). Think of it as everything that appears in our browser as source code.

Every HTML document ends with a tag </body> so if we want to add our own <foobar> tag to the end, we need to replace </body> with <foobar></foobar></body>. This can be done by using the PHP function `str_replace`:

```
$foobar = '<foobar></foobar>';
$body = str_replace('</body>', $foobar . '</body>', $body);
$app->setBody($body);
```

After modifying $body we can reinsert it back into Joomla by using the `JApplication::setBody()` method. That's it. As you can see, you only need about a dozen lines of PHP code to create a System Plugin, which replaces HTML code.

6.4   Skipping execution for the Joomla backend

By examining the source code in your browser, you should now be able to see the
`<foobar>` tag. It will appear in both the Joomla frontend and the Joomla backend. What if
we only want to include the tag in the frontend? We can simply add a check for this in our
code:

```
public function onAfterRender()
{
    $app = JFactory::getApplication();
    if ($app->isSite())
    {
        $body = $app->getBody();
        ...
        $app->setBody($body);
    }
}
```

With the method `isSite()`, we check whether the current application is in fact the
frontend application. We could also have added a check for the backend instead:

```
if ($app->isAdmin() == false)
```

However, the Joomla application can have more instances than just a frontend and a
backend (for instance API instances, the command-line and even daemons). To make sure
our code is only executed in the Joomla frontend, a check with the method `isSite()` is
preferred.

$application, $app or $this->app

As you can see, the code uses `$app` as variable name. In many examples you will see the
longer variable name `$application` instead. This requires more typing from your side.
In this book we simply choose for `$app`. If you want to opt for `$application` instead,
that is just fine. You can even just use `$a` but this will make your code harder to read –
better not do that.

I also mentioned earlier that Joomla 3.1 introduced the `$this->app` variable in every
plugin. If your plugin only needs to be compatible with Joomla 3.1 or higher, you might as
well just use `$this->app`. If you want to make use of `$this->app` though, you will first
need to initialize the `$app` variable at the top of your class (above your constructor) as
follows:

```
protected $app;
```

$db or $this->db

Similar to $app, you can also access the database using the JFactory class:

```
$db = JFactory::getDbo();
```

Again since Joomla 3.1, every plugin has this instance already available through $this->db, provided that you have initialized the $db variable as follows:

```
protected $db;
```

6.5 Example: Dealing with regular expressions

A common task for System Plugins is to replace some kind of tag within the page with dynamic output. For instance, users can be allowed to insert a tag like the following in content (articles, modules, etc) or the template:

```
{articletext id="42"}
```

The plugin will then replace this tag with the actual articles body (identified with ID 42).

In order for this to work, we can again use the onAfterRender() method. The body will be fetched, a regular expression is used to scan the body for the tag and the tags contents are then exploded to find its parameters.

 The full source code of this plugin can be found in the GitHub repository under the name **plg_system_articletext**.

Fetching the body and replacing tags

We are going to start with the same code as in the previous example. At the start of the method, we add a check to make sure our code is only executed in the Joomla frontend. The $body is fetched from the Joomla application. Next, we use a separate replaceTags() method to scan this $body for relevant tags.

```
class PlgSystemArticletext extends JPlugin
{
    public function onAfterRender()
    {
        $app = JFactory::getApplication();
        if ($app->isSite() == false)
        {
```

```
            return;
        }
```

```
        $body = $app->getBody();
        $body = $this->replaceTags($body);
        $app->setBody($body);
    }
}
```

The method `replaceTags()` has various tasks: First, it uses a regular expression to scan the body for tags. These tags are then converted into a nice usable array by using another `convertTagArgs()` method. This array is then passed through to the method `getArticleText()` to find the proper Joomla article in the database and output its article text. The original tag in the body is then replaced with this article text.

Task methods and helper methods

As you can see, we are using three additional methods besides the event method `onAfterRender()`. This way we can keep our code clean and organized. I like to call methods like `getArticleText()` and `convertTagArgs()` single task methods. They have only one task to perform and their method name describes this task. In this book, I will keep referring to similar methods as **task methods**. If there is a method that does something, however, it does not really classify as a task on its own, I will refer to this as a **helper method**. A method that assists in a certain task, for instance logging or debugging some task, is best referred to as a helper method.

The method `replaceTags()` is a task method. However, it has more than one task: It can be seen as the glue between the regular expression, the other two methods and the actual core task of this method (which is: replacing the tags in the given text):

```
protected function replaceTags($text)
{
    $regex = '/\{articletext\ ([^\}]+)\}/';
    if (!preg_match_all($regex, $text, $matches))
    {
        return false;
    }

    foreach ($matches[1] as $matchIndex => $match)
    {
        $tag = $matches[0][$matchIndex];

        $tagArgs = $this->convertTagArgs($match);
        $aText = $this->getArticleText($tagArgs);
```

```
        $text = str_replace($tag, $aText, $text);
    }


    return $text;
}
```

The regular expression

The regular expression here in `replaceTags()` is simple. However, if you are new to regular expressions, it can be overwhelming. We use the function `preg_match_all()` instead of `preg_match()`, because multiple tags can be included in the Joomla body and we want to replace all these tags, not just the first one. Using `preg_match()` will only work if the whole body contains only a single tag.

The function uses the following expression:

```
/\{articletext\ ([^\}]+)\}/
```

Here, all tags starting with `{articletext` and ending with `}` are matched, while the stuff that goes between these curly brackets can include any character, except for the ending curly bracket `}`. Backslashes are used to escape the `{}` curly brackets, making sure the expression treats these brackets as characters and not as commands for the expression itself.

Converting the tag arguments

The method `convertTagArgs()` takes the variable part of the tag (so everything between the curly brackets minus the `articletext` indicator) matched with the regular expression and converts it into an array. Let's insert the following tag into a Joomla article:

```
{articletext id="42"}
```

Here the regular expression matches with the following variable part:

```
id="42"
```

Instead of using another regular expression, we can simply separate the name `id` from the value `42` by using the = equal sign as separator. Let's complicate our example a little bit: Let's add in a new parameter `html` as well, which determines whether the article text identified by ID 42 should be inserted as HTML or as plain text. This way, users can determine whether to paste the original article as a whole or to strip all HTML tags.

We now have multiple arguments that need to be separated by a space first:

```
id="42" html="1"
```

Additionally, we want to make sure the syntax is flexible, so that all of the following variations should be allowed to work:

```
id="42" html="1"
id='42' html='1'
id=42 html=1
```

Because our arguments always have numerical values, this is pretty straightforward though. We simply strip the value part from all non-numerical characters, which will include spaces and quotes.

All of this logic is combined in the method as follows:

```php
protected function convertTagArgs($tagArgs)
{
    $args = array();
    $namevalues = explode(' ', trim($tagArgs));

    foreach ($namevalues as $namevalue)
    {
        $namevalue = explode('=', $namevalue);
        $name = $namevalue[0];
        $value = $namevalue[1];

        $value = preg_replace('/([^0-9]+)/', '', $value);
        $args[$name] = (int) $value;
    }

    return $args;
}
```

Fetching the article text

Now that the tag is converted into an array, this array can be used to find the correct article text. The method `getArticleText()` is responsible for this task. It first validates the ID. If the ID is 0, no article is returned. There is no point in making a database query either, so the method simply returns `null`. The `html` argument is also being checked upon, with `true` being its default.

After setting up both `$id` and `$html`, a database query is executed.

```php
protected function getArticleText($args)
{
```

```php
$html = (isset($args['html'])) ? (bool) $args['html'] : true;
$id = (isset($args['id'])) ? (int) $args['id'] : 0;

if (!$id > 0)
{
    return null;
}


$db = JFactory::getDbo();

$query = $db->getQuery(true);
$query->select($db->quoteName(array('introtext', 'fulltext')));
$query->from($db->quoteName('#__content'));
$query->where($db->quoteName('id') . '=' . $id);


$db->setQuery($query);
$row = $db->loadObject();

if (empty($row))
{
    return null;
}


$text = $row->introtext . $row->fulltext;

if ($html == false)
{
    $text = strip_tags($text);
}

return $text;
}
```

The results of the database query – being an article object – is then used to build the proper $text. The article fields introtext and fulltext are combined into a single string $text. If the flag $html is false, the PHP function strip_tags() is used to hack away all HTML tags from this text. Otherwise the text remains intact.

The $text is then returned to the replaceTags() method, which uses it to replace the original tag in the body with this text. The modified body is then returned by the replaceTags() method to the event method onAfterRender(), which inserts this modified body back into Joomla, right before the HTML document is sent to the client.

6.6 Using System Plugins instead of Content Plugins

With the previous examples, you have learned that you can modify the HTML output of Joomla in any way you want. For instance, you can add certain tags like {foobar} to your Joomla articles and let a System Plugin replace that tag with dynamic content. This is the functionality you can also add to a Content Plugin. However, Content Plugins only work on content like articles and weblinks, so using a Content Plugin is a little bit limited. A System Plugin will work on the entire page. The plugin tag might appear in regular content (articles, weblinks) as well as modules and even the template. Note that has a performance impact as well: A System Plugin is loaded on every page, while Content Plugins are only loaded on pages that offer content (articles, weblinks, some modules).

A good example of why System Plugins can be more useful than Content Plugins, is email cloaking. Email cloaking is a feature of the Joomla core in the form of a Content Plugin. If you have an email address in your Joomla article, this plugin allows you to translate that email address into a piece of JavaScript that is still completely readable by humans but harder to read by spam robots crawling your site. However, it does not protect other non-content extensions or content in your template. The email address you put in your template footer, or which is generated through some custom module, is still readable by any spam robot. Using a System Plugin allows you to overcome this issue.

 Generally speaking, the output of modules is not parsed by Content Plugins. The **Custom HTML** module is an exception to this. It offers a parameter **Prepare Content**, that allows its content to be parsed by Content Plugins.

Email cloaking for all your HTML

First of all, let's open up the file `emailcloak.php` in the folder `plugins/content/emailcloak` to see what kind of code lives there. When you scan the PHP code, you will see that the plugin implements the `onContentPrepare` event, to allow for the content to be replaced. However, it also has moved most of its logic to other methods, which are all set to be protected. This means that we can extend the original class and still make use of its original methods, without duplicating too much code. This is very convenient.

```
public function onContentPrepare($context, &$row, &$params, $page = 0)
{
    ...
    return $this->_cloak($row->text, $params);
}

protected function _cloak(&$text, &$params)
{
    ...
```

```
    return true;
}
```

 Note that the `_cloak()` method does not return the modified contents. It receives the `$text` argument by reference and just returns a boolean.

Let's start off with a new System Plugin. Instead of extending it from the `JPlugin` class, what we would normally do, we are going to extend it from the `PlgContentEmailcloak` class instead – the class contained in the original `emailcloak.php` file. Because Joomla might or might not be able to find this class, we are telling it where to find the class exactly. See the last chapter on a word on `JLoader::register()`.

```php
$path = JPATH_SITE.'/plugins/content/emailcloak/emailcloak.php';
JLoader::register('PlgContentEmailcloak', $path);

class PlgSystemEmailcloak extends PlgContentEmailcloak
{
    public function onAfterRender()
    {
        $ app = JFactory::getApplication();
        if ($app->isSite())
        {
            $body = $app->getBody();
            $params = new JRegistry();
            $this->_cloak(&$body, $params);
            $app->setBody($body);
        }
    }
}
```

The only thing left for us to do is to implement the code we wrote before for our `<foobar>` replacement, modify it a little bit and pass the `$body` through to the `_cloak()` method. Note that `$body` is passed through as a reference, so that the original variable living in the `onAfterRender()` method is modified directly by the `_cloak()` method.

Also note that the original `_cloak()` method expects a `$params` object but does not require any parameters to be in it. It does not use these parameters at all. Using an empty `JRegistry` object seems to be just fine, though it looks a bit hackish.

This plugin is available in the GitHub repository in the folder **chapter06** under the **name plg_system_emailcloak**.

Once this new System Plugin is created, you can install and enable it in Joomla. The original Content Plugin can be unpublished now – it is no longer needed. Make sure not to remove the original plugin though. That would remove also the parent class our System Plugin depends on.

6.7 System event onBeforeRender

The event `onAfterRender` is excellent for modifying the HTML code, after it has been rendered. The event `onBeforeRender`, on the contrary, allows you to hook into the Joomla boot procedure, just before that rendering takes place. The process of rendering begins with the Joomla document (the class `JDocumentHtml` in case of an HTML document) loading the Joomla template and parsing all the relevant Joomla `jdoc` statements:

```
<jdoc:include type="component" />
```

For each `jdoc` statement found, the relevant extensions are loaded (the component, assigned module instances) and executed. The extension output (read: HTML code) is then loaded into a document buffer until all extensions are rendered. The `jdoc` statements are replaced with the relevant buffers and the resulting HTML document is inserted as body into the Joomla application (`JApplication::setBody()`).

The most common modification that can be applied through a method `onBeforeRender()`, is to modify something in the document object. However, many of these modifications will most likely deal with the document header (read: JavaScript and CSS stuff), and for that, there is a separate event `onBeforeCompileHead` available, which is discussed in the next section. Put differently, all modifications that deal with the document header, should be dealt with through the `onBeforeCompileHead()` method, while all non-header modifications should be dealt with through the `onBeforeRender()` method.

What examples are there for usage of the `onBeforeRender` event? Well, actually I cannot think of any. Things like the language, the documents character set and the reading direction (left-to-right or right-to-left) are all part of the header logic, as are stylesheets and JavaScript. Looking at the code of the `JDocumentHtml` class itself, 95% of all the code deals with the header. As a result, most developers will not need this event. They will opt for the `onBeforeCompileHead` event instead.

6.8 System event onBeforeCompileHead

The event method `onBeforeCompileHead()` allows you to modify the `JDocumentHtml` object, right before it is used to generate the HTML code of the header. Its most common purpose is to modify scripts and stylesheets, which are added by other extensions. It assumes other extensions use the Joomla framework to properly add these scripts and stylesheets. The following examples are correct ways to do this:

```
JHtml::_('stylesheet', 'example.css');
JHtml::_('script', 'example.js');
JFactory::getDocument()->addStyleSheet('example.css');
JFactory::getDocument()->addScript('example.js');
```

Under the hood, these calls are used to add a new script or stylesheet to an internal array of the `JDocumentHtml` class. The event method `onBeforeCompileHead()` can be used to modify these arrays, before they are used to deliver actual output.

The following plugin shows this in action. It removes all scripts with the keyword `mootools` in their filename. Additionally, it replaces the core's jQuery library with its online jQuery CDN variation.

```php
class PlgSystemCustomscripts extends JPlugin
{
    public function onBeforeCompileHead()
    {
        $app = JFactory::getApplication();
        $document = JFactory::getDocument();
        if ($app->isSite() == false)
        {
            return;
        }

        $scripts = array();
        foreach ($document->_scripts as $name => $details)
        {
            if (strstr($name, 'mootools'))
            {
                continue;
            }

            if (strstr($name, 'js/jquery.min.js'))
            {
                $name = '//code.jquery.com/jquery-1.11.0.min.js';
            }
```

```
            $scripts[$name] = $details;
        }
        $document->_scripts = $scripts;
    }
}
```

Replacing the array or extending it

In this example, we created a new array and used it to replace the old array. You might be tempted to manipulate the old array directly with `unset()` and add in new values. Replacing the jQuery library in this way, would however result in a re-ordering of all scripts. By creating a new array, all previous ordering is maintained. An alternative way, that would still preserve the correct ordering, would be to simply change the corresponding array element, not remove it.

Keep the script ordering in mind, when manipulating the `$_scripts` array. Having a wrong order might cause JavaScript conflicts or other JavaScript errors.

Properties of the document object

The JavaScript files are contained in an array `$document->_scripts`, stylesheets are defined in an array `$document->_stylesheets`, separate JavaScript output is contained in `$document->_script`, separate CSS output in `$document->_style`, and the `$document->_custom` contains some custom tags like META tags. All these variable names start with an underscore.

Following generic PHP standards, this would mean they are either `private` or `protected`. Before PHP 5, the access modifiers `public`, `private` and `protected` did not exist and the underscore was used to indicate the method or property should not be accessed outside of the class.

In this case, these variables start with an underscore, suggesting they are either `private` or `protected`. However, they are `public`, allowing us to directly change them. Perhaps in the future, proper setters and getters will be introduced though, so keep up with how the Joomla API changes.

6.9   Modifying the incoming request

 The sources of the following example are available in the GitHub repository in the folder **chapter06** under the plugin folder **plg_system_ch06test02**.

Let's say you are receiving incoming requests from various affiliate sites, and these requests can be made for any page on your site. However, each affiliate request is always accompanied by an affiliate ID that is unique to each affiliate partner. An affiliate link can look like this:

```
http://JOOMLA/blog/21-article?affiliate_id=42
```

Your site needs to be able to track the affiliate_id and the current page. Rewriting a controller of a specific component for this does not make sense, because all pages served by all controllers of all components on your site need to be tracked. Writing a system plugin for this is the solution.

Let's start again with the basics of a system plugin.

```
jimport('joomla.plugin.plugin');
class PlgSystemCh06test02 extends JPlugin
{
}
```

onAfterRoute or onAfterInitialise

The first question that we will need to answer, is which event to catch. Do we want the affiliate ID to be fetched pretty early in the startup of Joomla, or at the very end? If the latter is the case, we can use the event onAfterRespond for this. This means we only save the affiliate ID to the Joomla database, once the request is completely dealt with and the HTML response has been sent back to the browser. When somebody is loading your webpage however and stops page execution halfway, it might be that the affiliate ID is never saved.

A better alternative is to use either the event onAfterInitialise or the event onAfterRoute - in other words, as early as possible in the Joomla boot procedure. There is a profound difference between the two events though, which lies in the routing mechanism used by Joomla. With the first event onAfterInitialise, the URL is not yet interpreted. However, with the second event onAfterRoute, it is.

Whether or not the URL has been interpreted, determines the calls we can use to fetch the variable from the URL. Let's start with using the event method onAfterRoute():

```
public function onAfterRoute()
{
    $app = JFactory::getApplication();
    $affiliate_id = $app->input->getInt('affiliate_id');
    $url = JURI::getInstance()->current();

    $this->trackAffiliate($affiliate_id, $url);
}
```

Only three lines of code. A lot is happening here though. First of all, the `JFactory::getApplication()` call is used to get an instance of the current application. This application contains the `JInput` object `$input`, which is used to fetch an integer from the current request. Note that this request can be either a POST request or GET request - in this case, we do not care.

With previous Joomla versions, an integer can be fetched with a call like `JRequest::getInt()`. Nowadays, the Joomla application uses an internal `$input` variable for this. The code in this event method `onAfterRoute()` is simple but also clean. The Joomla framework is used to perform all tasks and there is no dirty code present.

The nice thing about using the Joomla API here, is that the variable is cast automatically to an integer, thus protecting your site against SQL injection. If somebody was to enter `affiliate_id=SELECT * FROM #__users` in the URL, the affiliate_id would have a value of 0 (zero).

Another call `JURI::getInstance()` returns a reference to the JURI object, which represents the current URL. To get the exact URL that was called for, the `current()` method is used.

Method to log affiliates

The event method also shows that we use an internal method `trackAffiliate()` with two arguments. That method is using both arguments to insert all relevant information into a custom database table `#__affiliate_requests`:

```php
protected function trackAffiliate($affiliate_id, $url)
{
    $ip = $_SERVER['REMOTE_ADDR'];
    $referer = $_SERVER['HTTP_REFERER'];

    $db = JFactory::getDbo();

    $query = $db->getQuery(true);
    $query->insert($db->quoteName('#__affiliate_requests'))
        ->set($db->quoteName('affiliate_id') . '=' . $affiliate_id)
        ->set($db->quoteName('url') . '=' . $db->quote($url))
        ->set($db->quoteName('ip') . '=' . $db->quote($ip))
        ->set($db->quoteName('referer') . '=' . $db->quote($referer))
        ->set($db->quoteName('created_at') . '= NOW()')
    ;
}
```

We are logging the affiliate ID, the current URL, the visitors IP-address, the HTTP referrer and the current time. This code can be further enhanced by validating whether or not the given affiliate ID is recognized by the system. You probably get the point.

Using onAfterInitialise() instead of onAfterRoute()

As you can see, the code in the event `onAfterRoute` heavily relies on the Joomla framework. We can use `JURI` to access the current URL, and we use the application variable `$input` to convert the affiliate ID into an integer. Because Joomla has already routed the URL, we can also determine which component is being called upon and which view. This comes in handy, when we only want to track the affiliates on article pages:

```
$option = $app->input->getCmd('option');
$view = $app->input->getCmd('view');

if ($option == 'com_content' && $view == 'article')
{
    $this->trackAffiliate($affiliate_id, $url);
}
```

Instead of using `onAfterRoute()`, we can also use `onAfterInitialise()`. This way, our code is executed earlier in the Joomla boot procedure. However, this prevents us from using the Joomla framework to fetch all the information from the URL. Consider the following example:

```
public function onAfterInitialise()
{
    $app = JFactory::getApplication();
    $affiliate_id = $app->input->getInt('affiliate_id');
    $url = JURI::getInstance()->current();

    $option = $app->input->getCmd('option');
    $view = $app->input->getCmd('view');

    if ($option == 'com_content' && $view == 'article')
    {
        $this->trackAffiliate($affiliate_id, $url);
    }
}
```

While the code above is exactly the same as in our previous `onAfterRoute()` method, we will be unable to determine if the current page is displaying an article. This information is simply not available at this point. Because the URL is not routed yet, the `$option` and `$view` variables will always be empty.

To recapitulate: In your `onAfterInitalise()` method you can use the `JURI` class to access the URL. However, a SEF URL has not been converted yet into a system URL, so the relevant component (and its controller and/or view) will not have been determined yet.

Note that the `$affiliate_id` is already available though. It is added as a regular GET variable to the URL, and it will be known to the JURI class without the need for any SEF translation.

You might also be tempted to do it all the original PHP way:

```
$affiliate_id = (int)$_GET['affiliate_id'];
$url = $_SERVER['REQUEST_URI'];
$this->trackAffiliate($affiliate_id, $url);
```

This is definitely the least preferred way. The security mechanisms of Joomla (like converting a URL variable to an integer) are almost identical to the basic integer cast used above. However, if new security methods are introduced in Joomla, you will automatically benefit from them, as long as your code is written using Joomla standards. So, following the standards gives you a security benefit. Additionally, if your plugin is not just a random mix of Joomla code and generic PHP code, but a clean collection of Joomla-only code, it will be easier to read for other Joomla developers.

Modifying forms with System Plugins

Earlier, when discussing Content Plugins, we were able to see that you can modify any form in the Joomla application by using a method `onContentPrepareForm()`. You can use the method `onContentPrepareForm()` within System Plugin classes as well.

Using System Plugins to fetch any event

The reason for this lies within the code that is used to dispatch events to plugins:

```
JPluginHelper::importPlugin('user');
$dispatcher = JDispatcher::getInstance();

$arguments = array($form, $data);
$results = $dispatcher->trigger('onContentPrepareForm', $arguments);
```

This code shows how a Joomla component can allow plugins to hook into the form behavior of that component. The first line shows a call `JPluginHelper::importPlugin($group)` that seems to suggest that the event that is dispatched afterwards is only dispatched to plugins in the group `user`. This is not the case.

The event is dispatched to any plugin in any group, as long as that plugin is activated by

Joomla and contains the given method (in this case `onContentPrepareMethod()`).

Let's put the conclusion of the above a bit differently. When Joomla is dispatching events to plugins, it is simply dispatching the events and letting any plugin in any plugin group pick up on this event. However, this plugin needs to be loaded. If a plugin is not loaded, it will not do anything and it will not be able to pick up on this event.

In the early steps of starting up the Joomla application, the system event `onAfterInitialise` is thrown and right before this event is thrown, the System Plugins are loaded to capture this event. In other words, System Plugins are always loaded by Joomla. Because of this, you can use System Plugins to capture any event anywhere in the Joomla application. Our example component renders a form and explicitly loads the Content Plugins on top of this. Therefore, the form event can be caught with both System Plugins and Content Plugins.

Using a System Plugin for everything?

Because System Plugins are loaded at the very beginning of Joomla, you can say that you can use a System Plugin to use any event that occurs throughout the system. You can say that for any task that would require a Joomla plugin, writing a System Plugin would suffice. That is correct, however it defies the standards that Joomla tries to define.

A plugin dealing with user-related tasks should belong to the group of User Plugins. A plugin that handles authentication should belong to the Authentication Plugin group. It might also be that in the future Joomla tries to impose these standards more strictly, making it harder or even impossible to catch Joomla events belonging to one group by writing a plugin belonging to another group.

Using a System Plugin anyway

Can you use a System Plugin to modify a `JForm` form in Joomla? The answer is yes, you can. However, it is better not to do that. You can write a Content Plugin for this instead, following the standards of Joomla. Only if you have a strong reasons to put it into a System Plugin and not in a Content Plugin, go ahead – it is considered ok by many developers.

One very valid reason for writing a System Plugin that modifies a form, is because the plugin also needs to handle other events. In chapter 8, you will learn how to extend user forms and usergroup forms. These examples show you that you sometimes need to fetch multiple events to get you where you want. Having separate plugins for each event will annoy your users. In that case, it is better to bundle all event methods in a single plugin.

6.10 Alternative error handling

One interesting example of a System Plugin is the **System - Redirect** plugin. This plugin overrides the default error handling of Joomla and captures certain obsolete URLs, that throw a 404-error. It then allows these obsolete URLs to be redirected to a new page using a 301 status.

How Joomla does error handling

Joomla makes use of its own type of error handling, allowing you to generate errors through calls like `JError::raiseNotice()`, which just adds a session message, and `JError::raiseError()`, which completely stops page execution. This error handling can be modified using a System Plugin.

By default, the `JError` class interprets the error that is being handled and then displays the error page. You can also use your own static class plus method to introduce your own error handling. To do this, you simply need to set this class as early as possible in the Joomla boot procedure. And again System Plugins allow you to do just that.

Examining the System - Redirect plugin

The following segment shows how the **System - Redirect** plugin introduces its own `handleError()` method for error handling. First of all, the default constructor of the parent class `JPlugin` is being overridden. In our new constructor, we add two lines, that deal with error handling. `JError::setErrorHandling()` is the method that allows us to change error handling for Joomla specifically, while `set_exception_handler()` allows us to do the same in a generic PHP way.

```
public function __construct(&$subject, $config)
{
    parent::__construct($subject, $config);

    JError::setErrorHandling(E_ERROR, 'callback',
        array('PlgSystemRedirect', 'handleError'));

    set_exception_handler(array('PlgSystemRedirect', 'handleError'));
}
```

The `JError::setErrorHandling()` method has a first argument `$level`, which is set in the example above to `E_ERROR`. This refers to the PHP constants that are also used within the PHP configuration (`php.ini`) to set error reporting. You can replace this with `E_ALL`, which will also contain PHP notices and PHP warnings, or `E_ALL ^ E_NOTICE`, which contains all PHP messages but excludes PHP warnings.

The second argument `$mode` can be used for various things like logging. However, it is best to keep this at the value `callback` and use the third argument to refer to your own method instead, so you can deal with logging there.

JError and PHP exception handling

You can say that the `JError` object is called intentionally by the code, which generates the error. To give you an example: If an article is not found, the `com_content` component intentionally calls upon `JError` to generate an error. However, it can also be that an error occurs somewhere else, where it was not anticipated. In that case, the generic PHP exception handler is called, which then refers to the same class and method.

It can also be that the code (for instance, a model in a component that generates some kind of error) uses the PHP `try-catch` structure. Any error within the `try` block will not be forwarded to any exception handler. Instead, it will be handled by the `catch` block. Optionally, the `catch` block can also contain a `throw` statement, which again will channel the error back to the exception handler.

Constructor or onAfterInitialise?

Theoretically, you can use the `onAfterInitialise()` method in your plugin class to add the two error-handling lines as well. The event `onAfterInitialise()` is always the very first event that is thrown in Joomla. However, to call the `onAfterInitialise()` method, the plugin class is first instantiated and at that very point the class constructor is called. The following code, which resembles somewhat the code of the Joomla startup, illustrates this:

```
JPluginHelper::importPlugin('system');
$dispatcher = JDispatcher::getInstance();
$dispatcher->trigger('onAfterInitialise');
```

The first line instantiates all of the System Plugins and saves them in an internal plugin array for later usage. At this point the constructor of each plugin is executed. The third line calls the `onAfterInitialise()` method. Using the constructor guarantees that the new error handling is introduced as early as possible. If an exception occurs in the `onAfterInitialise()` method of another System Plugin, it will be caught using the new error handler. If an exception occurs in the constructor method of another System Plugin, that exception will still be caught by the new error handler, provided that your System Plugin is loaded with a lower ordering number (the ordering you can set within the Plugin Manager) than the other plugin.

Writing your own exception handler

Coding the exception handler method - in the case of the **System - Redirect** plugin, this is the `handleError()` method - is the same for Joomla as for any other PHP application.

The method has one argument $error, which contains an exception object. This object has a few methods like getCode() and getTrace(). It is easiest to debug the $error object with print_r() under the various circumstances to see whether it contains what you need.

One default exception handler only

It is only possible to have single exception handler. If you write your own System Plugin to handle exceptions, the **System - Redirect** plugin needs to be disabled. An exception can only be handled once.

6.11 **Alternate SEF handling**

When Joomla encounters a system URL (index.php?option=com_example) or SEF URL (/blog/42-example-article), it will translate that URL into input variables that define which extensions should be loaded on that page. For instance, the option variable defines which component is loaded. The Itemid variable defines which Menu-Item the current page is associated with, along with all the page assignments of modules and templates. A System Plugin can be used to change this workflow, by hooking into the onAfterRoute event and changing the URL variables. The plg_system_usergroup plugin of chapter08 uses this to reroute the current request to a different controller.

When a SEF URL is encountered, that URL first needs to be changed back to a system URL. Only the system URL contains enough information to properly route the request to the correct component. This translation of SEF URL to system URL (and back to SEF URL when HTML is being generated) is done by the SEF routing system of Joomla. Let's see how this works and what can be changed using plugins.

Explaining the core SEF plugin

The **System – SEF** plugin might seem very important to the entire SEF translation process, however it is not. When you disable this plugin, SEF will still work. The core plugin only provides you with two main tasks. First of all, it adds support for the canonical META tag in the header of your HTML documents. Second (and more vital for the usage of SEF), it hooks into the onAfterRender event to convert any remaining system URLs into SEF URLs, using the generic call JRoute::_($url). When you disable the plugin, your articles will still contain system URLs.

There are no other tasks. This plugin has nothing to do with the actual translation of SEF URLs into system URLs and back. It only applies the SEF mechanism that is already there. The working of SEF can actually be found in the JRouter class.

How Joomla builds a route

With the generic call `JRoute::_($url)` you can quickly translate any system URL to a SEF URL. Under the hood, an instance of the `JRouter` object is fetched and its `build()` method is called:

```
$router = JFactory::getApplication()->getRouter();
$uri = $router->build($url);
```

Within this `build()` method (contained in the file `libraries/cms/router/router.php`), two things happen. First of all, custom defined rules are applied. Second, the `build()` procedure continues to execute specific methods for either the system URL (`buildRawRoute()`) or the SEF URL (`buildSefRoute()`). These methods are empty in the `JRouter` class itself - they can be seen as interface methods. They are implemented though in the child class `JRouterSite` (`libraries/cms/router/site.php`), of which the `$router` object is an instance, assuming we are loading this code in the frontend.

Let's take a look at the class `JRouterSite`: The procedure for system URLs is to not do anything – the `buildRawRoute()` method is still empty. The procedure for SEF URLs contains something more interesting though. Within the method `buildSefRoute()` the component name is detected and from there the component's `router.php` file (for instance the file `components/com_content/router.php`) is included.

This component file `router.php` contains two functions. a function with postfix `BuildRoute()` and a function with postfix `ParseRoute()`. For instance, the functions are named `ContentBuildRoute()` and `ContentParseRoute()` in case of the com_content component. In the text below, we will dub these functions `XBuildRoute()` and `XParseRoute()`, where the X stands for the component's name.

With the com_content component the structure of the `router.php` is a little bit different. The file also defines a class `ContentRouter`. The functions `ContentBuildRoute()` and `ContentParseRoute()` rely on this class for routing instead. Similar approaches can be seen in other core components. It might be that the component routing changes to a class based approach in the future.

When the router executes its `buildSefRoute()` method, the component's `XBuildRoute()` function is called. In effect the component gets the chance to convert the `$query` argument into `$segments`, which is the main purpose of the `XBuildRoute()` function.

The `$segments` array is then converted into a string, with a slash separating each segment:

```
array('sample') => sample
array('sample', 'blog') => sample/blog
array('sample', 'blog', 'article') => sample/blog/article
```

It is the purpose of the component's `router.php` functions to convert `$query` variables into `$segments`. If there are any `$query` variables left, `JRouterSite` simply uses them as regular query arguments in the URL (`?foo=1&bar=1`).

When you are new to component development, routing can be complicated,. To get started with component routing, it is best to write a basic MVC component first. Make sure to create two separate views within that component, in order to navigate from one view to another.

The URLs you will be creating are system URLs. Once you start converting these system URLs into SEF URLs, you will need to create a `router.php` file.

Direct matches with Menu-Items

Keep an eye on the correlation of aliases and SEF URLs. If a system URL has query arguments that all match directly with the query arguments belonging to a specific Menu-Item, the system URL is in fact the same as the URL of that Menu-Item. There is a direct match. For instance, if we create a Menu-Item that points to an article with ID 14, and this Menu-Item is stored with ID 2 and alias `test`, the following system URL reflects this Menu-Item:

```
index.php?option=com_content&view=article&id=14&Itemid=2
```

If a direct match is found between the system URL and the Menu-Item, the building process becomes really simple. The alias of the Menu-Item (prepended with the aliases of any parent Menu-Items) is used to construct the SEF URL:

```
/blog/test
```

Because no additional query arguments exist for such a direct match, there is no need to build the URL any further either. The custom rules are therefore never used and the component's `router.php` file is never included either. In short: When the SEF URL is directly matched with a Menu-Item, the `router.php` file is never called upon.

How Joomla parses a route

When a SEF URL is used to call upon Joomla, the translation process needs to be reversed. The SEF URL needs to be translated back into the correct system URL. This is initiated by the `JApplication` class (or actually only the frontend version `JApplicationSite`) when it is started up. It calls upon the router again, but this time its `parse()` method:

```
$uri = clone JUri::getInstance();
$router = $this->getRouter();
$result = $router->parse($uri);
```

After these lines are executed, the `$result` (an associative array of input variables) is inserted into the Joomla `JInput` class. Next, the application triggers the event `onAfterRoute`.

Within the `parse()` method of the `$router` class, custom defined rules are applied. And again the router either executes a method specific to system URLs or a method specific to SEF URLs. This time, the system URL variation – the method `parseRawRoute()` - is not entirely empty. It contains logic to determine which Menu-Item is active at this point, set its `Itemid` accordingly and set the Menu-Item as active in the menu.

The `parseSefRoute()` method performs some checks to guarantee correct filtering of input values. There is some support for the language flags (`http://JOOMLA/en/`) and it tries to link the URL with one of the existing Menu-Items by matching the Menu-Item aliases.

If there are any URL segments left after the Menu-Item alias is subtracted from the incoming URL, the remaining segments are handed over to the component's `router.php` function `XParseRoute()`. For instance, take the following URL:

```
http://JOOMLA/blog/2-sample-article
```

If the URL is matched with a Menu-Item with alias `blog` (URL `http://JOOMLA/blog/`), the remainder of the URL (an array with value `2-sample-article`) will be handed over to the component's `router.php` file. A common approach is that the component router uses the number 2 to look up the article and then set the `view` and `layout` correspondingly.

Adding new routing rules

The `JRouterSite` architecture allows components to determine how a SEF URL should be constructed and interpreted. However, only a SEF URL that belongs to that component is interpreted by that component. How can you modify the routing mechanism of another component than your own? Let's say, you are using a third party component that is great in all its functionality except its routing – in other words, its SEF URLs are not the way you want them to be. Can you change them?

Yes, you can. The `JRouter` class has two methods `attachBuildRule()` and `attachParseRule()`, which allow you to extend the normal behavior of routing. Both methods receive a callback as an argument, which is either a direct function or a method in a class. With Joomla, we prefer the latter: a method in a class.

These rules are applied, before the component `router.php` is called upon. If the SEF URL needs to be parsed, the URI is passed through these custom rules, before the component's `XParseRoute()` function is called. If the SEF URL needs to be constructed, the `$query` array can be modified through custom rules, before being handed over to the component.

Note that the component is only called upon, when there is still something left to do. For instance, if the `$query` array is already emptied out by a custom rule, the component's `XBuildRoute()` function will no longer be applied.

Example: Adding a test variable to your SEF URLs

 The following code can be found in the GitHub repository in the subfolder **plg_system_ch06test03** in the parent folder **chapter06**.

Let's start with an example: Let's say we want to add our own variable to the `com_content` component. First of all, we start with listening to the event `onAfterInitialise`. Within this event method, we fetch the router object and add our callback to it:

```php
public function onAfterInitialise()
{
    $app = JFactory::getApplication();
    if ($app->isSite() == false)
    {
        return false;
    }

    $router = $app->getRouter();
    $callback = array($this, 'buildRoute');
    $router->attachBuildRule($callback);
}
```

The callback is a method `buildRoute()` in the same plugin class. Note that the method is not called directly from within the plugins method `onAfterInitialise()`. It is called by the routers `build()` method. The callback method should therefore be public, not protected or private.

The callback receives two arguments: the `$router` itself - an instance of the `JRouterSite` object - and `$uri` – a `JURI` instance of the URL that is going to be converted. The callback's return value is not relevant.

```
public function buildRoute($router, $uri)
{
    $uri->setVar('test', 1);
}
```

The example above sets a flag `test=1` to all SEF URLs, regardless of the component that builds the URL. You can preview this in your Joomla frontend easily. None of the component routers know how to translate this test value into a SEF-friendly segment, so the variable will remain a query variable and will be appended accordingly to the URL:

```
http://JOOMLA/blog/1-article?test=1
```

If you want to make sure the rule only applies to an article view, you can use the following code:

```
$routerClone = clone $router;
$vars = $routerClone->parse($uri);

if (isset($vars['view']) && $vars['view'] == 'article')
{
    $uri->setVar('test', 1);
}
```

We first clone the router object, so we do not have the original router anymore. The reason for this is that we want to call upon the routers method `parse()`, which translates the URI object into an associative array of query arguments. This method `parse()` can (theoretically) modify the original `$router` as well and we do not want that. Cloning the object makes sure the original object is not touched. Consider it a safety measure.

The router's `parse()` method returns an array that we can use to check for the proper view. In the example code, we are simply checking for the `view` variable. However, in a real-life plugin it is best to also check the component name and perhaps other variables as well.

Your custom build rule is applied to both SEF URLs and system URLs. If you want your logic to only apply to SEF URLs, you can check for the current router mode. Using the code below, you will have a `$sef` flag that can be used for this:

```
$mode = $router->getMode();
$sef = (bool) ($mode == JROUTER_MODE_SEF);
if ($sef)
{
    ...
}
```

Example: Removing numeric identifiers from URL slugs

 The following code can be found in the GitHub repository in the subfolder plg_system_ch06test04 in the parent folder **chapter06**.

The next example involves both a custom build rule and a custom parse rule. Let's say you have a small site and you want all URLs to be generated without any numbers in the URLs:

```
http://JOOMLA/blog/3-sample-article
```

Modifying the HTML source of all your pages through a System Plugin is a good first step. In the `onAfterRender()` method, it will replace all URLs with URLs without numbers:

```
http://JOOMLA/blog/sample-article
```

This will most likely result in a 404 error, because the component `router.php` of com_content does not know what to do with this article. We also need to change the route parsing by adding a custom parsing rule.

Let's start with the basic structure of a System Plugin. We hook into the `onAfterInitalise` event and add a callback to our custom build rule. We also add a new callback to a new custom parse rule:

```php
public function onAfterInitialise()
{
    $app = JFactory::getApplication();

    $router = $app->getRouter();
    $callback = array($this, 'buildRoute');
    $router->attachBuildRule($callback);

    $callback = array($this, 'parseRoute');
    $router->attachParseRule($callback);
}
```

Our `buildRoute()` method is now setup to remove any numerical ID from the URL:

```php
public function buildRoute($router, $uri)
{
    $query = $uri->getQuery();
    $regex = '/\&id=([0-9]+):([a-z0-9\-]+)/';
    $query = preg_replace($regex, '&id=\2', $query);
```

```
    $uri->setQuery($query);

    return;
}
```

We simply get the $query argument of the URL, which looks a little bit like the following:

```
option=com_content&id=3:sample-article&catid=6:blog
```

Next, we use a regular expression, so that the id part is changed to remove the numbers. The resulting $query that is inserted back into the URI object will now look like this:

```
option=com_content&id=sample-article&catid=6:blog
```

With this change, the URLs on your site should already be changing and generating 404 errors, because we have not applied a parsing rule yet. The Joomla router is unable to find the proper article for this URL without numbers. The parsing rule looks as follows:

```
public function parseRoute($router, $uri)
{
    $path = $uri->getPath();
    $segments = explode('/', $path);
    $alias = end($segments);

    if (preg_match('/^([0-9])\-/', $alias) == false)
    {
        $alias = preg_replace('/\-$/', '', $alias);
        $slug = $this->getSlugByAlias($alias);

        if (!empty($slug))
        {
            $path = str_replace($alias, $slug, $path);
            $uri->setPath($path);
        }
    }

    return array();
}
```

Here, the $path is extracted from the JURI object first:

```
blog/sample-article
```

We assume the last part of this path contains our alias (`sample-article`), so we chop the path in segments separated by slashes and use the last segment as our `$alias`. Next, we assume this `$alias` is unique in our database and is always an article. Note that assumptions like these make it easier to write this book, however the real world will be more complex.

With the alias, we can make a database query for the `#__content` table and select the article ID plus the article alias (referred to as the article slug). To make this code more readable, this logic is moved to its own task method `getSlugByAlias()`:

```
protected function getSlugByAlias($path)
{
    $db = JFactory::getDbo();

    $query = $db->getQuery(true);
    $query->select($db->quoteName(array('id', 'alias')));
    $query->from($db->quoteName('#__content'));
    $query->where($db->quoteName('alias') . '=' . $db->quote($path));

    $db->setQuery($query);
    $row = $db->loadObject();

    if (!empty($row))
    {
        return $row->id . ':' . $row->alias;
    }
}
```

If the `getSlugByAlias()` method returns a valid slug (ID plus semicolon plus alias), we use this slug to replace the old `$alias` in the path and insert this modified path back into the `$uri` object. This is seen in the last part of `parseRoute()` method.

Explaining some shortcomings

In the `parseRoute()` method you might have noticed the `preg_replace()` function that is added to remove a dash from the end of the `$alias`. When testing this plugin, every URL generated by the build process still contained a dash in the end. This is caused by the component's routers, that assume the ID to be a slug instead of just a number. The `preg_replace()` function is a quick workaround for something that likely needs fixing elsewhere.

Another issue: What if you also have third party components that generate URLs with a slug? The `buildRoute()` method would need to anticipate that as well. At this moment, our example only queried the database table `#__content` for detecting the ID of an article alias. Other components would require such a similar query as well. There is no generic way of fetching aliases.

The biggest shortcoming is that the alias always has to be unique, which is not 100% guaranteed by Joomla itself. Likely, you will want to modify backend forms to check for the uniqueness of the alias. Plugins still allow you to do this - it is just a lot of work.

I would not recommend you to take this code directly into production – it certainly needs additional tuning to make it stable. However, this book is not about showing you complete examples that you can simply copy and paste, it is more about showing you how you can develop even cooler things on your own.

Writing your own SEF engine

If you would like to replace the entire SEF mechanism of Joomla with your own, you will need to replace the `JRouterSite` class with your own by using the `JLoader` override methods. See the final chapter of this book for an explanation of how to create such an override. With your own SEF engine, you can add your own type of SEF URLs or allow for a template override of the component `router.php`.

6.12 **Summary**

This chapter gave you the ins and outs of System Plugins. You learned how to modify HTML or the document header. In addition, you learned how to modify the routing process of an incoming request, how to change the error handling of Joomla and how to modify the handling of SEF URLs. The chapter also gave an introduction on the various steps taken by the Joomla application to produce a webpage.

The next chapter deals with something completely different: Authentication.

7 Authentication Plugins

Authentication Plugins allow you to authenticate Joomla users against an authentication mechanism. By default, Joomla enables the Joomla Authentication Plugin, which authenticates users by using credentials stored in the Joomla database table #__users. However, there are many more authentication options out there: Gmail, LDAP, Facebook, PayPal Access. And what about Single Sign In and Single Sign On? It is all discussed in this chapter.

7.1 About authentication

Authentication versus authorization

Authentication and authorization are not the same thing. With **authentication**, we check whether the user who tries to login, is who he says he is – most commonly, this check is performed using username and password. As soon as the user is authenticated, the next step in the login process is to login that user, which is done partially by the Joomla core and partially by User Plugins (discussed in the next chapter).

As soon as the user is logged in, it also becomes important what privileges that user has. This part is called the authorization. In Joomla, this is managed through Access Control Lists (ACLs), which are rules that define who is allowed to do what.

Both authentication and authorization play a vital role in determining access. The situation can occur where a user is authenticated successfully, however the authorization rules define that the user is not allowed to do anything after being logged in.

Login procedure vs. authentication procedure

To distinguish between authentication and authorization a little bit more, we are going to introduce the terms **login procedure** and **authentication procedure**. The authentication procedure is the part we will focus on in this chapter. It covers all the steps Joomla takes to complete authentication. It is part of the login procedure, which covers all the steps needed to make sure a user is logged in.

With the login procedure, user interaction plays a major role. A module instance or component is used to display HTML code to the user, in order for the user to enter credentials. These credentials are then passed to the user component and the Joomla application itself.

The authentication procedure takes these credentials to validate them. Once validated, the User Plugins are called into action, including the **User - Joomla** plugin that sets up the user session. In the background, cookies are being set. Last but not least, the user can be redirected to a new page. At this point, the login procedure ends.

It is important to differentiate between the two procedures, especially when we are going to discuss things like OAuth and Single Sign On. The main point is that implementing for instance an OAuth login procedure, involves a lot more than just a single Authentication Plugin. The Authentication Plugin belongs to the authentication procedure. However, you will also need many more extensions (like a User Plugin and a module or component) to allow for the entire login procedure to be executed.

7.2　Core Authentication Plugins

The Joomla core comes with a couple of Authentication Plugins, of which the **Authentication - Joomla** plugin is the most important. It validates the username and password against the Joomla database table `#__users`. It is the only Authentication Plugin in the core that is enabled by default.

Another plugin, included with the Joomla core, is the **Authentication - LDAP** plugin, which allows authentication against a remote LDAP server. LDAP stands for Lightweight Directory Access Protocol and it allows for easy storage of name/value pairs in a tree-like system. It comes from the UNIX world, which might make you think that LDAP is rarely used. LDAP is used in archaic systems like Sun Directory Server and predecessors Netscape and Novell. However, LDAP is still very much alive. Microsoft Active Directory (MSAD), which is part of a Windows Domain infrastructure, uses LDAP at its core and because of this, the Joomla LDAP plugin allows authentication against Active Directory as well.

The **Authentication - Gmail** plugin allows you to authenticate with your Gmail credentials, in other words the credentials you would normally use to log into Google Mail. This authentication occurs without the Joomla user knowing that Gmail is actually used for this. The user simply enters the username and password belonging to his Gmail account into a Joomla login box, and the plugin tries to validate these credentials with Gmail under the hood.

The validation of the credentials is done via a simple trick. The plugin tries to load an Atom feed of the Google Mail inbox, which is only accessible by supplying the correct credentials. So, if the credentials that the user has entered, deliver a correct Atom feed, the Gmail credentials are correct and the plugin returns success. If the Atom feed returns an HTTP status other than 200, authentication has failed and the plugin returns false.

Last in line, the **Authentication - Cookie** plugin allows you to authenticate against a cookie. The cookie is set by Joomla, when a user logs in successfully using another Authentication Plugin. For instance, the **Authentication – Joomla** plugin. If the right cookie is set for the right user, authentication occurs. For this to work properly, the **System – Remember Me** plugin also needs to be enabled.

Disabling the Joomla Authentication Plugin

There are situations, where you might need to disable the Joomla Authentication Plugin. For instance, if there is a requirement that all authentication always occurs through a remote authentication server, like Active Directory. In this case, the Joomla Authentication Plugin might need to be disabled, to prevent bypassing this remote authentication server.

You should be aware that disabling the Joomla plugin will also have its effect on backend authentication. If the remaining Authentication Plugins fail, you might find yourself locked out of the backend. This can be quickly solved by temporarily toggling the `enabled` field in the #__extensions database table for the Joomla Authentication Plugin, so you can login again.

```
UPDATE `#__extensions` SET `enabled`=1
  WHERE `type`="plugin"
  AND `folder`="authentication"
  AND `element`="joomla"
```

When the Joomla Authentication Plugin is disabled, Joomla is no longer authenticating based upon the Joomla password in the #__users database table. Instead, a password stored on a remote system can be validated against. When a user wants to modify the password through his Joomla profile, it will not be sufficient to only modify this password in the #__users database. The password on the remote system needs to be synced also. To sync profile changes to a remote system, an additional User Plugin will be needed.

7.3 A basic Joomla authentication plugin

 The source code for the following plugin can be found in the **chapter07/plg_authentication_ch07test01** folder of the GitHub repository.

To write an authentication plugin, let's start with the basic structure again. We start off with an empty class:

```
jimport('joomla.plugin.plugin');
class PlgAuthenticationCh07test01 extends JPlugin
{
}
```

Next, within this class, we add a public method onUserAuthenticate() with three arguments, which will be explained in the next section. For now, we focus on the basic structure:

```
public function onUserAuthenticate($credentials, $options, &$response)
{
    $response->type = 'foobar';

    if (empty($credentials['password']))
    {
        $response->status = JAuthentication::STATUS_FAILURE;
        $message = JText::_('JGLOBAL_AUTH_EMPTY_PASS_NOT_ALLOWED');
        $response->error_message = $message;
```

```
        return false;
    }

if ($this->doAuthenticate($credentials) == true)
{
    $response->status = JAuthentication::STATUS_SUCCESS;
    $response->error_message = '';

    return true;
}
else
{
    $response->status = JAuthentication::STATUS_FAILURE;
    $response->error_message = JText::_('JGLOBAL_AUTH_FAIL');

    return false;
}
}
```

As you can see, the event method has mainly one task: To append information to the $response object, depending on whether the authentication was successful or not. Note that we use a task method doAuthenticate() to deal with the actual authentication logic. This is not mandatory at all. You can also place all your logic in the onUserAuthenticate() method.

Arguments, response and return

The three arguments are $credentials (an array containing the user credentials being posted), $options (an extra array with some options) and $response (a reference to an existing authentication response object). The purpose of the authentication plugin is to modify the $response object, which is a PHP reference. The return value is of no importance. However, it is good practice to return null, false or true, where appropriate.

As you can see, there are only two values that are inserted into the $response object: $status and $error_message. Of the two, $status is the most important. It tells whether authentication was successful or not, by setting the value to a constant of the JAuthentication class.

Besides the statuses used in our example, there are a few more statuses you can use:

```
STATUS_SUCCESS
STATUS_FAILURE
STATUS_CANCEL
STATUS_EXPIRED
STATUS_DENIED
STATUS_UKNOWN
```

Check the file `libraries/joomla/user/authentication.php` for a complete overview of these statuses.

Basic example of authentication

In our example, the `onUserAuthenticate()` method contains mostly generic Joomla logic. However, the real authentication takes place in the `doAuthenticate()` method. So, how are we going to use this method?

Let's take a simple example: An authentication that allows us to login with any credentials as long as we are accessing this site locally (from `localhost`).

```
protected function doAuthenticate($credentials)
{
    if ($_SERVER['REMOTE_ADDR'] == '127.0.0.1')
    {
        return true;
    }

    return false;
}
```

Whenever somebody tries to login from `localhost`, authentication succeeds, regardless of the given credentials. Normally, an Authentication Plugin will do something more useful with the credentials, but you can see the purpose of the `doAuthenticate()` method.

How Joomla authenticates

The `onUserAuthenticate` event is called when Joomla receives a request to authenticate. Most commonly, this happens when the user component receives a POST request from either the login module, or the login page of the user component itself. The controller of the user component will handle this POST request.

The controller then calls upon the Joomla application (`JFactory::getApplication()`) and executes the applications login method (`$app->login()`), which in turn triggers the Authentication Plugins. This can be seen in the Joomla code within the file `libraries/joomla/user/authenticate.php`, which holds the `JAuthentication` class and the method `authenticate()`.

Looping through plugins instead of using the dispatcher

When running the Authentication Plugins, it is not the event dispatcher that calls the plugins, which is normally the case with events and plugin event methods. The event dispatcher allows one result to be modified over-and-over again by plugins. However, this is not what is needed with Authentication Plugins.

If one Authentication Plugin sets the response to `STATUS_FAILURE`, the dispatcher will simply proceed to the next plugin instead. It can be that another Authentication Plugin allows for access. However, once a plugin returns a successful authentication, we want to break out of the loop and return the successful result. Instead of using the dispatcher, the `JAuthentication` class simply fetches a list of all the current plugin objects. It creates an instance of the plugin class of all plugins that are currently enabled. It then passes through the `$response` object to each plugin, until a plugin sets the status of that object to `STATUS_SUCCESS`.

What happens when one Joomla Authentication Plugin fails? Nothing. The plugin that succeeds makes sure that authentication as a whole succeeds. It does not matter if one of the other authentication procedures fails. However, when all Joomla Authentication Plugins fail, then authentication as a whole fails.

Master User plugin by Spiral Scripts

A great example of an Authentication Plugin is the **Master User** plugin by Spiral Scripts (**www.spiralscripts.co.uk**). It allows an administrator to login as another user, by using the username of that user, plus the password of the administrator (or the password of any user that belongs to the Administrators or Super Users group). While this is very convenient, it also poses a security risk. The plugin luckily also has an option for IP restriction.

To allow for the regular authentication to be bypassed, the plugin goes through various steps. After some validation checks, it loads all the user records of Super Users, takes the password out of the authentication credentials (which again originate from the POST request) and tries to match the given password with the password of one of the Super Users. If there is a match, authentication is successful.

The plugin gives a nice example of how the functionality of Authentication Plugins can be used to solve a different problem: How to easily review a site under another user account, without knowing that users password.

7.4 Authentication options

The `$options` array, which is passed as a second argument to the `onUserAuthenticate()` method of your Authentication Plugin, is passed through various parts of Joomla, before it arrives at your plugin. For instance, the `JApplication` object checks for a `$options['silent']` flag, which (if set to `true`) prevents notices or errors being given to the end user. Another example is the user component, which adds flags like `$options['remember']` (**Remember Me**) and `$options['return']` (the base64-encoded version of the URL to return to after successful login).

After the authentication plugins have finished their job, the same `$options` array is then passed on to the `onUserAfterLogin()` event, which is discussed in chapter 8. Right after the authentication has succeeded and just before the User Plugins are triggered, some additional values are added to `$options`: the `$user` object (instance of `JUser`), the `$responseType` containing the value `$response->type` set by the last Authentication Plugin in line (the one that gave a successful authentication), and some other values like a lifetime (a timeout).

Communicating between pluginsn

Unfortunately, there is no point to add additional values to the `$options` array from within the Authentication Plugin. The modified data is not picked up by the authentication mechanism (within `JAuthentication`) and it is not passed on to the User Plugins. Consider the `$options` array therefore read-only.

How can we pass variables from an Authentication Plugin to a User Plugin? I assume you are writing your own Authentication Plugin and your own User Plugin. The trick is to have some temporary storage available, where you can save some variables from within your Authentication Plugin and pick them up later from within your User Plugin.

This can be done using the configuration object that is returned by `JFactory::getConfig()`. Within your Authentication Plugin, you can use this object to temporarily save a value under some `$name`. Just make sure the `$name` is unique enough, to prevent it from interfering with other Joomla extensions.

```
JFactory::getConfig()->set($name, $value);
```

Then, in your User Plugin, you can fetch the value with code like this:

```
$value = JFactory::getConfig()->get($name);
```

An alternative is to set your variable in the input instead:

```
JFactory::getApplication()->input->set($name, $value);
```

Reading the value is done with this code:

```
$value = JFactory::getApplication()->input->get($name);
```

If for some reason your login procedure is not bound to a single web request, in other words, if your login procedure redirects to some other pages to continue the login procedure, like with Single Sign On, then these method do not work. The state of the application is lost. Approaches to solve this include separate cookies, database storage and file storage.

Do not try to store the variable within the application by using the `JApplication::getUserState()` and `JApplication::setUserState()` methods. While these are great in an MVC component, they rely on the current user session. However, this user session is refreshed halfway through the login procedure. The variables will therefore not remain in the session.

7.5   Adding a login hash

Let's say we want to authenticate users not only by using a username and password, but also by a third value, some kind of unique hash. This secret hash is known to the user and has to be entered by the user. We will refer to this hash as the login hash. To allow for such a scenario, a lot more has to be modified than just the Authentication Plugin. Let's take a look again at the login procedure of Joomla.

 The code in this example can be found under the name **plg_system_ch07test02** in the folder **chapter07** in the GitHub repository.

Adding the input field

First of all, the user logs in through a form generated by the `com_users` component (the login view) or the login module (`mod_login`). In this example, the login hash is a required value and it needs to be entered by the user, its input field needs to be added to either the component, the module or both.

The login hash we will be adding, looks like this:

```
<input type="password" name="login_hash" />
```

The `mod_login` module is based on MVC and therefore allows you to override the `default.php` file in your own Joomla template. Modify the HTML code and simply add the input field.

Changing the component is a little bit more difficult. The login view of the users component is based upon a mix between `JForm` and HTML. You can use a template override to simply modify the HTML code or alternatively create a System Plugin to override the `JForm` object before it is being outputted.

Changing the controller

Once the form is submitted, it is sent to the controller of the `com_users` component. To be more specific, this logic is contained in the file `user.php` in the folder `components/com_users/controllers`. Now things become more difficult. The controller receives our POST request, which contains our login hash. However, the controller will not do anything with it - it will simply disregard the login hash. We need to modify the controller's behavior, in order for the login hash to be validated and to make sure that login attempts without this hash fail. So, how to modify a controller?

Most HTML code in Joomla can be overridden using template overrides (also known as output overrides). However, Joomla does not offer such an override option for controllers. Controllers are locked inside the functionality of an MVC component. Because core hacks are evil, we cannot make a direct modification in the original controller code either.

There is a clean solution though. You can write a System Plugin that hooks into the `onAfterRoute` event, which represents the point in time where Joomla already knows to which component and which controller the request will be dispatched to. Using the event `onAfterDispatch` instead of `onAfterRoute` would be too late in the Joomla boot procedure to change anything.

Let's start with this: We create a new System Plugin with class `PlgSystemCh07test02`, start our class and add the `onAfterRoute()` method to this class:

```php
public function onAfterRoute()
{
    $input = JFactory::getApplication()->input;

    if ($input->get('option') == 'com_users'
        && $input->get('task') == 'user.login')
    {
        $input->set('option', 'com_customlogin');
        $input->set('task', 'login');
    }
}
```

The logic here is simple. The `JInput` object is fetched from the application, to allow us to easily access input parameters. The `option` parameter always contains the name of the component that the request will be dispatched to. The `task` parameter contains a reference to the controller within that component.

In the case of a login request in the Joomla core, this results in the `com_users` component and the task `user.login`, which leads to the controller file `controllers/user.php` and its method `login()`. Because we cannot override the controller file itself, we simply tell the Joomla application to dispatch the request to a different component instead: our own `com_customlogin` component with the task being set to `login`.

Note that the web request is not being redirected - there is no new HTTP request being made. It is only an internal redirect. When the Joomla application is finished with dealing all `onAfterRoute` events, it will dispatch the request to the component in question. It will determine this by looking at the `$option` variable. We simply modify the `$option` variable, in order for Joomla to look somewhere else instead.

A new login component

With the previous step, we forwarded the POST request, which contained all login credentials, including our own new login hash, to a new component. Now, we need to create that component. As this is a book about plugins and not components, we are going to create the component quickly and not get into details.

Creating a barebones component

Create the following folders:

```
administrator/components/com_customlogin
components/com_customlogin
```

Next, add an XML file within the `administrator/components/com_customlogin` folder called `customlogin.xml` with the following content:

```xml
<?xml version="1.0" encoding="utf-8"?>
<extension type="component" version="3.2" method="upgrade">
    <name>com_customlogin</name>
</extension>
```

This allows you to use the Joomla **Extension Manager** to discover and install the extension. Most likely, you will get some errors on a missing administration section in the XML. Our component does not have any administration section anyway, so we do not care about this. Just ignore these errors, it will install anyway.

Create the component's entry point

Within the site folder `components/com_customlogin`, we are going to add the entry point for this component: `customlogin.php`. It is again simple and to the point:

```php
<?php
defined('_JEXEC') or die;

$controller = JControllerLegacy::getInstance('Customlogin');
$controller->execute(JFactory::getApplication()->input->get('task'));
$controller->redirect();
```

The only purpose of this entry point is to get to the controller part.

Extending the original com_users controller

The controller is defined in a file `controller.php`. It can extend from the generic `JControllerLegacy` class and look something like this:

```php
<?php
defined('_JEXEC') or die;
class CustomloginController extends JControllerLegacy
{
    public function login()
    {
        // Your custom login procedure here?
    }
}
```

However, this means that we have to copy large chunks of code from the original com_users controller to this controller, just to mimic the original behavior. A better alternative is to extend the original controller class that we wanted to change initially. We will include this class (and its parent) and simply extend our class from it:

```php
<?php
defined('_JEXEC') or die;
require_once JPATH_SITE.'/components/com_users/controller.php';
require_once JPATH_SITE.'/components/com_users/controllers/user.php';

class CustomloginController extends UsersControllerUser
{
    public function login()
    {
        // Your custom login procedure here ...?
```

```
    $rt = parent::login();
    // ... or here?

    return $rt;
  }
}
```

The only thing left to do, is to modify the `login()` method to your needs.

Customizing the login() method

Unfortunately, the `login()` method of the original controller is not written in such a way that it can be easily extended. All code dealing with the login – including ways to fetch data from the request, constructing the credentials and passing the credentials to the authentication procedure – is stuffed into a single method `login()`. To modify this, we have to copy the entire chunk of code of the original `login()` method into our own controller and modify things from there.

 In the code below most of the original parts are left. See the repository for the full source code.

The original code looks like the following:

```
// Populate the data array:
$data = array();
$data['return'] = base64_decode($app->input->post->get('return', '',
'BASE64'));
$data['username'] = JRequest::getVar('username', '', 'method',
'username');
$data['password'] = JRequest::getString('password', '', 'post',
JREQUEST_ALLOWRAW);
$data['secretkey'] = JRequest::getString('secretkey', '');

...

// Get the log in options.
$options = array();
$options['remember'] = $this->input->getBool('remember', false);
$options['return'] = $data['return'];

// Get the log in credentials.
$credentials = array();
$credentials['username']  = $data['username'];
$credentials['password']  = $data['password'];
```

```
$credentials['secretkey'] = $data['secretkey'];
```

```
...
```

The code shows three parts that are of importance when extending the login procedure with your own custom fields:

o   The $data array is where information is extracted from the request (POST).
o   The $options array is where the options are gathered.
o   And the $credentials are where the credentials are constructed.

We can simply append our own $login_hash value to the $data and the $credentials array:

```
$data['login_hash'] = $this->input->getString('loginhash', '');
```

```
...
```

```
$credentials['login_hash'] = $data['login_hash'];
```

The $credentials array and the $options array are passed to the authentication procedure in the same method:

```
$app->login($credentials, $options)
```

As you can see, this approach of replacing the original controller also allows you to add new $options values to the authentication procedure.

Using the login_hash in our plugin

Thanks to this entire procedure, the field value for $login_hash is now available to our Authentication Plugin as part of the $credentials array:

```
public function onUserAuthenticate($credentials, $options, &$response)
{
    $login_hash = $credentials['loginhash'];
    ...
}
```

Instead of having credentials with two fields that can be validated, there are now three fields: the username, the password and the login hash. How this is implemented further, is up to you.

Shh, do not mention the secretkey yet

When you inspect the original code of the `com_users` controller, you might notice the mentioning of a `$secretkey` variable. This is part of the **Two Factor Authentication**, which we will discuss in more detail later on in this chapter.

Add request data directly to the Authentication Plugin

The approach of modifying the `$credentials` array within the login-method is clean and follows the Joomla standards in the correct way. It also requires the introduction of a new component and a new System Plugin, just to reroute the request to that new component.

It requires quite some effort to add just one single field. Instead of overriding the controller, you can also just read the request from within your authentication plugin. To do this, we simply add the following to our `onAuthenticate()` method:

```
public function onUserAuthenticate($credentials, $options, &$response)
{
    $input = JFactory::getApplication()->input;
    $login_hash = $input->getString('loginhash', '');
    ...
}
```

The bad thing about this approach is that we are assuming that the POST request is available within the Authentication Plugin, while in fact we have no guarantee for this at all. The most common scenario is that a user is logging in through a form on your site (login module or login view of the `com_users` component).

However, it might also be that the login request arrives from somewhere else – Single Sign On, a third party component that is used for logins, perhaps even a REST API call. Maybe you do not care about this too much, which might be ok for your site. However, taking the proper design of the Joomla application into consideration, the usage of request data (POST or GET) should be avoided when dealing with Authentication Plugins.

Another approach: everything from scratch

In the previous approach, we have been rewriting a whole bunch of core extensions with a whole bunch of new extensions. The HTML output was overwritten through output overrides in the Joomla template; a new System Plugin was used to reroute the POST request; a new component was used to override the original `login()` controller method – all just to add your own additional field. It is quite some work and still involves tight coupling with the old functionality. The original controller might change in time, which will break your own extensions.

Another approach is to clone the current code of the `com_users` component and login module and use these clones to write some fresh authentication mechanisms. Actually, this approach makes far more sense, when the authentication itself requires communication between Joomla and a remote server such as with OAuth. We will discuss this further on in this chapter.

With this approach, your authentication mechanism consists of much more than just a single Authentication Plugin. It can also include a Login Module, a Login Component and even a User Plugin.

Ehm, this sounds like Two Factor Authentication? Yes!

You might have already guessed it when you followed the previous sections and encountered the `$secretkey` variable. Adding a third field to the login procedure is now already part of the Joomla core in the form of **Two Factor Authentication**. The code of the `com_users` component revealed a `$secretkey`, which is used in this mechanism.

The reason we took all of this effort to explain you how to implement a third credential field, is that the TFA (Two Factor Authentication) is designed to add a third credential field, but not a fourth field, or a fifth field, etc. Also, TFA does not allow you to enforce the username to be an email address, in other words changing the behavior of the existing credential fields is not possible.

Once you start building your own login procedure, you might find that neither the Authentication Plugin mechanism nor the Two Factor Authentication mechanism fits your needs, and you need to rewrite parts of Joomla. The previous sections give you some clues on where to start.

7.6 Two Factor Authentication (TFA)

Here it is: TFA, short for Two Factor Authentication. In the previous section, the goal was to add a single field (or perhaps multiple fields) to the core login procedure. TFA does this for you.

What is Two Factor Authentication? What does Two Factor Authentication exactly do? Matt Cutts, head of Google's Webspam team, defined it as follows: "Two Factor Authentication is a simple feature that asks for more than just your password. It requires both **something you know** (like a password) and **something you have** (like your phone)."

Instead of just requiring you to enter a password, Two Factor Authentication also adds in a thing like a PIN number or a randomly generated digit that is sent to you by SMS or generated by an app. Within the core login procedure, this additional code is what the `$secretkey` variable is referring to.

Core TFA plugins

There are two TFA plugins included in the Joomla core: the Google Authenticator plugin and the YubiKey plugin.

The Google Authenticator plugin allows you to communicate with the Google Authenticator, an app available for iOS and Android, which generates secret keys every time you want to login. This secret key can be used in the Joomla login form, which contains an additional field for this, once the Google Authenticator plugin is enabled. Entering a value for this secret key is optional. The user is free to skip the usage of this TFA. When the user decides to enable TFA, it can be done through the user's profile, where a three step procedure guides the user through the required steps to link the Joomla profile with the Google Authenticator app.

The YubiKey plugin allows you to generate the additional secret key through a small USB device – the YubiKey developed by Yubico (**http://www.yubico.com/**) - which is inserted in your computer and generates a random code specific to your own profile. Again there is a setup procedure that can be followed from within the user profile. Authentication does not only take place with the USB device. The remote Yubico servers are also contacted to validate the `$secretkey` that is entered by the user.

One time passwords (OTP)

The basic concept of both the YubiKey plugin and the Google Authenticator plugin is to add an additional `$secretkey` to the existing set of username plus password, thereby making authentication (who you are) more secure. Additionally, the `$secretkey` is regenerated for every login attempt. This mechanism is commonly referred to as One Time Passwords (OTP) and the term OTP pops up in the code many times.

The Google Authenticator plugin even claims that it is compatible with other OTP mechanisms than the Google Authenticator app. However, at the time of writing the usage of the Google API was still hard-coded.

Events for a TFA plugin

A TFA plugin is part of the plugin group `twofactorauth`. Its plugin class has the following layout:

```
class PlgTwofactorauthTest07 extends JPlugin
{
    public function onUserTwofactorIdentify(
    ) {}

    public function onUserTwofactorShowConfiguration(
        $otpConfig, $user_id = null
    ) {}

    public function onUserTwofactorApplyConfiguration(
        $method
    ) {}

    public function onUserTwofactorAuthenticate(
        $credentials, $options
    ) {}
}
```

The main purpose of the event `onUserTwofactorShowConfiguration` is to modify the user's profile, in order for the user to be guided into configuring his profile for the plugin's TFA. With both core plugins, the profile page is modified using HTML code in an additional `tmpl` subfolder within the plugin folder.

Once the profile is saved, the event `onUserTwofactorApplyConfiguration` is called upon. This event allows for the information that is being submitted with the profile, to be saved correctly. The event does not store information itself, but rather returns an OTP configuration object (`$otpConfig`).

OTP configuration object

This OTP configuration object `$otpConfig` is a classless object (not an instantiated class), with properties telling the TFA mechanism how to handle this TFA attempt. The `$otpConfig` is passed around by the various plugin methods and it is also used outside the scope of TFA plugins. It appears in the `com_users` backend, the `com_users` frontend and in the Joomla Authentication Plugin (where it is initially created).

Note that the Joomla login procedure only hooks into the TFA procedure through the Joomla Authentication Plugin (`plugins/authentication/joomla/joomla.php`). TFA is not available when the Joomla Authentication Plugin is disabled. If you want TFA to still be available once the core Joomla Authentication Plugin is disabled, you will need to copy code from the Joomla Authentication Plugin to your own plugin.

Usage of Framework on Framework (FoF)

Both TFA plugins include code of the **Framework-on-Framework** (FoF) library – a Rapid Application Development (RAD) library written by Nicholas Dionysopoulos (AkeebaBackup) and are included in the Joomla core since Joomla 3.1. FoF allows for quick creation of extensions by automatically applying certain behaviors. With components, there are specific MVC classes available in FoF. With plugins, there are not. Still, the FoF libraries allow you to use tricks that are convenient for plugins. One example being the template overrides, which are explained below.

To initialize FoF, the following is added to the plugins constructor:

```
if (!defined('FOF_INCLUDED'))
{
    include_once JPATH_LIBRARIES . '/fof/include.php';
}
```

After this `include_once` statement, all FoF libraries are available in the plugin. At the time of writing, the Google Authenticator plugin (with the technical name `totp`) heavily depends on the FoF framework-class `FOFEncryptTotp` to apply the actual OTP authentication in Joomla.

```
$totp = new FOFEncryptTotp(30, 6, 10);
```

FoF template overrides

A FoF trick that is very useful with plugins is the usage of template overrides. If your plugin produces bigger chunks of HTML, it is logical to create a layout file for this output instead – similar to what components and modules do within their MVC architecture. If your plugin uses a layout file, it is good practice to also allow a template developer to make an override of this layout file in the Joomla template. We call these copies **output overrides** or **template overrides**.

In chapter 13, we will discuss the concept of template overrides with plugins in more detail. For now, we will focus on what the YubiKey plugin does to fetch its override folder:

```
$overridePath = FOFPlatform::getInstance()
    ->getTemplateOverridePath('plg_twofactorauth_totp', true);
```

The `$overridePath` now contains the full path to the template override-folder `templates/TEMPLATE/html/plg_twofactorauth_totp`. Next, a simple `if-else` check will establish whether a template file exists in that override folder. If not, the original (placed in the plugins `tmpl` folder) is used instead.

```
if (file_exists($overridePath . '/default.php') == false)
{
    $path = __DIR__ . '/tmpl/default.php';
}
```

7.7   IMAP login

The Gmail Authentication Plugin gives you an interesting example of how an Authentication Plugin is used to authenticate against remote systems. Such a remote system only needs to support a simple call with a username, a password and a return value that indicates whether authentication was successful or not. Gmail offers a remote system. It allows for the Gmail credentials to be posted within an `HTTP Authorisation` header (which is equal to the CURL option `CURLOPT_USERPWD`) and it returns an HTTP status that indicates whether authentication succeeded or not.

Other systems offer similar methods. The IMAP protocol is a good example. It allows a simple login using username and password, through a secured connection (SSL) or insecure connection, on a remote IMAP server. The PHP function `imap_open($mailbox, $username, $password)` allows you to open up a certain IMAP folder `$mailbox` with a `$username` and `$password`. If this succeeds, you have validated the credentials. When this fails, the credentials are wrong. We are going to create an Authentication Plugin that uses IMAP as an authentication protocol.

Plugin parameters

To allow for the authentication to take place with a specific IMAP server, the IMAP server details need to be configured within the plugin settings. We will add some parameters to this plugin by adding the following XML `<fields>` structure to the plugins XML manifest:

```
<fieldset name="basic">
    <field type="text" name="server" />
    <field type="text" name="port" />
    <field type="list" name="ssl" default="1">
        <option value="1">JYES</option>
        <option value="0">JNO</option>
    </field>
</fieldset>
```

The port number is usually 143 (IMAP v2), 220 (IMAP v3) or 993 (IMAP secure). However, it might also be a custom port, so we will use a plain textfield for input. The server is either a Fully Qualified Domain Name (FQDN) like mail.example.com or an IP-address.

 Note that the fields are missing labels and descriptions - it improves readability but violates standards. The full source code plg_authentication_imap contains all tags to make the plugin comply to Joomla standards. Check out its source in the folder **chapter07** in the GitHub repository.

Plugin class

The structure of the plugin class is the same as our previous basic example. The onUserAuthenticate() contains logic to deal with the $response object. For the actual authentication, the doAuthenticate() method is used:

```
protected function doAuthenticate($credentials)
{
    $username = $credentials['username'];
    $password = $credentials['password'];

    $server = $this->params->get('server');
    $port = (int) $this->params->get('port');

    if ($this->params->get('ssl') === '1')
    {
        $suffix = '/ssl/novalidate-cert';
    }
    else
    {
        $suffix = '/notls';
    }

    $mailbox = "{" . $server . ":" . $port . $suffix . "}";
    $mbox = imap_open($mailbox, $username, $password);

    if ($mbox === false)
    {
        return false;
    }

    return true;
}
```

Depending on the parameter `ssl`, the `$mailbox` parameter also gets a specific suffix indicating whether SSL (TLS) is used or not. When SSL is used, the SSL certificate that is used on the IMAP server can be a signed certificate, but it could also be unsigned or self-signed. If you do not care if the certificate is actually valid or not, you can also add the IMAP flag `novalidate-cert`.

Knocking on the door might block your IP

Whether this authentication method actually offers a solid way of authenticating users, is something that is questionable. Every time IMAP authentication fails, there is a login attempt that might have been logged by some intrusion detection system (IDS). It can be that IDS is secured in such a way that 10 failed logins result in a temporary or permanent blocking of the originating IP. Because the login attempt is made from the Joomla site and not the user's origin, the Joomla IP will be blocked, making it impossible to do any IMAP authentication from that point onwards.

In general, mechanisms that knock on the remote server's door to see if authentication credentials are valid, only work when the remote server does not implement a blocking mechanism. Because such a blocking mechanism is a smart thing to have security-wise - a popular example of such a mechanism is Fail2Ban - the entire knocking on the door might not be the best idea.

7.8 **Actually not Authentication Plugins**

HTTP Authentication Plugin

Personally, I have written and released a plugin under the name **HTTP Authentication Plugin**. However, it is not an Authentication Plugin but a System Plugin. The name of the extension is **HTTP Authentication**, so the keyword **Authentication** belongs to the plugin name, not the plugin group. It refers to using **HTTP Basic Authentication** – the browser popup asking for a username and password - to require users to login before being able to access the site.

To put it differently: It replaces the normal Joomla login module or login component, while still applying the normal login procedure to authenticate and login users. When the **HTTP Basic Authentication** is checked, the username and password are passed on to the Joomla application, which calls upon existing Authentication Plugins.

The plugin is very simple in architecture. It has two methods: an event method `onAfterInitalise()` and a task method `showHttpAuth()`, which is called from `onAfterInitalise()`. The sources of this plugin can be found on GitHub: **https://github.com/yireo/plg_system_httpauth**

Facebook Authentication

When dealing with Authentication Plugins, you might come up with the idea to authenticate against Facebook. Facebook has various developer guides that help you implement their **Facebook Login API** in your own site.

True. However, this does not mean it can be done with an Authentication Plugin. An Authentication Plugin takes a set of credentials (read: username and password) and tries to validate these credentials. However, this also assumes these credentials were entered by the user in some Joomla form (generated by a Joomla login module or a Joomla login component). This is not the case with Facebook Login.

With Facebook Login, the user opens up a new webpage, loaded from the Facebook website, within a new browser window, and enters his credentials within that non-Joomla page. The Facebook credentials never touch the Joomla application. Therefore, Authentication Plugins can never be put to work. What is possible though, is to have a System Plugin, which receives a specific request placed by Facebook, which tells Joomla that a specific user has been logged into Facebook using the Facebook Login API and now also needs to be logged into Joomla.

Currently, it does not seem like Facebook offers an API that allows a simple POST of login credentials, and that returns `true` in case the credentials match and `false` in case the credentials do not match. Only if such an API would exist, would it be possible to create an Authentication Plugin.

Twitter Authentication

The same answer that applies to Facebook also applies to Twitter. Twitter offers a login method. However, this login method is not meant for usage within an Authentication Plugin. The Twitter Login method opens up a new webpage, served by Twitter itself, that allows the user to enter credentials. These credentials are never touched by Joomla. Twitter does not offer an API that allows for posting credentials and getting a validated response back.

Emulating a browser

There are some workarounds that allow you to login using Twitter or Facebook though. You can emulate a browser from within a plugin. When you log in to Twitter or Facebook manually, your browser loads a specific login page, enters the credentials in the form on that page, and posts this form back to the server. The end result is that the browser is redirected back to the same page with an error displaying (if authentication failed) or to the account page (if authentication succeeded).

This exact process can be replayed in your Joomla plugin by using custom CURL requests and parsing the resulting HTML output. As long as the webpages of Twitter or Facebook do not change that much, this is a hack that works.

It is a hack: It does not involve some API that guarantees compatibility. Instead, it relies on what the Twitter and Facebook frontend developers do in their HTML. There are a couple of third party Joomla plugins listed in the JED (Joomla Extension Directory), that take this approach.

Application authentication using OAuth

Do not confuse the technology of **user authentication** with the technology **application authentication**: Both Twitter and Facebook allow application developers to hook into their API. This makes it possible to build a Joomla extension that for instance fetches tweets or Facebook updates. To make sure the application is able to access certain parts of the API, authentication is used and this authentication is based upon OAuth: a standardized authentication protocol that is pretty popular these days.

With OAuth, the application (read: your Joomla extension) first sends a request with OAuth credentials to the remote server to obtain a certain token. This token is similar to a PHP session. However, note that the token is not authorized by your own server but by the remote server instead. As long as this token is valid, the token can be used to access other resources. The OAuth credentials (frequently called an API key and an API secret) resemble Joomla credentials (username and password) but are not the same. They are meant to identify your application and are generated on the API website of either Facebook or Twitter. This is what **application authentication** refers to.

The description above is a simplified version of how OAuth works. Implementing OAuth can be tricky. However, it offers many opportunities. Nowadays, many APIs (Twitter, PayPal Access, Microsoft Live Connect, Facebook, to name a few) authenticate using OAuth. OAuth is becoming increasingly popular.

On behalf of your visitors

Things get more difficult when you want your Facebook integration to behave not only on your behalf (you as a site developer) but also on behalf of your visitors. A good example of this is the Facebook Login API. In order for this to work, your users also need to authorize you as intermediate party, which requires more OAuth communication between your server and the remote server. Most commonly, the user is asked in a popup window to grant your application access to the remote resources, using additional permissions.

Typically, complex OAuth scenarios require the usage of a Joomla component. This is especially true, in case the OAuth remote server also needs to contact the Joomla site, as part of the OAuth communication. There is no clean way for intercepting remote calls to Joomla, except for using an MVC component, with a specific controller dealing with the OAuth handshaking.

7.9 Authentication Bridges

A whole different type of authentication is offered by bridges. Bridges are sets of extensions, that bring the functionality of another application like WordPress or Magento into Joomla, or vice versa. When the visual output of one application (say WordPress) is combined in the other (say Joomla), a common desire is to also have the logins synchronized so you can login into both Joomla and WordPress using the same credentials. This concept is known as **Single Sign In**.

To get Single Sign In working, you need to have an Authentication Plugin installed in Joomla that is able to contact (the API of) the other application such as WordPress. This is only part of the solution. What if the other application does not offer an authentication API? Then the bridge needs to add an API as well to this other application (for instance, in the form of a WordPress extension).

In the other application, Joomla needs to be contacted as well for authentication. Additionally, in case the username or password changes on one side, this change needs to be synced to the other side as well – and vice versa. There are many things to do when building a bridge.

MageBridge

One example of a bridge is MageBridge, of which I am the main developer. MageBridge connects Joomla and Magento in a user-friendly way. It comes with a MageBridge Authentication Plugin for Joomla. It also offers Joomla authentication for Magento through an additional Magento extension. This allows for authentication in either direction.

There is a MageBridge User Plugin and a Magento extension offering equivalent functionality in Magento. MageBridge also offers a complete visual integration of both applications, plus search integration, after-sales actions and many other tricks.

The MageBridge suite includes over 90 extensions for Jooma! and a couple of Magento extensions. This shows you how many extensions there can be, once you start thinking about a full integration.

JFusion

Similar to MageBridge, JFusion bridges applications using a set of extensions instead of just a single plugin. Instead of supporting just a single application like MageBridge does, it supports many applications (phpBB, Gallery2, Dokuwiki, Mediawiki, Moodle and more).

The JFusion package features authentication plugins, bi-directional user synchronization and even a visual integration of output from either side of the bridge.

Single Sign In (SSI) vs Single Sign On (SSO)

When working with bridges, the terms **Single Sign In** (SSI) and **Single Sign On** (SSO) frequently popup. Sometimes they are confused. Here is the true meaning:

Single Sign In refers to the concept of the same credentials being used in both applications. So for instance, the username and password in Joomla also work in Magento. This immediately requires a solution for user profile synchronization, because when a user changes his password in Joomla, it also needs to be changed in Magento. If the user logs into Joomla, the concept of SSI does not mean that the user is simultaneously logged into Magento. SSI requires the user to also explicitly log into Magento.

Single Sign On refers to the concept that when a user logs into Joomla, he is also automatically logged into Magento – and vice versa. SSO requires SSI to be working. However, SSO allows for things to be a lot more user friendly. Besides the features of SSI, SSO also makes sure the same user session is shared between the two applications.

One technique to make this happen is through cookie sharing. The Joomla cookie is reused in the Magento application and vice versa. Because browsers do not allow cookies to be used across different domains, Magento and Joomla either have to live on the exact same domain or in subdomains of the same domain. There are other approaches to bypass this restriction. For instance, sessions can be synchronized using the bridge itself (an approach taken in MageBridge).

When applying the terminology of SSI and SSO to Joomla plugins, an Authentication Plugin can be used for SSI purposes. When a user logs into Joomla, the Authentication Plugin is able to contact Magento to guarantee the user is able to login using Magento credentials. A User Plugin can be used to synchronize the password between the two applications.

SSO is made possible using a User Plugin that for instance deals with certain cookies as soon as the user logs in. This can involve cookie sharing or cookie bridging. To receive feedback from the other application to complete the bridge, either a System Plugin or a component can be used.

7.10 **A word on authentication protocols**

This chapter on Authentication Plugins is filled with topics, that actually do not involve the Authentication Plugins at all. However, these topics still apply to Joomla authentication and are therefore useful to bring to your attention. For instance, **authentication protocols**. Earlier, we have touched on the topic of OAuth. OAuth is an authentication protocol, which defines how the applications on either side of the connection should exchange information, in order for authentication to be done in a secure way.

Another good example of an authentication protocol is Kerberos, which is used in open source projects like CUPS, as well as Microsoft Active Directory (based on LDAP) and Apple Open Directory (also based on LDAP). The main difference between OAuth and Kerberos is that Kerberos is typically used in a so-called controlled environment, where all servers are controlled by the same entity (read: the same company). OAuth however allows for authentication in an open environment (read: the Internet) with various entities. You can say that Kerberos is centralized and OAuth is decentralized.

Is Kerberos something to use within a Joomla plugin? Perhaps. PHP contains a `Kerberos V` library with functions to connect to a Kerberos database. This allows Joomla to act either as a Kerberos client or as a Kerberos server. However, just like with OAuth, Kerberos only provides the technology. It gives you a car and a road but not a destination to drive to. The question is what you want to connect with Joomla using Kerberos.

If you want an Authentication Plugin to connect to a Microsoft Active Directory server (which again uses Kerberos and LDAP), perhaps you are tempted to use Kerberos. You do not need to use this though. The LDAP bindings in PHP already contain support for Kerberos and you only need to base your plugin upon these LDAP functions. Kerberos is used automatically and in such a way that you never need to know about it.

7.11 Some events that we skipped

An Authentication Plugin can have more event methods than just `onUserAuthenticate()`. There are in total three events that belong to this group:

```
onUserAuthorisation
onUserAuthorisationFailure
onUserAuthenticate
```

These events will be discussed more thoroughly in the next chapter on User Plugins.

7.12 Summary

This chapter focused on authentication and Authentication Plugins. It did not only tell you the basics of an Authentication Plugin, but it also uncovered details of the Two Factor Authentication, as well as some concepts of bridged authentication. What it did not cover is the process that is executed once authentication succeeds: This is discussed in the next chapter on User Plugins.

(8) User Plugins

Whenever a user is logging in, whenever he is logging out, or whenever his profile is being changed, User Plugins come into action. User Plugins can be used to extend the user profile, or to allow for synchronization of Joomla profiles with another remote application. This chapter covers the events of this plugin group and also shows you some useful examples of how to implement your own User Plugin.

8.1   User Plugins in the Joomla core

There are three plugins included in the Joomla CMS (**User - Joomla**, **User - Profile** and **User - Contact Creator**) of which the **User – Joomla** plugin is the most important. The **User - Joomla** plugin is responsible for logging in the user. It should normally not be disabled, unless another User Plugin completely takes over its functionality. It also offers automatic user creation (if enabled), sends registration mails and enables cookie logins.

The **User – Profile** plugin can be seen as optional. It extends the regular Joomla user profile with additional fields, which can be activated through the plugins parameters in the **Plugin Manager**. To extend the profile, the plugin makes use of two events, which do not belong to the plugin group `user` but to the plugin group `content`:

- `onContentPrepareForm` to load the additional fields into the profile form
- `onContentPrepareData` to load the additional stored values into the profile form or profile view

Normally, you would modify forms using Content Plugins. However, when the profile forms are loaded, the User Plugins have already been initialized in the Joomla boot procedure. Therefore, the `onContent` events can be intercepted by the **User – Profile** plugin. It is kind of a trick that works quite well.

The third core plugin **User – Contact Creator** automatically creates contact information for new users. It hooks in on the `onUserAfterSave` event and uses parts of the `com_contact` component to insert the user data into the contact tables as well.

8.2   Events of User Plugins

The three core plugins show you some solutions you can create using User Plugins. There is a lot more to do, due to the fact that there are a lot of different events within the plugin group `user`. To learn what can be done with what event, it is best to group the events by their functionality.

The following events allow you to react on the saving and deleting of user records:

```
onUserBeforeSave
onUserAfterSave
```

```
onUserBeforeDelete
onUserAfterDelete
```

The following events allow you to deal with usergroups being added or removed:

```
onUserAfterSaveGroup
onUserBeforeSaveGroup
onUserBeforeDeleteGroup
onUserAfterDeleteGroup
```

The following events allow you to react on logging in and logging out users:

```
onUserLogin
onUserLogout
onUserLoginFailure
onUserLogoutFailure
onUserAfterLogin
onUserAfterLogout
```

To confuse you, the following events allow you to hook into the authentication and authorization process. Even though they have the onUser prefix, they still require an Authentication Plugin to work and should therefore be placed in the plugin group authentication instead. This will be explained later:

```
onUserAuthorisation
onUserAuthorisationFailure
onUserAuthenticate
```

The events onUserLogin and onUserAfterLogin are really User Plugin events. However, because these events always occur after authentication, you can use these two events in an Authentication Plugin as well. I hope you are still with me.

```
onUserLogin
onUserAfterLogin
onUserLoginFailure
```

There are some more methods that have a prefix onUser, yet are not really known to be User Plugin events:

o   All events starting with onUserTwofactor: These plugins deal with the Two Factor Authentication mechanism, which is discussed in chapter 7.
o   onUserAvatar: This event stands a little bit on its own. It is discussed at the end of this chapter.

8.3   Saving and deleting users

In general, the four events that deal with changing a user record (saving and deleting), allow you to synchronize this change with another mechanism. For instance, you can store additional userdata in another database table or even another application.

```
onUserBeforeDelete
onUserAfterDelete
onUserBeforeSave
onUserAfterSave
```

It is important that you know whether to hook into the `before` or the `after` variation of the event. If you want Joomla to proceed with saving or deleting, regardless of what your plugin does, the `after` variation should be used. If your plugin should prevent saving or deleting, the `before` variation should be used.

Preventing saving user data

The event `onUserBeforeSave` receives three arguments: `$user` (an array with existing user data), `$isnew` (a boolean flag to determine whether this is a new record or not) and `$data` (an array with new user data). If you only want to do something in your plugin when certain fields are changed, you can compare the values of `$user` with the values of `$data` to detect this change.

The return value of this event is very important. If you want the user data to be saved, your method must return `true`. If you want to prevent the user data from being saved, your method must return `false`. Returning nothing or `null` will default to true. If you forget about the return value, no harm is done. Good practice is to return either `true` when the user is allowed to be saved, or `false` when the user is not allowed to be saved.

```php
public function onUserBeforeSave($user, $isnew, $data)
{
    if (preg_match('/@example.com$/', $data['email']))
    {
        JError::raiseWarning(500, 'PLG_USER_TEST_WARNING');
        return false;
    }

    return true;
}
```

The example above checks whether the email address ends with `@example.com`, and if so, prevents the record from being saved. It is also kind enough to display a warning to the user showing why things failed.

Preventing deleting user records

The event method `onUserBeforeDelete()` is similar to the `onUserBeforeSave()` method. It is executed just before a user record is deleted. However, the return value of the event is not used. In other words, Joomla does not offer a solid method to prevent user records from being deleted. A hack would be to simply stop the current request and redirect to another page. It is still a hack though.

```
public function onUserBeforeDelete($user)
{
    $app = JFactory::getApplication();
    $url = JRoute::_('index.php');

    $app->redirect($url);
    $app->close();
}
```

Another hack is to set the ID of the $user to 0. This way the selection of the user record in the database will fail, so no deletion will occur.

Correcting user data

Instead of changing the return value of the onUserBeforeSave() method you can also change the user data. Let's take the example of really stupid users who enter their email address with spelling mistakes - so annoying. Personally, I witnessed it many times that somebody entered his email address as **john@hotmail.co** instead of **john@hotmail.com**. We can autocorrect this through a User Plugin:

```
public function onUserBeforeSave($user, $isnew, $data)
{
    $regex = '/@hotmail.co$/';

    if (preg_match($regex, $data['email']))
    {
        $email = $data['email'];
        $email = preg_replace($regex, '@hotmail.com', $email);
        $data['email'] = $data;
    }

    return true;
}
```

A different example: The **User – Profile** plugin allows you to add additional fields to the profile, including a website field. If you want to guarantee that the entered URL starts with either `http://` or `https://`, you can use a method like this:

```
public function onUserBeforeSave($user, $isnew, $data)
{
    if (isset($data['website']))
```

```
{
    $regex = '/^(http|https):\/\//';

    if (preg_match($regex, $data['website']) == false)
    {
        $data['website'] = 'http://' . $data['website'];
    }
}

return true;
}
```

Whenever a URL is entered without an HTTP prefix, the value http:// is simply prepended to it.

After a user has been saved or deleted

You have seen some examples of onUser events that allow you to deal with the user data before it is being saved or deleted. Now let's take a look at the events that allow you to manipulate things after they have been saved: onUserAfterSave and onUserAfterDelete.

```
public function onUserAfterSave($data, $isNew, $result, $error)
{
}
```

```
public function onUserAfterDelete($data, $result, $error)
{
}
```

In both methods, the return value is disregarded by Joomla. You can set it to be true, false or null - it will not change anything in the behavior. Changing $user or $data will not have any effect either. The after keyword indicates the data has already been altered in the Joomla database. Because of these characteristics, these events are typically used to synchronize Joomla user data to another system (a third party Joomla database table; another bridged application).

onAfterUserSave() arguments

The arguments of the onUserAfterSave() method are $data (an array with the user values), $isNew (a flag indicating whether the user record was newly created or not), $result (a boolean that equals the return value of the JTableUser::store() call) and $error (a string value if the user model returned an error).

Note that the $data array is the same array as the $data array that is used as a fourth argument to the `onUserBeforeSave()` event. The only difference is that the various User Plugins might have modified this `$data`.

onUserAfterDelete() arguments

The arguments of the `onUserAfterDelete()` method are `$data` (an array of the user data being removed), `$result` (a boolean being set to `true` in case the user was indeed removed correctly) and `$error` (a string value in case the user-model returned an error). As you can see, the arguments are the same as the `onUserAfterSave()` arguments, except for the flag `$isNew`, which is no longer present.

When you read the source of `plugins/user/joomla/joomla.php`, you will see that the arguments are named differently. This may confuse you. With PHP the naming of arguments can change in each method.

In the **User - Joomla** plugin the `onUserAfterDelete()` method looks as follows:

```
public function onUserAfterDelete($user, $success, $msg)
{

}
```

Personally, I think the names `$user` and `$msg` are confusing. The variable `$user` is used normally as an instance of the `JUser` object . The user is no longer available when this event is thrown and therefore the `$user` does not contain a reference to the user itself. It contains a copy of the original data that no longer exists. A name like `$data` or even `$originalData` would be better.

The variable name `$msg` suggests that it can also contain some kind of session message when the deletion went ok (`$success` is set to `true`). However, this is not correct: The `$msg` variable is always empty unless it contains an error (and `$success` is set to `false`). Naming the variable to `$error` would seem more appropriate.

When a user is not saved correctly

When the user data is not saved correctly to the database, the third argument `$result` of the method `onUserAfterSave()` is set to `false`. Likely, the `$error` variable also contains some hint on what went wrong. Do not take this for granted though. In most (if not all) cases the `$error` string contains the result from the `JUser::getError()` method, which again contains the output of the `JTableUser::getError()` method, which again is filled with `JTableUser::setError()` method, which always uses `JText::_()` to translate the actual system error.

In short, the `$error` variable contains a system error that is translated. It should not be used for investigating what caused the actual error. The error might be English, it might be Spanish, it might be Tamil.

```
public function onUserAfterSave ($data, $isNew, $result, $error)
{
    if ($result == false)
    {
        echo $error;
        // Output in French: Veuillez entrer une adresse e-mail valide
    }
}
```

Because the only other piece of evidence is the $result flag itself (which is only true or false), you can simply state that a User Plugin should not be used to investigate why the saving of a user failed. It should only be used to connect things to each other. It is the responsibility of either the model or the table class to figure out what went wrong where for what reason.

Of course you can still use the User Plugin to pass through the $error message to some other place. For instance, you can log it to a database table:

```
public function onUserAfterSave ($data, $isNew, $result, $error)
{
    if ($result == false)
    {
        $db = JFactory::getDbo ();
        $query = $db->getQuery (true);

        $columns = array ('user_id', 'email', 'type', 'error');
        $logType = 'onUserAfterSave failed';
        $logUserId = (isset ($data ['id'])) ? $data ['id'] : null;
        $logEmail = (isset ($data ['email'])) ? $data ['email'] : null;
        $values = array ($logUserId, $logEmail, $logType, $error);

        $query->insert ($db->quoteName ('#__user_log'))
            ->columns ($db->quoteName ($columns))
            ->values (implode (',', $values));

        $db->setQuery ($query);
        $db->execute ();
    }
}
```

When the user data cannot be saved, the component controller that was responsible for the attempt to save user data will typically redirect the current user (either the Joomla user trying to save his or her own data, or some kind of Super User) to the same form with the $error set in a message box.

8.4   Using non-user events in User Plugins

In earlier chapters we already learned that as long as the plugin group is loaded (meaning all plugin classes of that group are instantiated), the plugins of that group will be able to listen to any event and not just the event of that group. Once the System Plugins are loaded (which is true for any Joomla request), a System Plugin can include all the events that belong to User Plugins. And you can use any System Plugin event within a User Plugin.

Within the Joomla core you can find various examples of this. The **System – Language Filter** plugin uses various `onUser` events, while a couple of Authentication Plugins call upon the event `onUserAuthenticate`. Also the **User – Profile** plugin calls upon a couple of `onContent` events to allow the user form to be extended.

It is easiest to refer to a User Plugin as a way to respond to `onUser` events. At least you now know this statement is actually not entirely true.

8.5   Extending user profiles

 The code for this plugin can be found online in the GitHub repository accompanying this book. Check for the folder **chapter08** and then the plugin folder **plg_user_firstlast**.

When you want to add new fields to the user profile and you want these fields to be populated with the right profile values, you can use a single User Plugin to make this happen. However, this User Plugin will also need to implement a couple of events borrowed from other plugin groups.

As an example, we are going to build a User Plugin named **Firstlast**, which is extending the user profile with a **firstname** and a **lastname** field. It is quite some work. However, most of the code involved has been discussed before. Let's start with an outline of the plugin file:

```php
<?php
defined('_JEXEC') or die;

jimport('joomla.plugin.plugin');

class PlgUserFirstlast extends JPlugin
{
    protected $autoloadLanguage = true;

    public function onContentPrepareForm($form, $data)
    {
        // Add the extra input fields to the form
```

```
    }

    public function onContentPrepareData($context, $data)
    {
        // Populate the extra input fields with extra user data
    }

    public function onUserAfterSave($data, $isNew, $result, $error)
    {
        // Save the extra input into the database
    }

    public function onUserAfterDelete($data, $result, $error)
    {
        // Remove the extra data when removing the user
    }
}
```

As you can see, there are four events used in the plugin class: onContentPrepareForm, onContentPrepareData, onUserAfterSave and onUserAfterDelete. The last two belong to the user group and the first two belong to the content group. In the code outline above, each event method contains a comment to show you what the purpose is of that event.

The protected variable $autoloadLanguage is used here to make sure that the plugins language file en-GB.plg_user_firstlast.ini is always loaded by Joomla in both the frontend and the backend.

Adding fields to the profile form

We will start with the onContentPrepareForm() method, which will add our new fields to the form. Also we are going to define our own XML file with a fieldset for two extra fields – firstname and lastname. This is discussed after the PHP code in the plugin method.

```
public function onContentPrepareForm($form, $data)
{
}
```

The event method has two arguments: $form and $data. To add our fields to the form, we only need to use the $form object. Theoretically, some code can call for this event with $form being an array. However, this is useless in our case. To make sure this does not give weird PHP Fatal Errors, we simply check whether the $form argument is indeed an instance of the JForm class. If it is not, we cannot extend it either, so we return false.

```
if (!($form instanceof JForm))
```

```
{
     $this->_subject->setError('JERROR_NOT_A_FORM');

     return false;
}
```

Because `JForm` instances are all over the place with Joomla, we want to make sure that our fields are only added to the profile forms and not to others forms like a Menu-Item form or an article form. To check for the right form, we fetch the form's name using the `JForm::getName()` method and then check whether it is the one we need:

```
$context = $form->getName();
if (!in_array($context, $this->allowedContext))
{
     return true;
}
```

This contextual check is also being used elsewhere in our plugin. To prevent code duplication, we move the allowed contexts to a private array that is defined at the top of our class:

```
private $allowedContext = array(
     'com_users.profile',
     'com_users.user',
     'com_users.registration',
     'com_admin.profile',
);
```

In the last part of the method, the `JForm::loadFile()` call is used to load our XML file and insert its form definitions into the current form. With the `JForm::addFormPath()` call we tell `JForm` to search the plugins subfolder `form/` as well for form definitions. The argument to `loadFile()` - in our case `form` – is a reference to the file itself (`form.xml`).

```
JForm::addFormPath(__DIR__ . '/form');
$form->loadFile('form', false);

return true;
```

After the XML is added, we are done and we return `true`.

Defining the extra fields in XML

The file `plugins/user/firstlast/form/form.xml` contains our `JForm` definition:

```xml
<?xml version="1.0" encoding="utf-8"?>
<form>
    <fields name="firstlast">
        <fieldset name="firstlast" label="PLG_USER_FIRSTLAST_FIELDS">
            <field
                name="firstname"
                type="text"
                id="firstname"
                description="PLG_USER_FIRSTLAST_FIELD_FIRSTNAME_DESC"
                label="PLG_USER_FIRSTLAST_FIELD_FIRSTNAME_LABEL"
                filter="string"
            />
            <field
                name="lastname"
                type="text"
                id="lastname"
                description="PLG_USER_FIRSTLAST_FIELD_LASTNAME_DESC"
                label="PLG_USER_FIRSTLAST_FIELD_LASTNAME_LABEL"
                filter="string"
            />
        </fieldset>
    </fields>
</form>
```

It is not a complex form. A new set of fields named `firstlast` is defined. This means that `JForm` will generate HTML code that looks a little bit like this:

```html
<input type="text" name="firstlast[firstname]" />
<input type="text" name="firstlast[lastname]" />
```

The new fields are inserted into an array `firstlast`. We need to remember this when we are dealing with the POST values of the profile. The fieldsets `name` is of no importance here. It is only used to visually place the fields somewhere on screen. Fieldsets do not change the way that the POST values are being handled.

The `$autoloadLanguage` flag in the plugin makes sure that all labels and descriptions are available to be translated correctly by Joomla.

Once you are done with this step - both the `onContentPrepareData()` method and the XML file - you can activate the plugin. This adds a new tab to the user's profile in the Joomla **User Manager**.

Saving our data to #__user_profile

The next step is to have our data saved to the database. This is done using the onUserAfterSave() method we have discussed earlier in this chapter. The method looks like this:

```
public function onUserAfterSave($data, $isNew, $result, $error)
{
    return true;
}
```

Our new fields will need to be stored somewhere. Because the #__users table is not really designed for storing extra fields, we are going to store them in the same place where Joomla already includes support for extra profile fields of the **User – Profile** plugin: the table #__user_profile. In this table, a new row will be created for each unique combination of user ID (user_id), field name (profile_key) and field value (profile_value). For instance, a row might contain the following fields:

```
user_id = 42
profile_key = firstname
profile_value = John
```

The $data argument of the event method contains a copy of all the user data. Within this user data, the user ID can be found, which we need for storing data in the #__user_profile table. We can extract the user ID from the $data array with the following code:

```
$userId = isset($data['id']) ? (int) $data['id'] : 0;
```

This works fine. We can also use a specific Joomla call JArrayHelper::getValue() to do exactly the same thing. Either approach is fine:

```
$userId = JArrayHelper::getValue($data, 'id', 0, 'int');
```

There are a couple of conditions that need to be satisfied to make sure our additional fields are stored correctly. First of all, we require that the $userId is higher than 0 (which is the same as the $userId is true), because otherwise we do not know for which user to save the field values.

We also want to check whether the $result is true, meaning the user data was saved correctly to the #__users table. The last check is to see whether our fieldgroup firstlast indeed contains values. If all three checks are successful, we have made sure saving these values to the #__user_profile table makes sense. The three checks combined look like this:

```
if ($userId && $result
    && isset($data['firstlast'])
    && (count($data['firstlast']))))
```

```
{
    ...
}
```

Within this `if` structure (replacing the dots), we are going to save the data to `#__user_profile`. There are various ways to do this. We can query the table to see whether values already exist for each of our fields and then use either an `INSERT` (in case no values exist for that field) or an `UPDATE` (in case values already exist for that field). However, having two fields `firstname` and `lastname` this would require four queries in total. A more efficient way is to simply remove all values that belong to our plugin and then use only `INSERT` queries. With this approach, only three queries are needed.

Instead of placing all these queries directly in our `onUserAfterSave()` method, we are going to keep our code lean and mean, and place each query in its own method: `deleteFields()` and `insertFields()`. The additional code in the event method is therefore still readable:

```
try
{
    $this->deleteFields($userId);

    $ordering = 0;
    foreach ($data['firstlast'] as $fName => $fValue)
    {
        $this->insertField($userId, $fName, $fValue, $ordering);
        $ordering++;
    }
}
catch (RuntimeException $e)
{
    $this->_subject->setError($e->getMessage());
    return false;
}
```

Fetching errors

The code above contains a `try-catch` statement. If for some reason, something goes wrong when executing our queries, which causes a PHP exception to occur, this exception will be caught by the `catch{}` structure.

```
$this->_subject->setError($e->getMessage());
```

Here we bump into a new class variable `$this->_subject`. This is an instance of the class `JEventDispatcher`, which will be discussed at the end of this book in chapter 12. It is the object that actually generates the event, on behalf of the component or other code segment that istriggering the event. We refer to this object as the dispatcher.

Because the plugin has no clue in which application it is being executed (CMS, another web application, command line), it is bad practice to let the plugin deal with error handling. Instead, the code above hands the error back to the dispatcher and lets the dispatcher deal with it. Good riddance.

Database helper for removing data

We use helper functions for all database interaction. Perhaps things can be optimized even more by reusing the MVC classes of some core component. In our plugin we are also using raw queries. This might mean our code will crash if the table structure of `#__user_profile` changes. Or to put it differently: Whenever the table structure of `#__user_profile` changes, our plugin needs an update as well. If the profile component offers API calls, we should use those instead.

In our event method the two task methods `deleteFields()` and `insertField()` are called upon. We still have to create them. First we are going to define the `deleteFields()` method. It only needs one variable to process the right query: the $userId. We construct the query in an object-oriented way by using the `JDatabaseQuery` class (instantiated here as $query):

```
protected function deleteFields($userId)
{
    $db = JFactory::getDbo();

    $query = $db->getQuery(true)
        ->delete($db->quoteName('#__user_profiles'))
        ->where($db->quoteName('user_id') . '=' . (int) $userId)
        ->where($db->quoteName('profile_key')
            . ' LIKE ' . $db->quote('firstlast.%')
            )
    ;

    $db->setQuery($query);
    $db->execute();
}
```

This will generate a database query similar to the following:

```
DELETE FROM `#__user_profiles`
  WHERE `user_id` = "1234"
  AND `profile_key` LIKE 'firstlast.%'
```

Adding a prefix to your profile data

With the `deleteFields()` method, we are only removing records that have a `profile_` key starting with `firstlast`. The **User – Profile** plugin uses the exact same table. However, it uses the prefix `profile` instead. By using prefixes, multiple extensions can use the same `#__user_profile` table while not getting in each other's way. Make sure you always use a unique prefix in the `profile_key`!

Database helper for inserting data

Next, we are going to create a helper function for inserting data. All records include a `$userId`, a `$name` and `$value` (our field names and field values) and an `$ordering`. In the `onUserAfterSave()` method this `$ordering` was set. However, it is just following the ordering of the fields as defined in our XML file. The first field being `firstname` with ordering 0, the second field being `lastname` with ordering 1.

The `JDatabaseQuery` object allows us to define the columns and the values as arrays. Earlier, we mentioned the prefixes used in both our plugin and the **User – Profile** plugin. The `profile_key` field gets the prefix `firstlast` plus a dot, so that the `profile_key` for the firstname becomes `firstlast.firstname`.

```
protected function insertField($userId, $name, $value, $ordering)
{
    $db = JFactory::getDbo();

    $columns = array(
        'user_id',
        'profile_key',
        'profile_value',
        'ordering'
    );

    $values = array(
        $userId,
        $db->quote('firstlast.' . $name),
        $db->quote($value),
        $ordering
    );

    $query = $db->getQuery(true)
        ->insert($db->quoteName('#__user_profiles'))
        ->columns($db->quoteName($columns))
        ->values(implode(',', $values));

    $db->setQuery($query);
```

```
    $db->execute();
}
```

Database helper to fetch data

We are going to add a third database helper, while we are at it. When we are loading our saved data in the next step, we need to fetch all our fields from the database again using a SELECT statement. We are going to use a function getFields() for this.

```
protected function getFields($userId)
{
    $db = JFactory::getDbo();
    $query = $db->getQuery(true);

    $columns = array('profile_key', 'profile_value');

    $query->select($db->quoteName($columns));
    $query->from($db->quoteName('#__user_profiles'));
    $query->where($db->quoteName('profile_key')
        .' LIKE '.$db->quote('firstlast.%'));
    $query->where($db->quoteName('user_id') . '=' . (int) $userId);
    $query->order('ordering ASC');

    $db->setQuery($query);
    $results = $db->loadRowList();

    return $results;
}
```

Note that again the prefix firstlast. is used to only fetch our own fields, not the fields used by other extensions.

Loading our data back into the form

The next major step in our plugin is to load data from the table and insert this data into our form again. The method that we are going to create for this, looks like this:

```
public function onContentPrepareData($context, $data)
{
    return true;
}
```

First, we are going to check for the right context again, just like with the onContentPrepareForm() method:

```
if (!in_array($context, $this->allowedContext))
{
    return true;
}
```

Next, we are extracting the $userId from the $data, in order for us to load all user-specific data from the #__user_profile table using our helper function getFields():

```
if (is_object($data))
{
    $userId = isset($data->id) ? $data->id : 0;

    if (!isset($data->firstlast) and $userId > 0)
    {
        try
        {
            $fields = $this->getFields($userId);
        }
        catch (RuntimeException $e)
        {
            $this->_subject->setError($e->getMessage());
            return false;
        }
        ...
```

Now that we have our custom values ($fields), we will merge them with the user data ($data). Remember that each profile_key fieldname still has the prefix firstlast (plus a dot) so we need to remove that prefix first.

```
...
$data->firstlast = array();
foreach ($fields as $field)
{
    $fieldName = str_replace('firstlast.', '', $field[0]);
    $data->firstlast[$fieldName] = json_decode($field[1], true);

    if ($data->firstlast[$fieldName] === null)
    {
        $data->firstlast[$fieldName] = $field[1];
    }
}
```

There is no need to return the $data. Returning true is just fine. The original user data is modified directly, because $data is a reference by default.

Autocompleting the firstname and lastname

Now that we have a method in place to store the `firstname` and `lastname` and load them again from the database, it is time to make things a little bit more user friendly. Our new fields will confuse people. First you ask them to enter a **Name** (the original name field of `#__users`) and then you also ask them for a firstname and lastname. It would be much better if the firstname and lastname would be extracted from the name itself.

Many people in western countries will have a name similar to **John Doe**, where the first part of their name is the firstname (**John**) and the rest is the lastname (**Doe**). What we can do is split the name into segments separated by spaces (using the PHP function `explode()`), use the first array element as `firstname` and the rest again as `lastname`. This way the lastname will also include any middle name of prefix to the lastname. This will not work in all cases – some people have multiple firstnames, and in some cultures the names are reversed (not John Doe but Doe John). But hey, it is better than nothing.

```
if (empty($data->firstlast['firstname'])
        && empty($data->firstlast['lastname'])
        && !empty($data->name))
{
    $name = explode(' ', $data->name);
    if (count($name) >= 2)
    {
        $data->firstlast['firstname'] = trim(array_shift($name));
        $data->firstlast['lastname'] = trim(implode(' ', $name));
    }
}
```

Perhaps one more improvement would be to hide the original `name` field altogether and only require a user to enter a `firstname` and `lastname`. To hide the original name field using CSS rules is an option. Constructing the real name from the firstname and lastname is simple as well:

```
if (!empty($data->firstlast['firstname'])
        && !empty($data->firstlast['lastname'])
        && empty($data->name))
{
    $data->name = $data->firstlast['firstname']
        . ' ' . $data->firstlast['lastname'];
}
```

Greeting the user with his firstname

Interestingly, the plugin as it is now also shows our new fields in the frontend when a user is viewing his own profile – not just when he is editing his profile. For the read-only view, the same `JForm` approach is being used. No additional work is required here.

Now that we have both a full name and a firstname available, we can also go through the Joomla application and see where the full name is still ok or where a firstname display would be more appropriate. The login module is a good example.

The file `modules/mod_login/tmpl/default_logout.php` contains the following code segment:

```
echo JText::sprintf('MOD_LOGIN_HINAME',
    htmlspecialchars($user->get('name')));
```

The user is greeted with his full name. It would make more sense to greet the user with his `firstname`, if it exists. To modify this, we can make a template override of the file by copying the file to the location `templates/YOURTEMPLATE/html/mod_login/default_logout.php`. Let's change the code a little bit:

```
$greetingName = trim($user->get('firstname'));
if (empty($greetingName)) $greetingName = $user->get('name');
$greetingName = htmlspecialchars($greetingName);

echo JText::sprintf('MOD_LOGIN_HINAME', $greetingName));
```

Now we are setting the greeting name to the `firstname`, unless that value is not set, in which case we fallback to the `name` (the full name).

Inserting extra fields when loading a user

There is one major problem here. It does not work. The `firstname` value is not included into the `$user` object (`JFactory::getUser()`) when the user is being loaded from the database. Even worse: There is no plugin event that allows you to hook into the process of loading a user. There is no event like `onUserLoadAfter` or something similar.

Luckily, we are coders and we can create such an event for ourselves anyway. It is not even that hard. We can add an output override of the template file `default_logout.php`. Within this override, just below the `_JEXEC` statement, we can insert a single line:

```
JEventDispatcher::getInstance()->trigger('onUserLoad', array($user));
```

This will trigger a new user event called `onUserLoad`, and all plugins loaded at this moment will be able to listen to it. Now we can implement this event `onUserLoad` in our plugin as well:

```
public function onUserLoad($user)
```

```
{
    return true;
}
```

The plugin method will start with some validation to make sure the user record is there and is not a guest record (with an ID of zero).

```
if (empty($user) || empty($user->id))
{
    return false;
}
```

Next, we use our existing getFields() method to fetch the extra fields from the database:

```
try
{
    $fields = $this->getFields($user->id);
}
catch (Exception $e)
{
    $this->_subject->setError($e->getMessage());
    return false;
}
```

These extra fields are merged into the $user object:

```
foreach ($fields as $field)
{
    $fieldName = str_replace('firstlast.', '', $field[0]);
    $fieldValue = $field[1];
    $user->set($fieldName, $fieldValue);
}
```

Once this is done, the $user object in the template override will include a property firstname:

```
$user->get('firstname');
```

Improvements on autoloading data

There are some improvements to be made here. The getFields() method now only fetches all fields belonging to our plugin (prefix firstlast), while it can be useful to load other profile fields as well.

Also, the plugin method is run on every page where the **Login Module** is being displayed and this will cause an extra SELECT query on every page. To increase performance, it is an idea to add the extra user data to the user session instead. This way, the SELECT query is only executed once per user session. Of course, when the user data is changed during the session, the stored data need to be refreshed as well.

Cleaning up data again

To finalize our firstlast plugin example, we still need to catch one more event -onUserAfterDelete() - to make sure we clean up the database when the user is removed. The code is very similar to methods we have seen before.

The method is defined with three arguments: $data, $result and $error. When the $result flag is set to false, the removal for the user failed for some reason and we must assume that the user record is still there. Therefore, there is no need to remove the additional data either, so we return false.

```
public function onUserAfterDelete($data, $result, $error)
{
    if (!$result)
    {
        return false;
    }
```

Next, we extract the $userId from the data again and use it to call upon our task method. Because we have the deleteFields() method already in place, the code in the onUserAfterDelete() method is short and to the point.

```
$userId = JArrayHelper::getValue($data, 'id', 0, 'int');

if ($userId)
{
    try
    {
        $this->deleteFields($userId);
    }
    catch (Exception $e)
    {
        $this->_subject->setError($e->getMessage());
        return false;
    }
}

    return true;
}
```

Easier version of the same plugin?

Instead of introducing our own field group `firstlast`, we also could have used the existing field group `profile`. This would require the **User – Profile** plugin to be enabled for our plugin to work. If this additional requirement is an option, it allows for a lot of code to be skipped.

The `onContentPrepareForm()` still needs to be used to allow for our own XML fields to be loaded. However, all other events can be skipped. Including all task methods and helper methods, except for the part in the `onContentPrepareData()` method that autocompletes the `firstname` and `lastname` based upon the existing name value.

8.6 Extending usergroups

Most of the tricks that can be applied to user data can also be applied to usergroup data. We can hook into usergroups using the following events:

```
onUserAfterSaveGroup
onUserBeforeSaveGroup
onUserBeforeDeleteGroup
onUserAfterDeleteGroup
```

As with users, we can also hook into `onContent` events to modify existing forms. Let's take the example of adding an extra field `description` to the usergroup forms. This optional description allows backend users to keep better track of which usergroup was created for what purpose.

The plugin code for this usergroup example will not be shown here in detail. The source resembles for the most parts the code of the firstlast plugin in the previous sections - it would be a waste of paper to include the same code again.

To migrate the plugin you can simply rename the events `onUserAfterSave` to `onUserAfterSaveGroup` and `onUserAfterDelete` to `onUserAfterDeleteGroup`.

The full code of this plugin is available on GitHub through the books repository. Look in the folder **chapter08** for the plugin **plg_system_usergroupdescription**. The reason why this is not a User Plugin but a System Plugin will be explained in the following sections of this book.

Storing data in your own database table

There is no existing table for storing usergroup related information, so we are going to create our own table manually. Our plugin will only support one field `description` and therefore the table has only two columns:

```
CREATE TABLE IF NOT EXISTS `#__usergroup_fields` (
  `usergroup_id` int(11) NOT NULL,
  `description` varchar(255) NOT NULL,
  UNIQUE KEY `usergroup_id` (`usergroup_id`)
);
```

Task methods

With the `firstlast` plugin of the previous section, the plugin class included three task methods: `getFields()`, `deleteFields()` and `insertField()`. The task methods are copied to this new plugin and are modified accordingly, to match the new database structure.

The `SELECT` query for instance now looks like this:

```
$columns = array('description');
$query->select($db->quoteName($columns));
$query->from($db->quoteName('#__usergroup_fields'));
$query->where($db->quoteName('usergroup_id')
    . '=' . (int)$usergroupId);
```

Extending the form

The events `onContentPrepareForm` and `onContentPrepareData` are again used to modify the form. To match the proper usergroup form, the `$allowedContext` definition changes:

```
protected $allowedContext = array(
    'com_users.group',
);
```

Again, the logic here is that we use the `onContentPrepareForm()` event method to extend the existing `$form` object with our own additional XML file `form.xml`. The `onContentPrepareData()` event method is then used to add the additional `description` to the usergroup data.

Creating a template override ... with our plugin?

There is only one major problem. The template file that is converting the XML form into an

actual HTML form is `administrator/components/com_users/views/group/`
`tmpl/edit.php`. While many `JForm` templates allow for automatic detection of fieldsets
and fields, this template does not. It does not allow any additional fields to be displayed
automatically. It only supports the default fields `title` and `parent_id`. Even though we
will have added the new `description` field correctly using our plugin, it will never show
in the backend.

To overcome this issue, a template override can be used. We simply create a new override
folder `administrator/templates/TEMPLATE/html/com_users/group` - make
sure to replace `TEMPLATE` with the name of your admin template, for instance `hathor` or
`isis`. Next, we copy the `edit.php` to this override folder and modify things from there.
Within the `edit.php` file, move out the blocks that hard-code the two fields `title` and
`parent_id` and replace them with a more dynamic code version that shows all the fields
defined in the `$form` object.

This template override is placed within the current Joomla admin template. This adds an
extra requirement for an additional file in a non-plugin folder. What if somebody wants
to use our plugin and chooses to use a different backend template? It is much nicer if our
plugin simply includes our template override as well. Whoever uses our plugin can simply
use our template override as well.

Joomla is cool. This can be done. We can create a template override from within our plugin
and allow for the component view to look in our own plugin folder instead when searching
for the layout file `edit.php`.

Before we start going down this path, I have to warn you that this approach is kind of
hackish. It does not use core hacks but rather uses a lot of tricks to implement something
that we would have liked to be very simple. It would be great if every view would generate a
plugin event to change the layout path - in other words, the folder containing our modified
`edit.php` file - before rendering the view. Unfortunately, there is no such event. We will
need to create a workaround for this to work – and it is a rather large workaround.

Changing from User Plugin to System Plugin

To allow for creating a template override with our plugin, we are going to tell Joomla to
look for a different `JView` class when it displays the usergroup form. This way, we replace
the original `JView` class with our own and add our own layout path to it. Because of this
additional layout path, our template override is loaded instead of the original `edit.php`
file.

We have seen such rerouting of classes before in chapter 6, when we were dealing with
System Plugins. Actually, this type of rerouting can **only** be done with a System Plugin. We
need to convert our User Plugin to a System Plugin:

We move all the files in `plugins/user/usergroupdescription` to `plugins/system/usergroupdescription` and change the class name. The overview of the class now looks like this:

```
class PlgSystemUsergroupdescription extends JPlugin
{
    public function onAfterInitialise()
    {}

    public function onContentPrepareForm(
        $form, $data
    ) {}

    public function onContentPrepareData(
        $context, $data
    ) {}

    public function onUserAfterSaveGroup(
        $context, $data, $isNew
    ) {}

    public function onUserAfterDeleteGroup(
        $usergroup, $success, $msg
    ) {}

    protected function getFields(
        $usergroupId
    ) {}

    protected function deleteFields(
        $usergroupId
    ) {}

    protected function insertField(
        $usergroupId, $name, $value
    ) {}
}
```

As you can see, we also add the `onAfterInitialise()` method that allows us to make some routing changes. Because System Plugins are always loaded in the Joomla system, we can safely use the original `onContent` and `onUser` events as well.

Rerouting the form page to our own JView class

The form is normally displayed using the class `UsersViewGroup`, which is located in the file `view.html.php` in the folder `administrator/components/com_users/views/group/`. The `onAfterInitalise()` method allows us to display the form not using this original class, but our own class instead.

First, we check for the correct URL using the `$input` variable. We make sure we are dealing with the component `com_users`, the view `group` and the layout `edit`. In other words, we make sure we are dealing with the correct request:

```
public function onAfterInitialise()
{
    $input = JFactory::getApplication()->input;

    if (JFactory::getApplication()->isAdmin()
        && $input->getCmd('option') == 'com_users'
        && $input->getCmd('view') == 'group'
        && $input->getCmd('layout') == 'edit'
    ) {
        JRequest::setVar('view', 'groupextra');
        JLoader::register('UsersViewGroupextra',
            __DIR__ . '/views/group/view.html.php');
    }
}
```

After we have made sure that we are hooking into the correct request, we tell Joomla to use the new view `groupextra` instead. The new value `groupextra` of the `view` variable will be picked up by the `com_users` controller and it will construct the class name `UsersViewGroupextra` based upon this `view` variable. Joomla will try to locate this class `UsersViewGroupextra` in the component's folder by default. Obviously, Joomla will not find our new class in that location and this will cause an error. However, we are going to register the new `view` class here in the `onAfterInitialise()` method as well. This way Joomla has no problem locating the new class in the file that we include with our plugin:

```
plugins/system/usergroupdescription/views/group/view.html.php
```

We could have used any path and any filename for this. However, it seems like a good idea to copy the folder structure of the `com_users` component.

Extending the original JView and JModel

The main reason for creating a new `view.html.php` file is to define our new class `UsersViewGroupextra` inside this file. Initially, we simply want to copy the behavior of the original view. Because we do not want to copy a lot of code, we simply extend the new class from the original `UsersViewGroup` class. The only method that needs changing is `display()`. For this, we define the method ourselves, add some code and then call upon the parent's original.

```
class UsersViewGroupextra extends UsersViewGroup
{
    public function display($tpl = null)
    {
        ...
        return parent::display($tpl);
    }
}
```

At this point, we have messed up the component's normal logic. The component is unable to find the original class `UsersViewGroup`. To make sure the parent class is found, we use the `JLoader::register()` call to tell Joomla where to look for this class.

```
<?php
defined('_JEXEC') or die;

$comUsersPath = JPATH_ADMINISTRATOR . '/components/com_users/';
$viewPath = '/views/group/view.html.php';
$modelPath = '/models/group.php';

JLoader::register('UsersViewGroup', $comUsersPath . $viewPath);
JLoader::register('UsersModelGroup', $comUsersPath . $modelPath);

class UsersViewGroupextra extends UsersViewGroup
{
    public function display($tpl = null)
    {
        $this->addTemplatePath(__DIR__ . '/tmpl/');

        return parent::display($tpl);
    }
}

class UsersModelGroupextra extends UsersModelGroup
{
}
```

As you can see, we are also messing with the model. The `com_users` component is following the MVC (Model-View-Controller) pattern, and because of this, the view gets its data from a model. Because we renamed the original view, the component is now looking for an alternative model as well: `UsersModelGroupextra`.

We have no special need for this model, so we simply extend the original model class, like we extended the original view class. Again, because Joomla is unable to find the original model class `UsersModelGroup`, we use `JLoader::register()` to tell Joomla where to look for the class.

Finally ... the override itself

The only reason we created all the code above, was to introduce one line into the view class:

```
$this->addTemplatePath(__DIR__ . '/tmpl/');
```

With this line, we are able to tell the view to look for the `edit.php` file in our own location, instead of the original template path. The `edit.php` file is not changed dramatically. It already used the `JForm` library to generate a form. However, it was used to explicitly generate two fields. We are going to replace this with a `foreach()` loop that fetches all fields in the form:

```php
<?php foreach ($this->form->getFieldset() as $field) : ?>
<div class="control-group">
    <?php if ($field->hidden == false) : ?>
    <div class="control-label">
        <?php echo $field->label; ?>
    </div>
    <div class="controls">
        <?php echo $field->input; ?>
    </div>
    <?php endif; ?>
</div>
<?php endforeach; ?>
```

With this new layout in place, the plugin shows us the additional fields that we have inserted into the `JForm` object, using the two `onContent` methods. Once the form is saved, the `onUser` methods are called, allowing us to save the form data.

8.7   Reacting to logins and logouts

With the events in the User Plugin group you can also react to user logins and logouts.

```
onUserLogin
onUserAfterLogin
onUserLoginFailure
onUserLogout
```

```
onUserAfterLogout
onUserLogoutFailure
```

There are also some events in Authentication Plugins that I want to add in here. Note that these events can only be used within an Authentication Plugin and not within a User Plugin:

```
onUserAuthenticate
onUserAuthorisation
onUserAuthorisationFailure
```

 This pretty much extends from what we have seen in the chapter on Joomla Authentication Plugins. Chapter 8 was mostly about the authentication process itself. These sections are best seen as a continuation of that chapter.

After a login request has been posted to Joomla, the `JApplication::login()` method calls upon Authentication Plugins to determine whether the user credentials are correct or not. This call is named `onUserAuthenticate`, which is only handled by Authentication Plugins as we have seen before. After this initial authentication, the various login events are triggered.

Authorizing a login

When the credentials are found to be correct, in other words when authentication is a success, the next step is the authorization of the user. Here the event `onUserAuthorisation` is triggered. At this point, both User Plugins and Authentication Plugins have been initialized, so you can use both to intercept this event.

```
public function onUserAuthorisation(array $response, array $options)
{
}
```

The method receives two arguments: `$response` and `$options`. The `$response` is an array with the same values as the `$response` object that is part of the authentication procedure. The `$response['status']` therefore contains a status `JAuthentication::STATUS_SUCCESS` (which has a value of 1).

The `$response` also contains a `type` property (referring to the Authentication Plugin that gave successful authentication). Most commonly, the relevant Authentication Plugin also sets additional values in the `$response` array like `email`, `fullname` and `language`.

The second argument - `$options` – is the exact same as the `$options` argument for Authentication Plugins, with values like `silent` (for authentications that should occur in the background) and `remember` (when a cookie needs to be set for cookie-based logins).

What can we do with this new event? Well, there are no core plugins that make use of this event. And the workings of this event are very similar to `onUserAuthenticate` event. So, we can even skip this event and use the event `onUserAuthenticate` instead. So why would we still use it. This event is still interesting because it allows for double authentication. For instance, even though a user's credentials are correct, there might be other reasons to reject the login: Perhaps, this is a testing site, we do not want regular users to have access to. Perhaps, logins are not allowed on Sundays.

The `onUserAuthorisation()` method is able to change the status of the `$response` object, which again is picked up by the login process. When the status is set to either `JAuthentication::STATUS_EXPIRED` or `JAuthentication::STATUS_DENIED`, the login is denied.

For instance, we can require that people login using a valid login (`onUserAuthenticate`) and a valid IP (`onUserAuthorisation`). To do this, we first set the login status to denied, when the IP does not match:

```
public function onUserAuthorisation(array $response, array $options)
{
    if ($_SERVER['REMOTE_ADDR'] != '127.0.0.1')
    {
        $response['status'] = JAuthentication::STATUS_DENIED;
    }
}
```

Once the authorization is either denied or expired, the login process stops and by default, an error is given. Before this happens, an additional event `onUserAuthorisationFailure` is triggered. You can use this to redirect the user to a page with login instructions.

```
public function onUserAuthorisationFailure($authorisation)
{
    $denied_page = JRoute::_('index.php?Itemid=1');
    $expired_page = JRoute::_('index.php?Itemid=2');
    $other_page = JRoute::_('index.php?Itemid=3');

    $status = $authorisation['status'];

    if ($status == JAuthentication::STATUS_DENIED)
    {
        $redirect = $denied_page;
    }
    elseif ($status == JAuthentication::STATUS_EXPIRED)
```

```
    {
        $redirect = $expired_page;
    }
    else
    {
        $redirect = $other_page;
    }

    $app = JFactory::getApplication();
    $app->setRedirect($redirect);
    $app->close();
    exit;
}
```

Handling a successful login ... or denying access anyway

When the credentials are validated (so onUserAuthenticate delivers a success) and there are no other plugins objecting to the login either (so onUserAuthorisation does not change things), the next step in the login process is reached. The event onUserLogin is triggered.

```
public function onUserLogin(array $response, array $options)
{
    return true;
}
```

With Authentication Plugins, only one plugin needs to make sure the credentials are correct. With User Plugins, this is different: All plugins are responsible for a success. All onUserLogin() methods need to return true. If one plugin returns false, the whole login process fails.

A good example of this can be found within the **User – Joomla** plugin, which is responsible for validating Joomla users the Joomla way. When authentication is a success (for instance, using a GMail plugin to validate the credentials against Google Mail), it might still be that a login needs to be denied. For instance, because the user is blocked by a flag in the #__users table, or because the user belongs to a usergroup that simply is not allowed to login. The **User – Joomla** plugin checks for these conditions and returns false if the user should be denied access. The plugin is also responsible for keeping track of user sessions in the Joomla database, so it is pretty vital to have this plugin enabled in your Joomla site.

Interestingly, the **System – Language Filter** plugin also catches this event onUserLogin. It uses it to set the user specific language, if it differs from the current language.

After a successful login

In case all User Plugins return `true` upon the event `onUserLogin`, the event `onUserAfterLogin` is triggered. This is the only event that you can use when you need to be absolutely certain that the user login was successful.

```
public function onUserAfterLogin($options)
{
}
```

The **User – Joomla** plugin uses this event to set a cookie for cookie-based authentication. When you are writing your own Single Sign On method, this would be a good method to use as well. Most likely, you do not want the normal Joomla login to fail, when the remote Single Sign On (logging the user into a remote application automatically) fails. One failure is already bad enough. The SSO procedure is best placed in `onUserAfterLogin()` and not `onUserLogin()`.

After a failed login

In case all of the Authentication Plugins return `false` upon the event `onUserAuthenticate`, the event `onUserLoginFailure` is triggered:

```
public function  onUserLoginFailure($response)
{
}
```

The **System – Log** plugin uses this event to write the login failure to the Joomla logs. You can also use this event, when you have some cleaning up to do. Say that you have written a custom Authentication Plugin that authenticates through some remote system. When authentication succeeds, you might set some additional cookies for later usage. If the login fails in a later stage, these additional cookies are best removed. A perfect example for applying the `onUserLoginFailure()` method.

Handling logouts

When a logout occurs, the logout process is initiated by the `JApplication` class – this time the `JApplication::logout()` call is used. First, the `onUserLogout()` method is called upon with a `$parameter` array, containing an `id` and `username` of the user to be logged out.

```
public function onUserLogout($parameters, $options)
{
    return true;
}
```

Just like with the `onUserLogin()` method, the return value of the `onUserLogout()`

method is of great importance: All plugins need to return `true`, for the logout process to be completed. If one plugin returns `false`, the entire logout process fails.

When `onUserLogout` fails, the event `onUserAfterLogout` is triggered. It is important to realize that the Joomla session is already destroyed during the `onUserLogout` event, so calls to the session are pointless. When the logout process fails, it does not mean that the login is restored.

The method is useful for these cases, where you absolutely need to make sure that the method is only executed when the logout really happened, for instance for cleaning up cookies.

```
public function onUserAfterLogout($options)
{
}
```

When the `onUserLogout()` method of one of the plugins returns `false`, so when the logout process has failed, the `onUserAfterLogout` event is skipped and the `onUserLogoutFailure` event is generated instead:

```
public function onUserLogoutFailure()
{
}
```

This is a little bit weird. As mentioned earlier, when logging out a user, the session becomes invalid and the original login is effectively destroyed. It is not possible to restore the login upon failure.

Also, a logout is not much more than the removal of the user session. Why on earth would it fail? Good point: The Joomla source itself does not implement this method. I have not found any extension on the web, that uses this event. I also looked hard for any plugin using the `onUserLogout()` method to return `false` and generate this condition in the first place. However, I was unable to find any. It was probably added to Joomla, because of standardization. There already was an `onUserLoginFailure` event as well.

8.8   Blacklisting users by IP

A practical use case for some of these login related events, is a simple mechanism that allows you to blacklist users by IP. When a user succeeds to login, everything is fine. Whenever a user fails to login and keeps trying for say ten times, we are going to assume this is not a valid user attempt but a hack attempt from a certain IP. In this case, any further attempts from that IP will be blocked.

The source code for the following plugin can be found in the **chapter08/plg_authentication_blocker** folder of the GitHub repository.

For all of this to work, our plugin needs to be an Authentication Plugin, not a User Plugin. This is mainly because in earlier Joomla versions only Authentication Plugins were able to catch the event `onUserLoginFailure`. To make our plugin compatible with these versions, we create an Authentication Plugin.

The plugin will get the following layout:

```
class PlgAuthenticationBlocker extends JPlugin
{
    public function onUserAuthenticate(
        $credentials, $options, &$response
    )
    {
        return false;
    }

    public function onUserLoginFailure()
    {
        // When a user fails to login, the failure is logged
    }

    protected function checkDeny($username)
    {
        // When a user is blocked, give an error
    }

    protected function countFailedAttempts($username)
    {
        // Return number of failed attempts from this IP
    }

    protected function logAttempt($username)
    {
        // Log the failed attempt to the database
    }
}
```

The presence of the `onUserAuthenticate` method might confuse you. Our plugin does not deal with the actual authentication of users, it only deals with what comes afterwards. So, why do we need this event?

Joomla will call upon the `onUserAuthenticate` method of our plugin, because it will call upon the `onUserAuthenticate` method of all Authentication Plugins – call it a bug, call it a feature. Without the method, we would encounter a **PHP Fatal Error**, because the method `onUserAuthenticate` method cannot be found in our plugin. We bypass this problem by simply defining the method once. It does not do anything. It only returns `false` for now.

Logging a failed login attempt

The first step is to log a failed login attempt to our own database table. We are going to name our table `#__user_login_attempts`, because we are not going to store whether or not somebody is blacklisted, we are only going to store the actual login attempts. Perhaps we can later enhance our plugin to also log attempts that were successful, possibly offering ways to whitelist users. For now, we always will set the flag `success` to 0 (failed).

```sql
CREATE TABLE IF NOT EXISTS `#__user_login_attempts` (
  `id` int(11) NOT NULL AUTO_INCREMENT,
  `username` varchar(150) NOT NULL,
  `ip` varchar(15) NOT NULL,
  `success` tinyint(1) NOT NULL DEFAULT '0',
  `date` datetime NOT NULL,
  PRIMARY KEY (`id`),
  KEY `username` (`username`,`ip`)
)
```

Note the key for the combination `username` and `ip`. Every time a user tries to login, we will look up username and IP. The `SELECT` statement will be used a lot and needs to be well optimized.

To write to this table, we are going to implement a method `logAttempt()`. The method only receives the `$username` argument and a flag `$success` for logging either a login failure (default) or a login success (which we are not going to implement).

The values for the IP address and the date will be determined by the method itself:

```php
protected function logAttempt($username, $success = 0)
{
    $db = JFactory::getDbo();
    $ip = $_SERVER['REMOTE_ADDR'];

    $columns = array('username', 'ip', 'success', 'date');
    $values = array(
        $db->quote($username),
        $db->quote($ip),
        $success,
```

```
        $db->quote(JFactory::getDate()->toSql()),
    );

    $query = $db->getQuery(true)
        ->insert($db->quoteName('#__user_login_attempts'))
        ->columns($db->quoteName($columns))
        ->values(implode(',', $values));
    $db->setQuery($query);
    $db->execute();
}
```

To implement this method we are going to use the Authentication Plugin event
onUserLoginFailure. The method is basic. It only includes a call to our
logAttempt() method:

```
public function onUserLoginFailure($response)
{
    $this->logAttempt($response['username']);
}
```

You should be able to test out the functionality now. Every time the login fails, due to a
wrong username or password, a new log entry should appear in the database.

Checking for previous attempts and blocking access

Now that all failed login attempts are logged, the next step is to check for these previous
attempts, whenever a new attempt occurs. To do this, we first implement a task method
countFailedAttempts() that allows us to easily fetch the number of failed attempts
for a specific username and IP from the database.

```
protected function countFailedAttempts($username)
{
    $db = JFactory::getDbo();
    $query = $db->getQuery(true);
    $ip = $_SERVER['REMOTE_ADDR'];

    $columns = array('id');
    $query->select($db->quoteName($columns));
    $query->from($db->quoteName('#__user_login_attempts'));
    $query->where($db->quoteName('username')
        .' = ' . $db->quote($username));
    $query->where($db->quoteName('ip') . '=' . $db->quote($ip));
    $query->where($db->quoteName('success') . '=0');

    $db->setQuery($query);
```

```
    $db->execute();

    return $db->getNumRows();
}
```

Next, we are going to create the method checkDeny(), that checks these values to see whether there have been too many failed attempts for a certain username and certain IP, in order for this combination to be blocked.

```
protected function checkDeny($username)
{
    $failed = $this->countFailedAttempts($username);
    $failedTreshold = 10;

    if ($failed > $failedTreshold)
    {
        $error = JText::_('JGLOBAL_AUTH_ACCESS_DENIED');
        JError::raiseError(403, $error);
    }
}
```

Last but not least, the most vital part of our plugin: We need to call upon the checkDeny() method to see whether a certain login attempt should be blocked. This has to occur at some point in the login procedure, in order for no further authentication to occur. Unfortunately, there is no pre-authenticate event. We can either use a system event for this, which would mean the checkDeny() method is triggered for every incoming event, or we put it as early as possible within the authentication procedure: the onUserAuthenticate event.

While I told you previously the onUserAuthenticate() method of this plugin was only going to return false, we are now going to add a call to checkDeny() anyway:

```
public function onUserAuthenticate($credentials, $options, &$response)
{
    if (isset($credentials['username']))
    {
        $this->checkDeny($credentials['username']);
    }

    return false;
}
```

This works. There are of course some improvements to be made. All failed attempts remain in the database ... forever. A failed attempt from years ago will still count as dangerous, and without doubt, a lot of honest users will find their account blocked some day. Some kind of cleaning up would be nice here.

Also the threshold of login attempts is now a static number 10. It would be nicer to define this as a plugin parameter.

8.9 Event onUserAvatar

The `onUserAvatar` event is used in only one place in the Joomla source and that is in the file `libraries/fof/form/field/user.php`. It is used by third party extensions though, such as Akeeba Subscriptions. The event is part of the **FoF** library (**Framework-on-Framework**) and is thrown when a user field is being rendered. When a form is created using `FOFForm`, and this form includes a field of type `user` and it is used to display a list of users, that list will include the avatars of these users and the `onUserAvatar` event allows you to determine the avatar.

Or in a shorter version: The `onUserAvatar` event allows you to return the URL of the user's avatar. If no URL is made available through the event, **Gravatar** is used instead.

The event is only used in one single place in the current Joomla sources and it has never been used in a User Plugin that I encountered. The architecture is there though. It might be that future Joomla changes will allow this event to also be used in the user's profile and in other places.

8.10 Summary

In this chapter, you have learned what you can do with User Plugins: e.g. react on events when users are being saved or deleted. We have also discussed the login procedure a little bit more thoroughly.

We will now move away from users and authentication. Chapter 9 deals with search: basic search, Smart Search and external search engines.

Extending search

Most components that deal with content also need to deal with the ability to search for that content. Search Plugins are therefore among the most common plugins written for Joomla. This chapter covers how to write both Search Plugins and Smart Search Plugins. It also addresses external search mechanisms like Solr or Sphinx. In short: Here is all you need to know about search in Joomla.

9.1 Explaining normal search and Smart Search

The first thing we need to discuss when it comes to search in Joomla, is the difference between regular search and Smart Search. Regular search is the search functionality that has existed in Joomla since Mambo times. Smart Search is a newer search mechanism. It was first developed as a third party extension, called **Finder**. Then, with the release of Joomla 2.5, it was integrated in the core. Currently, it is named Smart Search, while in the code its old name `finder` is still used.

When you implement search into a Joomla site, you need to make a choice between regular search or Smart Search. Depending on this choice, you implement either the `com_search` component or the `com_finder` component. For module output, you implement either the `mod_search` module or the `mod_finder` module. You use a set of plugins that belong to either the `search` group or the `finder` group. The main difference between the two is the way search results are fetched - either in real-time or from a pre-built index. This chapter explains the difference between the two search mechanisms in more detail and shows you how you can create a plugin for either mechanism.

How regular search works

When the regular search is used by a visitor to search for a keyword, the initial search request is made through the `com_search` component (optionally linked through a Menu-Item) or the `mod_search` module. The controller of the `com_search` component receives this incoming request, initializes the `view` class, which calls upon the search model to perform the search query. To retrieve search results, the model initializes plugins in the group `search` and calls upon the event `onContentSearch`. Each plugin can use this event to run their own queries on certain database tables and return results. Typically, this all happens in real time.

Each search plugin is meant to represent its own type of content that can be searched for. The **Search - Content** plugin searches for articles, the **Search - Categories** plugin searches for categories (that is: article categories, not other categories) and so on. The core comes with a search plugin for each type of content. When you are using a third party extension to generate content, you will probably also look for a search plugin belonging to this third party extension.

The search can be limited to certain types of content (articles, weblinks, etc) by enabling only these plugins and disabling the rest. You can also use search parameters to specify which type of content needs to be searched for. This is referred to as a **search area**. Within the search form of the search component, you can select the search areas to narrow down your search results. Each search plugin is able to define one or more search areas through the event `onContentSearchAreas`, which should return a basic array.

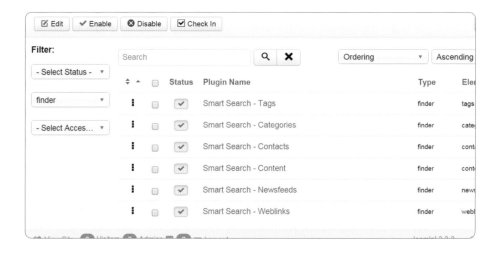

How Smart Search works

With Smart Search (also known as finder), the search process is quite different. The main difference is that it uses a separate search index that is initially constructed as a batch process.

Instead of the regular search component and search module, you will be using the finder equivalents. Similar to the regular search, a search request is first sent to the controller, which initializes a view, which again calls upon the model. Instead of letting the model call upon all finder plugins, which would again query their database tables in real time, the model fetches the search result from a set of database tables (prefix #__finder), that hold the search results in optimized chunks.

To get something out of these database tables, you need to put something in first. Within the **Smart Search** backend, you can use the **Index** button to index all content. This indexing process uses the Smart Search Plugins to fetch the search results from the original database tables, and stores these results into the finder tables. When indexing, the event method index() of each Smart Search Plugin is called upon.

One of the benefits of this indexing mechanism is that complex search queries are no longer performed. They are replaced with faster queries to optimized database tables. Additionally, the index tables provide a uniform search interface that treats all content types the same. However, this approach of using indexed searches gives an additional challenge: Every time an article changes, the indexes need to be updated as well. Instead of rebuilding the entire index again and again, you can use the **Content – Smart Search** plugin to make changes within the index for only those parts that change. If an article changes, this plugin makes sure that the indexed references to this article are changed as well. When you are using Smart Search on your site, it is best to have this plugin enabled at all times.

While creating a regular search plugin is fairly easy, creating a finder plugin is more complicated. You need to implement the index() method. However, you also need to implement various other methods that are used by the **Content** plugin, to keep the index up to date when your content changes. We will cover everything in this chapter.

Which is better?

Regular search uses the original content tables. Smart Search uses separate index tables that contain the search results for all types of content. For example, suppose you have five types of content (for example articles, weblinks, contacts, categories and newsfeeds), with regular search, you would need to search through five different database tables. With Smart Search, you would almost think that only the index tables need to be used, so less database queries would be required. This is not true however. Smart Search uses more database queries to return search results. It can even be a little bit slower on a default Joomla site with demo data installed!

With a small site, when you look at performance, it does not matter much which search mechanism you use. Both regular search and Smart Search are fine. With medium sites (say up to 10,000 small articles), Smart Search becomes more and more efficient, thanks to the indexing technology. When you have a large site (say above 10,000 articles or when your articles are much larger in size), using Smart Search also begins to give you headaches (timeouts, performance issues) so consider the usage of external search engines.

There is another benefit to Smart Search: Like regular search, Smart Search has the ability to refine search results by selecting specific search areas. However, with Smart Search, this tuning is far more advanced. With regular search, you can decide to search for either weblinks or articles or both. However, you cannot specify that you only want to search for articles in a specific category.

Smart Search adds the concept of content mapping, where all content is placed into various branches (categories, authors, languages). It allows you to search for a specific keyword in articles, placed into a specific category, written by a specific person, in a specific language. It allows for much more filtering than regular search does.

Another cool feature is that Smart Search is able to give search suggestions as well. Searching for a word like **examp** would return zero results, however it would also give you the suggestion to search for **example** instead.

Most sites do not pay a lot of attention to their search pages. The primary search that visitors will be using is Google Search anyway. This should not mean that designing Joomla search pages can be skipped. It looks bad if your search is a mess, while all other pages look fine. If you do not want to put too much time into search, use the simpler regular search instead of tuning Smart Search.

Keep in mind that - while the **Content – Smart Search** plugin does a great job in keeping the finder indexes up to date – it is still recommended to rebuild the entire index once in a while (**Purge** then **Index**). This adds another task to your todo list. (We will discuss the CLI tool of Finder later in this chapter.)

In most situations, you can choose between Smart Search and regular search. However, there are some situations that require different solutions. With really large sites, it becomes almost impossible to rebuild the index from scratch – it will take hours (or days) to complete. Another issue might be disk space - index tables usually take up more space than the regular content tables. In these scenarios, it is best to offload the entire search to a dedicated search application such as Solr or Sphinx.

9.2   Creating a regular search plugin

When creating a regular search plugin, your plugin class needs to implement two methods. The method onContentSearch() should return an array, containing your search results. The method onContentSearchAreas() is optional, but recommended. It should return an array of the search types that your plugin provides.

The plugin layout looks like this:

```
class PlgSearchExample extends JPlugin
{
    public function onContentSearch(
        $text, $phrase='', $ordering='', $areas=null
    )
    {}

    public function onContentSearchAreas()
    {}
}
```

We will focus on getting the onContentSearch() method up and running first.

Our example plugin: A song catalog

We are going to build a search plugin. Because Joomla already includes search plugins for each core component, it is not likely that we will write a search plugin for the Joomla core. It is more likely that you need a search plugin for your own custom component. Because developing a component is not covered by this book, we are going to assume that you already have a custom component with its own type of content. This non-existent component is called com_music and will have its own set of database tables, of which we will create the structure.

The source code for the following plugin can be found in the **chapter09/plg_search_music** folder of the GitHub repository.

As an example, we will assume the existence of a component that generates a catalog of music with some kind of hierarchy (classical, pop, rock) and tracks (the actual songs). Each song is stored in a database table #__music_songs and has a `title`, a `text` (a description) and a `state` flag (to allow the song to be published or unpublished). It also has a reference to an artist (stored in a second table #__music_artists) and a reference to the category (for which the core category system is used).

The songs table looks like this:

```
CREATE TABLE `#__music_songs` (
    `id` int(11) NOT NULL AUTO_INCREMENT,
    `category_id` int(11) NOT NULL,
    `artist_id` int(11) NOT NULL,
    `title` varchar(255) NOT NULL,
    `text` text NOT NULL,
    `state` tinyint(1) NOT NULL,
    PRIMARY KEY (`id`)
);
```

The artists table looks like this:

```
CREATE TABLE `#__music_artists` (
    `id` int(11) NOT NULL AUTO_INCREMENT,
    `name` varchar(255) NOT NULL,
    PRIMARY KEY (`id`)
);
```

The database table is very basic. In real life, it is best to have some additional fields like `alias`, `params`, `hits` and `ordering` – you can inspect the database tables of core components to find some good examples. To keep things simple and to focus on creating a search plugin only, we are skipping these parts. All component code is skipped as well. We are simply assuming that we have a backend to manage entries like songs, artists and categories, and a frontend to display these entries.

Returning search results

The `onContentSearch()` method returns a list of search results. Typically, a database query is used to perform this search. To know what to search for, the method has four parameters:

o $text: The actual search request being made;
o $phrase: The value of the Search For field in the search form;
o $ordering: The value of the Ordering field in the search form;
o $areas: an array of the selected areas that should be searched;

We can now create a basic database query that searches our #__music_songs table for the $text string. The other parameters are ignored for now.

```
$db = JFactory::getDbo();

$query = $db->getQuery(true);
$query->select($db->quoteName('s.*'));
$query->from($db->quoteName('#__music_songs', 's'));
$query->where($db->quoteName('s.title')
    .' LIKE '.$db->quote('%'.$text.'%'));
$query->where($db->quoteName('s.state') . '=1');

$db->setQuery($query);
$results = $db->loadObjectList();

return $results;
```

In this code sample, we fetch the current database object and get a fresh query from it (the getQuery() method with true argument). Next, we fill this query object in order to select data from our database. If the $text variable had the value **example**, the SELECT statement would look similar to this:

```
SELECT s.* FROM `#__music_songs` AS s
  WHERE s.`title` LIKE '%example%';
```

You can see that this code executes a query, which returns some results and these results are displayed on screen right away. It works!

Fields to return to the search component

The code above shows some results. However, it also generates some PHP notices, caused by missing properties in our search results. When the search component renders the output of search results, all search results are treated the same – articles, weblinks, songs. To make sure they can all be displayed in the same way, the component expects your search results to have the following properties defined per search item:

o   `title`: The title of your item.

o   `section`:An indication of the section of the item. If your content has a very basic structure, you can use just a static value for all your content items. If you have categories, you can include the category name and even the category path (the category name plus the names of its parents). Customize it at will.

o   `text`: The complete text of your item. If you are using an `introtext` and `fulltext` like Joomla articles, concatenate them into a single `text`.

o   `created`: A string describing the creation date of your item (YYYY-MM-DD HH:MM:SS).

o   `href`: The system URL of your item. This value will be printed using a call to `JRoute::_()`, so there is no need to use `JRoute` yourself.

o   `browsernav`: This value is used for one thing. If it is set to 1, the link to the content item will open up in a new browser screen (the link target is set to `_blank`). Omitting this property will generate a PHP notice, so make sure to include it and set the value 0 by default.

Do not use a wildcard in your SELECT statements

In our earlier SQL statements the star wildcard (*) was used to select all fields from the table:

```
SELECT * FROM table
```

While this is convenient, it also downgrades performance. Our example table has only six fields and three of them definitely need to be selected (id, `title`, `text`). While tuning has not that much effect on our example, selecting three fields costs less effort than selecting all six fields. As soon as you have more fields or your table contains more entries, the performance gain will become more evident. The following query will perform better:

```
SELECT id,title,text FROM table
```

 Forgive me that this book will still contain wildcards, instead of selecting individual fields. It is just to make sure you can still read the code.

Selecting specific fields is faster than selecting fields with a star wildcard. The benefit is greatest when you are skipping `TEXT` fields or `BLOB` fields when they are not needed in your results. However, in our case, the field `text` (of type `TEXT`) is needed in the search results, so here this argument does not hold water.

Often, Joomla tables include all kind of meta-data that is relevant for CMS functionality. However, it will be less relevant to search results: `checkout_out`, `hits`, `params`, etc. Other fields might not be needed for displaying the search results, but can still be needed for making sure the right results are shown under the right circumstances. The fields related to the access rights are a good example here (`asset_id`, `access`, `created_by`).

It is also important how you implement the `WHERE` statement in your query to select specific rows and how this `WHERE` statement relates to the table indices. A full text search is always slower than other queries. This is important to know when you setup search queries. However, in this case, a full text search is exactly the setup we are after. We will go into the issue of full text searches later on in this chapter when we discuss non-Joomla solutions like **Sphinx**. There are some other arguments that matter too (like PHP memory consumption).

Checking for the correct area

When you go back to the search component form and filter the results by selecting only the search area **Articles**, the results from our music table are still shown. The reason for this is that the `$areas` argument is not used in our code yet.

A check needs to be added to match our own areas with the `$areas` argument. If it does match, we make our query and return the results. If it does not match, somebody is not searching for our content and our plugin should not return any results.

```php
public function onContentSearch(
    $text, $phrase='', $ordering='', $areas=null
)
{
    if (is_array($areas))
    {
        $arrayKeys = array_keys($this->onContentSearchAreas());

        if (!array_intersect($areas, $arrayKeys))
        {
            return array();
        }
    }

    $db = JFactory::getDbo();
    ...
    $results = $db->loadObjectList();

    return $results;
}
```

Specifying the search areas

In the previous code segment, we saw a PHP call to the method
`onContentSearchAreas()`.
We use it as an internal method. However, the method is also called by the search
component to display the **Search Only** field in the search form. Hence, the method is
actually an event method.

The method returns a list of the areas that are part of our component. In most cases, it
involves little more than the declaration of an array variable, which is used as return value:

```php
public function onContentSearchAreas()
{
    static $areas = array(
        'songs' => 'PLG_SEARCH_MUSIC_AREA_SONGS',
    );

    return $areas;
}
```

The array contains a translatable string `PLG_SEARCH_MUSIC_AREA_SONGS`, so it is
a good idea to include a language file with your plugin. To allow this language file to be
automatically loaded as well, we add the `$autoloadLanguage` flag to the top of the
class:

```php
protected $autoloadLanguage = true;
```

Adding a second search area

So far, we have been adding a single content type **Song** to the regular search. Let's
complicate things a little bit by adding a second content type **Artist**. Earlier, we created
two tables for this already:`#__music_songs` and`#__music_artists`. Now, we also
modify our plugin to allow to search artists as well:

```php
public function onContentSearchAreas()
{
    static $areas = array(
        'songs' => 'PLG_SEARCH_MUSIC_AREA_SONGS',
        'artists' => 'PLG_SEARCH_MUSIC_AREA_ARTISTS',
    );

    return $areas;
}
```

We also need to fit in a second database query. To make sure this new code is not cluttering up the method too much, we are going to move all query code to separate task methods.

Within the main onContentSearch() method we only need to check whether the areas requested in the search query match either songs or artists. If no areas are given, we are going to search for both songs and artists, merge the results and return the combined set of results. Or if areas are specified, we are going to match them with the selected areas.

Search results for the area songs are returned by the getSongs() method, search results for the area artists are returned by the getArtists() method.

```php
public function onContentSearch(
    $text, $phrase='', $ordering='', $areas=null
)
{
    if (is_array($areas))
    {
        $array_keys = array_keys($this->onContentSearchAreas());

        if (!array_intersect($areas, $array_keys))
        {
            return array();
        }
    }

    $results = array();
    if (empty($areas) || in_array('songs', $areas))
    {
        $songs = $this->getSongs($text, $phrase, $ordering);

        if (!empty($songs))
        {
            $results = array_merge($results, $songs);
        }
    }

    if (empty($areas) || in_array('artists', $areas))
    {
        $artists = $this->getArtists($text, $phrase, $ordering);

        if (!empty($artists))
        {
            $results = array_merge($results, $artists);
        }
    }
```

```
    }

    return $results;
}
```

The `getSongs()` method still contains our original code:

```
protected function getSongs($text, $phrase='', $ordering='')
{
    $db = JFactory::getDbo();
    ...
    $results = $db->loadObjectList();

    return $results;
}
```

The `getArtists()` method has the same logic as `getSongs()`, but uses a different query:

```
protected function getArtists($text, $phrase='', $ordering='')
{
    $db = JFactory::getDbo();

    $query = $db->getQuery(true);
    $query->select($db->quoteName('a.*'));
    $query->from($db->quoteName('#__music_artists', 'a'));
    $query->where($db->quoteName('a.name')
        .' LIKE ' . $db->quote('%'.$text.'%'));

    $db->setQuery($query);

    $results = $db->loadObjectList();
}
```

Fixing the search results for songs

Earlier, we mentioned that with the code so far, our search results are shown on screen just fine. However, they will also generate a PHP notice due to some missing properties. The search component expects each search result (`$result`) to have a `href` field (`$result->href`) as well as a `section` field and a `created` field.

We need to enhance our plugin a little bit to add these extra fields to the results before returning them to the search component. For the songs, this leads to the following code:

```
protected function getSongs($text, $phrase='', $ordering='')
{
    $db = JFactory::getDbo();
    ...
    $results = $db->loadObjectList();

    foreach ($results as $result)
    {
        $result->href = 'index.php?option=com_music&view=song';
        $result->href .= '&id=' . $result->id;
        $result->section = JText::_('PLG_SEARCH_MUSIC_AREA_SONGS');
        $result->created = 'today';
    }

    return $results;
}
```

Each URL points to the com_music component (of which we assume has already been created). The section variable has a static value. Translated into English it says **Songs**. You can enhance the plugin by adding a JOIN to the SQL query, so that the category title can be included in each $result: This way, the section variable can have a value like **Songs / Rock**.

Similarly, the created field should reflect the date at which the song entry was created (or perhaps the date on which the artist wrote the song). The value is passed through the JDate class, which uses strtotime() to turn your date string into a UNIX timestamp. If you do not have a valid date in your table, you can just use now or today. Using such a dummy value is technically wrong - your code should simply include a creation date - however it prevents a PHP notice. In our case, our database table is too simple to have a date field. Hence, we are just adding the dummy value today.

Fixing the search results for artists

When completing the results for the artists, we apply the same fields. However, the #__ music_artists table does not use a title field, but a name field instead. The search results will not display this field by default, so we copy the name value to a new title value. Similarly, an artist does not even have a text value, so we reuse the name value for that as well.

```
protected function getArtists($text, $phrase='', $ordering='')
{
    $db = JFactory::getDbo();
    ...
    $results = $db->loadObjectList();
```

```
foreach ($results as $result)
{
    $result->title = $result->name;
    $result->text = $result->name;
    $result->href = 'index.php?option=com_music&view=artist';
    $result->href .= '&id=' . $result->id;
    $result->section = JText::_('PLG_SEARCH_MUSIC_AREA_ARTISTS');
    $result->created = 'today';
}

return $results;
}
```

Instead of fixing the name field in a loop, you can also opt for rewriting the query. In our query, a few pages back, we used the star wildcard (a.*) to fetch all fields. This degrades performance slightly. We can also rewrite the SELECT statement to include only the fields we need, plus rename the field name to title.

```
$query->select(array(
    $db->quoteName('a.id'),
    $db->quoteName('a.title', 'name'),
    $db->quoteName('a.alias'),
));
```

Adding ordering

We are not done yet. We have not implemented the $ordering argument. The $ordering argument has one of the following values:

o   (empty)
o   newest
o   oldest
o   popular
o   alpha
o   category

Because our table does not contain any of the default core fields (created, modified, hits), we cannot order songs by their date entry or popularity. In this example, we will use a default ordering. We can order by title and category though. To add the ordering conditionally, we use a switch statement, so that $query->order can be applied to the database query before it is being executed.

```
switch ($ordering)
{
    case 'alpha':
        $query->order('title ASC');
        break;

    case 'category':
        $query->order('category_id ASC');
        break;

    case 'popular':
    case 'oldest':
    case 'newest':
    default:
        break;
}

$db->setQuery($query);
```

Switching per phrase

Let's move on to the argument $phrase. The $phrase argument determines whether the search word $text needs to be taken literally or not. It can be one of the following:

o   any (default)
o   all
o   exact

For example, if our table contains a song called **Gangnam Style**, we could enter the search word **gangnam style**, which would result in the following query:

```
SELECT * FROM #__music_songs
   WHERE title LIKE "%gangnam style%"
```

A direct match, of course. However, if somebody were to enter a search phrase **style gangnam** (switching the two words), this query would return no results:

```
SELECT * FROM #__music_songs
   WHERE title LIKE "%style gangnam%"
```

The search query makes an exact match between the search phrase and the returned search results. Therefore, this is the query that needs to be performed when $phrase is set to exact. We can even decide that an exact match should match the complete title, and not just part of it. When the complete title needs to be matched, the LIKE statement transforms into an **is-equal** statement (=).

```
SELECT * FROM #__music_songs
  WHERE title = "gangnam style"
```

It just depends on how you interpret the word **exact**. Most core plugins use the method with LIKE and taking the search phrase as a whole string.

When $phrase is set to any or all, we can make the search query more intelligent like this:

```
SELECT * FROM #__music_songs
  WHERE (title LIKE "%gangnam%" OR title LIKE "%style%")
```

In the case of $phrase being set to any, the song is matched when any of the search words is matches using the SQL OR condition. However, when we want the song to match all of the search words - so if $phrase is set to all - we would replace OR with AND.

```
SELECT * FROM #__music_songs
  WHERE (title LIKE "%gangnam%" AND title LIKE "%style%")
```

Important here is that the original $text value is split into pieces using a space as a separator - in other words, the original search phrase (containing spaces) is split into separate search words. The simplest way to do this is, to use explode(). However, if somebody enters more than one space between words in the search phrase, this might give issues with our database query, so we need to clean up spaces around $words as well.

```
$words = explode(' ', $text);

foreach ($words as $wordIndex => $word)
{
    $word = trim($word);

    if (empty($word))
    {
        unset($words[$wordIndex]);
        continue;
    }

    $words[$wordIndex] = $word;
}
```

By using the array of $words, we can construct the query. We can use a switch statement to switch between the different $phrase values. When $phrase has the value exact, we can add the original WHERE statement using the $text value. When $phrase has the value any or all, we can add a WHERE statement for each $word in the $words array.

In addition, we add the ability to search both the title field and the text field. Both fields have content that is relevant while searching. Here we go:

```
$searchFields = array('title', 'text');
$where = array();

switch ($phrase)
{
    case 'exact':
        foreach ($searchFields as $searchField)
        {
            $search = $db->quote('%'.$text.'%');
            $searchField = $db->quoteName('s.' . $searchField);
            $where[] = $searchField.' LIKE ' . $search;
        }
        break;

    case 'all':
        foreach ($searchFields as $searchField)
        {
            $searchField = $db->quoteName('s.' . $searchField);

            $wordWhere = array();
            foreach ($words as $word)
            {
                $search = $db->quote('%'.$word.'%');
                $wordWhere[] = $searchField . ' LIKE ' . $search;
            }

            $where[] = '(' . implode(' AND ', $wordWhere) . ')';
        }
        break;

    case 'any':
    default:
        foreach ($searchFields as $searchField)
        {
            $searchField = $db->quoteName('s.' . $searchField);
```

```
            $wordWhere = array();
            foreach ($words as $word)
            {
                $search = $db->quote('%'.$word.'%');
                $wordWhere[] = $searchField . ' LIKE ' . $search;
            }

            $where[] = '(' . implode(' OR ', $wordWhere) . ')';
        }
        break;
}


$query->where('(' . implode(' OR ', $where) . ')');
```

Debugging the query

The query code turned complex pretty quickly by implementing the arguments $phrase and $ordering. It might be a little bit overwhelming. Because of this, it might be best to start off with a basic example that only performs a basic query and start hacking things from there. Once the query contains multiple WHERE statements, mistakes are made quicker.

To allow for more efficient troubleshooting, you can add the following line just after the $db->setQuery($query) statement:

```
echo str_replace('#__', $db->getPrefix(), $db->getQuery());
```

This will print your query on the search page.When your $query variable is not a string but a JDatabaseQuery object - as it should be - you can even make this more simple:

```
echo $query->dump();
```

Now, you can open up phpMyAdmin or a similar database management tool and run the query manually to see what the query actually does.

9.3 Creating a Smart Search plugin

When writing a Smart Search plugin, you will reuse little of the code of a regular plugin, except perhaps for the database queries. To show you how a finder plugin is created, we are going to reuse the example of songs from the previous sections. With Smart Search, this means that we will write a plugin that allows the com_finder component to index our content and then fetch that content again from the index when asked.

The source code for the following plugin can be found in the **chapter09/plg_finder_song** folder of the GitHub repository.

Normally, it involves a lot of code to allow all the parameters and filters to be implemented in your plugin. To help you with this, you can extend the plugin class from the parent`FinderIndexerAdapter` class instead of the regular `JPlugin` class. While this allows you to write your code more efficiently, a first glance at the plugin layout might overwhelm you. There are quite a lot of methods to implement and also a bunch of class variables to define.

```
$comFinder = JPATH_ADMINISTRATOR . '/components/com_finder/';
require_once $comFinder . 'helpers/indexer/adapter.php';

class PlgFinderSong extends FinderIndexerAdapter
{
    protected $context = 'Song';
    protected $extension = 'com_music';
    protected $layout = 'song';
    protected $type_title = 'Song';
    protected $table = '#__music_songs';
    protected $state_field = 'state';
    protected $autoloadLanguage = true;

    protected function index(
        FinderIndexerResult $item, $format = 'html'
    ) {}

    protected function setup() {}

    protected function getListQuery($query = null) {}

    public function onFinderCategoryChangeState(
        $extension, $pks, $value
    ) {}

    public function onFinderAfterDelete($context, $table) {}

    public function onFinderAfterSave($context, $row, $isNew) {}

    public function onFinderBeforeSave($context, $row, $isNew) {}

    public function onFinderChangeState($context, $pks, $value) {}
}
```

To explain the layout of this class: The `require_once` statement at the top is needed to include the parent class `FinderIndexerAdapter`. Next, a bunch of protected class variables is defined. All variables are specific to the finder plugin, except for the `$autoloadLanguage` flag. They allow the core methods to do their magic:

- `setup()` - a method that is called before `index()` is executed.
- `index()` - a method that is called for each content item when it is being indexed.
- `getListQuery()` - a method returning a `JDatabaseQuery` object.

We will focus on getting these three core methods up and running first. The plugin methods starting with `onFinder` can be seen as optional. They represent the events that are fired by the **Content – Smart Search** plugin and can be implemented at a later stage.

A separate Search Plugin per content type

In our example, we use two different database tables, each with their own type of content: songs and artists. When you peek at the class variables, you might notice four variables that are specific to each content type: `$context`, `$layout`, `$type_title` and `$table`. In our code, these variables point to songs. Therefore, the plugin is specific to songs and not to artists.

Smart Search tries to make our life easier by automating the way that queries are used to access our tables. Apart from the method `getListQuery()`, which allows you to define a query that returns a list of all content items, our plugin will not hold any SQL code. The parent classes of our plugin take care of the actual queries. Because one class can only contain one `getListQuery()` method, one Smart Search plugin is specific to one content table.

Our component `com_music` offers two types of content. Therefore, we should write two plugins. This is also the reason why the name of the regular search plugin was `music`, while the name of this plugin is `song`. Also, note that the `$context` variable is **Song**, and not **Music**.

Starting with the setup() method

When the indexer is run, the `com_finder` controller initializes all finder plugins and calls upon their `onBeforeIndex()` event. There is no need to implement this event method though. The method `onBeforeIndex()` of the parent class `FinderIndexerAdapter` calls upon the `setup()` method and this is the method we should implement:

```
protected function setup()
{
}
```

After the plugins are initialized and the `setup()` method of all plugins is run, the indexer fetches a list of all the content items to index. This is done with the help of the `getListQuery()` method. The indexer then loops through all the content items and runs the `index()` method for each of them.

If you have some kind of helper that you want to include using `require_once`, it is not efficient to call `require_once` every time the `index()` method is run. It is best to place this in the `setup()` method.

A common use case for such a helper is the component's helper class, which determines the proper URL of a content item. For instance, our `com_music` can have a helper class `MusicHelperRoute`, which perhaps contains a static `MusicHelperRoute::get SongRoute()` method that allows us to generate a proper system URL for each song. Including this helper looks like this:

```
protected function setup()
{
    require_once JPATH_SITE.'/components/com_music/helpers/route.php';
}
```

It may also be that your component does not have such a helper class. The `setup()` method has no requirement to do anything. It can be empty. And its return value is not picked up by the indexer. It is ignored.

Even if the `setup()` method is not doing anything and its return value is ignored, you cannot omit the method. The parent class `FinderIndexerAdapter` defines the `setup()` method as abstract, which means that you have to implement it in your plugin class.

Determining what to index through getListQuery()

Before we can start indexing things, we first need to tell the indexer which content items should be indexed. Instead of letting our plugin run the actual query for this, the query is run by the indexer. The main reason for having such a mechanism is that the indexer indexes all content items in batches. Within the Joomla backend, you can see an example of how these batches are used when the progress bar is showing how many items have been completed. Under the hood AJAX calls are made to the JSON controller of the `com_finder` component.

What should the `getListQuery()` method do? It should return a `JDatabaseQuery` object. This method will look similar to the `getSongs()` method we created earlier for the regular search plugin. The `WHERE` statements to search for a specific text are removed, because we will be indexing all items. All content items will have relevant content, even those items that are currently unpublished.

```
protected function getListQuery($query = null)
{
    $db = JFactory::getDbo();
    $query = $db->getQuery(true);
    $query->select($db->quoteName('a.*'));
    $query->from($db->quoteName('#__music_songs', 'a'));
    return $query;
}
```

Note that #__music_songs gets an alias a. This is a requirement for the indexer to identify your primary data and you cannot change this alias. The alias should always be the letter a.

Also note that the wildcard (a.*) is better replaced with a list of all the fields you actually want to have indexed (a.id, a.title, a.alias, etc). Being specific about the fields you want to select, increases performance. This is even true if the number of fields is large - say 20 fields.

For now, we will focus on getting a basic example going, so this query is all we need.

Actually indexing things

To index your content items, the index() method is run. The main purpose of the method is to make the call $this->indexer->index($item). In its basic form it looks like this:

```
protected function index(FinderIndexerResult $item, $format = 'html')
{
    /*if (JComponentHelper::isEnabled($this->extension) == false)
    {
        return;
    }*/

    $this->indexer->index($item);
}
```

When the component is not available (disabled or not installed), there is no need to index the component's items anyway. In the code above, the component check is commented out, because our example does not include an existing component com_music. We only fake the component by creating its database tables and referring to URLs like index. php?option=com_music, which is all we need to get our example up and running.

With your own extension, you most likely have both the plugin and the component in place. In this case, you will want to remove the code comments and activate the check.

Testing the plugin from the command line

We are now ready for testing the plugin in its basic form. In the **Extension Manager**, you can install and publish the plugin. Next, you can start indexing your content from within the Smart Search backend.

There is one common problem here, that many developers encounter: When things go wrong, when your code contains a PHP error or when the database query fails, it is hard - if not impossible - to troubleshoot this properly through the Joomla backend. The indexer uses AJAX and it requires additional work to debug the relevant errors properly. To allow for better troubleshooting, I recommend you use the PHP command line instead.

Open a shell (either a terminal when you are working locally or an SSH connection), browse to the root of your Joomla folder and run the `cli/finder_indexer.php` script.

```
php ./cli/finder_indexer.php
```

If there are any PHP errors, they will be printed on screen. You might get some PHP notices about a missing `HTTP_HOST` variable on screen as well. To hide these notices, simply append a dummy `HTTP_HOST` to the command:

```
HTTP_HOST=localhost php ./cli/finder_indexer.php
```

The output should be something like the following:

```
Starting Indexer
Setting up Finder plugins
Setup 2 items in 0.103 seconds.
 * Processed batch 1 in 1.005 seconds.
Total Processing Time: 1.109 seconds.
```

Debugging can be made easier by printing text in your plugin code. For instance, we can print the `$query` in the `getListQuery()` method, just before the `$query` is returned.

```
echo "[SONGS]\n".$query->dump()."\n[/SONGS]\n";
return $query;
```

The `$query` variable is an object and normally objects cannot be printed to screen. However, thanks to the magic methods of the `JDatabaseQuery` class, the `$query` can be flattened to a string without any issues. When the command line indexer is now run, we can preview the query:

```
Starting Indexer
[SONGS]
SELECT a.*
```

```
FROM `iq8e3__music_songs` AS a
[/SONGS]
Setting up Finder plugins
Setup 2 items in 0.102 seconds.
[SONGS]
SELECT a.*
FROM `iq8e3__music_songs` AS a
[/SONGS]
 * Processed batch 1 in 0.977 seconds.
Total Processing Time: 1.079 seconds.
```

Once the indexer has run, you should be able to find your indexed content within the Smart Search backend under **Indexed Content**.

Preparing an item for indexing

So far, we have seen a basic example of the plugin, where the `$item` was not modified at all but simply passed through to the indexer. There is more to do in the `index()` method though: We need to prepare the item for indexing. Certain fields need to be set in the content item. Some fields are optional, some fields are required.

We will cover the required fields in this section:

- `title`
- `url`
- `route`
- `description`
- `published`
- `state`
- `access`
- `language`
- `publish_start_date`
- `publish_end_date`
- `extension`

  All of these fields have a purpose in the Smart Search mechanism. If our database table does not include some of these fields, the `index()` method allows us to offer a work around.

  For instance, if our content item has a `name` but no `title`, we can create the `title` here:

```
$item->title = $item->name;
unset($item->name);
```

Note that we also unset the old variable. The `$item` object is serialized and stored in the database table `#__finder_links`. Old variables that are not needed in the indexing process or in the search results, are best removed to prevent this taking up unneeded memory and disk space.

Setting access

If you have tested the example code so far, you might have noticed that the songs are showing up as indexed content in the backend. However, they are not showing up in the frontend. This is because the indexer expects each item to have an `access` field.

If the `access` field is not returned as a result of the `getListQuery()` method, its default value is 0. The value 0 is insufficient to show that item on the frontend. A simple hack would be to set `access` to 1. A better approach is to include the `access` field in your database table and allow managers to properly set the access level through your component.

```
$item->access = 1;
```

Handling URLs

Another issue with the `$item` that we have indexed so far, is the URL. It points back to a Smart Search page, which should actually be a page of our component instead. To make sure the search results point to the correct song page, we need to set its URL.

Our plugin's parent class `FinderIndexerAdapter` offers the following method for this:

```
protected function getURL($id, $extension, $view)
{
    return 'index.php?option=' . $extension . '&view='
        . $view . '&id=' . $id;
}
```

The `getURL()` method tries to generate the URL using a generic MVC approach. The method can be called from within our own `index()` method as follows:

```
$route = $this->getURL($item->id, $this->extension, $this->layout);
$item->route = $route;
```

This is equivalent to the following:

```
$item->route = 'index.php?option=com_music&view=song&id=' . $item->id;
```

If your component has a non-standard routing, you can either construct the URL directly when declaring `$item->route` or by overriding the `getURL()` method in your plugin class.

Dealing with layouts

If you look closely at the code of the getURL() method, you might be confused about the usage of the $this->layout variable. It is used as an argument to getURL() and then it is used to fill in the component's view. However, views and layouts are completely different things in the Joomla MVC model.

This is confusing. The $this->layout variable actually does not refer to your MVC component at all. Instead, it refers to a layout file that can be used to style the search results page. Because $this->layout is set to **song** in our case, the com_finder component will try to locate a template file default_song.php. When it does not find such a file, it will use the default template default_result.php instead.

```
components/com_finder/views/search/tmpl/default_result.php
```

Adding your own layout file in the same folder classifies as a core hack, so it should not be undertaken. To add your own layout file specifically for songs, a template override is needed:

```
templates/TEMPLATE/html/com_finder/search/default_song.php
```

Having a layout file specifically for one content type, opens up many opportunities. You can add additional fields to your items, that will then be indexed. Next, you can show these additional fields again using a specific layout file for songs. For example, you can add a thumbnail of the album that contains the song, the year in which the song was released and of course the name of the artist.

Working with URLs

While defining a variable $item->route is enough to get your search results showing in the frontend, the URL will not show in the Smart Search backend. To allow for the URL to show there as well, the $item->url variable is used. Even though the code in some core finder plugins suggests otherwise, both variables can have the same value:

```
$item->url = $item->route;
```

Yet another URL occurs in the code: The SEF equivalent of the same URL. The $item->route variable will contain a system URL (starting with index.php?option=com_music) and this URL will be converted into a real-life SEF URL using JRoute::_(). If you do not define an $item->path, the indexing will just use your $item->route instead. In other words, if you omit this $item->path property, you have nothing to worry about.

In some cases however, the usage of $item->route leads to unwanted results. Perhaps your component's router contains some strange logic that does not work with Smart Search. Or generating URLs simply takes a lot of time, while you may want the search results to be lightning fast. You may be tempted to do something like this:

```
$item->path = JRoute::_($item->route);
```

Do not do this! This will definitely not work. When running the indexer through either the backend or the command-line, the Joomla application will not be the same application as the frontend. If you run `JRoute::_()` in the backend, it will generate a backend URL, not a frontend URL. Luckily, the Smart Search component offers a way to generate the correct frontend URL, regardless of which application you are currently using:

```
$item->path = FinderIndexerHelper::getContentPath($item->route);
```

Probably in most cases this line of code is not needed.However, you may include it. It does no harm.

Adding new taxonomies

With the regular search, there is only one type of search filter to be made: the content type (defined as search areas). With Smart Search, a content type can be used as a **taxonomy**, a way of categorizing content.

With Smart Search you are not limited to one taxonomy. You can add several. To get you started, we are going to extend the existing taxonomy **Type** and add our own type **Song** to it. This way people can search for articles or weblinks or songs.

For this, we add the following to the `index()` method:

```
$item->addTaxonomy('Type', 'Song');
```

We can also add new taxonomies that normally do not exist in Smart Search. Our songs include an `artist_id` that refers to the `#__music_artists` table. If we extend our `SELECT` query to make a `JOIN` with this second table, we can add the `artist` name to our content items:

```
$query = $db->getQuery(true);
$query->select('a.*');
$query->select('p.name AS artist');
$query->from($db->quoteName('#__music_songs', 'a'));
$query->innerJoin($db->quoteName('#__music_artists', 'p')
    . ' ON (' . $db->quoteName('a.artist_id')
    . '=' . $db->quoteName('p.id') . ')'
);
```

Next, we add a new taxonomy **Artist**, so that people can filter search results not only by type (**Content, Weblink, Song**), but also by artist (**Frank Sinatra, Michael Jackson, Amir Diab**):

```
$item->addTaxonomy('Artist', $item->artist);
```

On the frontend, the string `PLG_FINDER_QUERY_FILTER_BRANCH_S_ARTIST` is now shown. It is automatically created by Smart Search. To translate this new string, we add the following to our language file `en-GB.plg_finder_music.ini`:

```
PLG_FINDER_QUERY_FILTER_BRANCH_S_ARTIST="Artist"
```

What if we want to search for the artist name as well? That is simple. Assuming that our `getListQuery()` method also returned values for the field `artist` (coming from a database JOIN with the `#__music_artists` table), we can simply instruct the indexer to include this field in the search as well:

```
$item->addInstruction(FinderIndexer::META_CONTEXT, 'artist');
```

The class constant `META_CONTEXT` is defined in the class `FinderIndexer` and is used to add more relevance to the search results. There are more context constants that can be used.Additionally, there are some fields linked to each context by default. The following gives a listing of the available contexts and which fields are linked to this context by default:

```
FinderIndexer::TITLE_CONTEXT = title, subtitle, id
FinderIndexer::TEXT_CONTEXT = summary, body
FinderIndexer::META_CONTEXT = meta, list_price, sale_price
FinderIndexer::PATH_CONTEXT = path, alias
FinderIndexer::MISC_CONTEXT = comments
```

As you can see, there is no need to add a new instruction to link the field `title` to the `TITLE_CONTEXT` constant. It is already available. However, if you have new fields that you want to add to your indexed content, you should add a new instruction for the.

Each context can be found in the Joomla backend under the **Options** of the Smart Search component. There, a multiplier is given to each context. Each search result is given a relevance score, which shows how relevant the result is to the given search phrase. The most relevant results will be shown at the top. The relevance score of each search result is determined by a combination of the multipliers of each field. If you think the artist name should have the same relevance as the song title, you could give the **Meta Data Weight Multiplier** the same value as the **Title Text Weight Modifier**. If you want to solve this in the code, you should use the `TITLE_CONTEXT` instead of the `META_CONTEXT`:

```
$item->addInstruction(FinderIndexer::TITLE_CONTEXT, 'artist');
```

Dealing with languages

When your content items are multilingual, it is a good idea to allow for multilingual setups as well. For this to work properly, your `$item` needs an additional property `language`. The value of this property should contain the relevant language code (en-GB or nl-NL). If your component supports multiple languages, you should be able to add the `language` field to the query in the `getListQuery()` method (a.language).Alternatively, if the item applies to all languages or if there is only one language available, the wildcard * can be used as the value:

```
$item->language = '*';
```

An alternative to this is to use the `setLanguage()` method. It receives no arguments, but simply detects whether the language is empty or set to the wildcard *, in which case the default language is used instead:

```
$item->setLanguage();
```

It is recommended (but optional) to add the language as a taxonomy to your indexed items. This way, users can filter search results by language as well:

```
$item->addTaxonomy('Language', $item->language);
```

Extending the $item using onPrepareFinderContent()

One more thing that you can add to the `index()` method, is the following:

```
FinderIndexerHelper::getContentExtras($item);
```

This allows your `$item` to be extended using other plugins with the event `onPrepareFinderContent`. While for your own plugin, you can easily add the `$item` properties within the `index()` method, this also shows you a completely different scenario: You can extend any other indexed content item (articles, contacts, weblinks) using your own plugin.

Take for example a scenario where you add a new field `teaser` to each article form. In the previous chapters, you have already seen how to do this. When you want to modify the frontend to display this new teaser on article pages, you might also want to consider adding the teaser to search results. This event allows you to accomplish exactly that. By implementing the event method in your plugin, you can index the content of each article's teaser. Using a template override, you can display that teaser in your search results.

Handling different item states

If you are following Joomla standards, you have a `state` field in your database table that can be either 0 (disabled) or 1 (enabled). However, there is no requirement to stick to this standard and you may have good reasons to use a different field name instead. For instance, your table may contain a field `enabled`.

To make sure the indexer knows how to interpret your table, you can define which table field toggles the item's state:

```
protected $state_field = 'enabled';
```

Suppose, your content has multiple states, for example, where the number 0 still represents a state of **disabled**, the number 1 represents a state of **enabled**, but the number 2 means **pending**. Then if pending items should not be indexed, you will need to tell the indexer not to index items with state 2.

The default logic is defined in the `translateState()` method of the `FinderIndexerAdapter` class. To change it, you can override this method in your plugin class. The method receives two arguments: `$item` and `$category`. While the name may suggest an object, the parameters are two integers referring to the item state and category state.

```
protected function translateState($item, $category = null)
```

```
{
    if ($item == 2)
    {
        return 1;
    }

    return parent::translateState($item, $category);
}
```

This example changes the default behavior slightly. Normally, the indexer interprets the state 2 as archived content, which should be indexed. In our case, it refers to a pending state, which should not be indexed. We reset 2 to 0 (and not to 1 as the original method did).

Method getStateQuery()

Another important method to keep an eye on is the `getStateQuery()` method, which is used under the hood by the indexer with some of the `onFinder` events. If you do not override it, the default method from the `FinderIndexerAdapter` class will be used. This method is expected to return a mapping between primary keys and the state they are in.

If you have content items with default field names (`a.id`, `a.access`) and a relation with categories (`a.catid`), this will work out of the box. Our example code is far too simple and therefore does not work with this default implementation. We replace it with a simpler query, that forgets about `access` and categories. It only returns the IDs with their `state`:

```
protected function getStateQuery()
{
    $db = $this->db;

    $query = $db->getQuery(true);
    $query->select($db->quoteName('a.id'));
    $query->select($db->quoteName('a.' . $this->state_field)
        . ' AS '.$db->quoteName('state'));
    $query->from($db->quoteName($this->table, 'a'));

    return $query;
}
```

Finder events - onFinderChangeState

The main functionality of the Smart Search plugin has been built now. However, it is not really flexible: Every time the content changes, we have to rebuild the entire index manually. To improve this, the Smart Search approach takes a little bit more work. We can implement the various onFinder event methods in our plugin.

Let's assume that we use a component to modify our songs and artists and that this component is dispatching content events properly. How you can incorporate these onContent events into your own component is explained in chapter 11. If your component is throwing onContent events properly, the **Content – Finder** plugin will be notified every time your component's content is changed. We will discuss the onContentChangeState event first.

When the component is used to disable a content item, the component will initialize the onContentChangeState event, which again triggers the onFinderChangeState event. If the component's model is based on either JModelAdmin or FOFModel, this is all done automatically when calling upon the publish() method.

The onFinderChangeState() method is simple. It receives the following arguments:

- $context - an identifier, mentioning where we are exactly in the application
- $pks - an array, containing all the IDs of content items that will be changed
- $value - the integer identifying the new state

There is not much to do, except for matching the $context with our own component. If a match is found, it calls upon the parent method $this->itemStateChange().

```
public function onFinderChangeState($context, $pks, $value)
{
    if ($context == 'com_music.song')
    {
        $this->itemStateChange($pks, $value);
    }

    if ($context == 'com_plugins.plugin' && $value === 0)
    {
        $this->pluginDisable($pks);
    }
}
```

The second part needs some explaining: When a Finder Plugin is disabled in the **Plugin Manager**, the plugin will attempt to remove all indexed items that belong to that plugin. For example, if we disable the **Finder – Content** plugin, the plugin's own onFinderChangeState() method will be called, which again calls the pluginDisable() method to remove all indexed articles.

This only works if the getStateQuery() method is correctly implemented and if the context of the plugin ($this->context) matches the actual plugin name (the element in the #__extensions table).

When the Finder Plugin is activated again, the indexer needs to be run again (through cron or manually), to make sure all content items are added to the index again.

Finder events - onFinderCategoryChangeState

Just as the content item can change state, the category containing all these items can also change state. This is dealt with by the event onFinderCategoryChangeState, which is called in response to the onCategoryChangeState event.

Our component does not implement the feature of having categories. However, if it did and if the getStateQuery() method included these categories, theonFinderCategoryChangeState() method could be implemented like this:

```
public function onFinderCategoryChangeState($extension, $pks, $value)
{
    if ($extension == 'com_music')
    {
        $this->categoryStateChange($pks, $value);
    }
}
```

Finder events – onFinderBeforeSave and onFinderAfterSave

Before a content item is saved, the onContentBeforeSave event is triggered. Again, this is picked up by the **Content - Finder** plugin and this triggers the onFinderBeforeSave method in our plugin:

```
public function onFinderBeforeSave($context, $row, $isNew)
{
    if ($context == 'com_music.song' && $isNew == false)
    {
        $this->checkItemAccess($row);
    }

    if ($context == 'com_categories.category' && $isNew == false)
    {
        $this->checkCategoryAccess($row);
    }
}
```

The checkItemAccess() method queries the database for the value of the access field of the content item `$row` and stores the value in a temporary variable `$this->old_access`. Similarly, the `checkCategoryAccess()` method checks on the `access` field of the category, which contains the content item `$row`, and stores the value in a variable `$this->old_cataccess`. Both methods create a temporary variable.

The real purpose of these temporary variables can be understood when we look at the `onFinderAfterSave` method, which is triggered by the `onContentAfterSave` event:

```
public function onFinderAfterSave($context, $row, $isNew)
{
    if ($context == 'com_music.song')
    {
        if (!$isNew && $this->old_access != $row->access)
        {
            $this->itemAccessChange($row);
        }

        $this->reindex($row->id);
    }

    if ($context == 'com_categories.category')
    {
        if (!$isNew && $this->old_cataccess != $row->access)
        {
            $this->categoryAccessChange($row);
        }
    }
}
```

As in the `onFinderBeforeSave()` method, we do something for content items (songs) and we do something for categories. Let's focus on the content items first. The only reason we implemented the `onFinderBeforeSave()` method earlier was to keep track of the original `access` value by storing it in a temporary variable, `$this->old_access`. The `onContentAfterSave` event holds a copy of the modified data, but not a copy of the original data. Therefore, the workaround with the temporary variable is needed in order to know what changed and what did not.

Only if the `access` value has changed is the `$this->itemAccessChange()` method called. Next, the `$this->itemAccessChange()` method updates the indexed `access` value for the content item in the `#__finder_links` tables accordingly.

```
if (!$isNew && $this->old_access != $row->access)
{
    $this->itemAccessChange($row);
}
```

Finally, the item is reindexed. The `reindex()` call runs the `setup()` method to make sure everything is initialized correctly. It then removes the current `$item` from the index (removing its record from the `#__finder_links` tables) and then runs `index()` again to index every aspect of the item.

```
$this->reindex($row->id);
```

Personally, I think this does not make sense. First, the indexer updates entries in `#__finder_links` using the `itemAccessChange()` method. Now, using the `reindex()` method, it removes all these entries anyway to reindex the content item from scratch. The entire checking for `access` changes should simply be skipped and only the `reindex()` call should remain.Currently, it just adds a pointless extra `UPDATE` query, that is performed right before a `DELETE` query wipes out that same change. Alternatively, the partial reindexing of access should remain and the `reindex()` call should be removed. Perhaps this will be changed in the core at some point.

Let's move on. When the category is modified and its `access` field is changed, it needs to be matched with in the finder plugin, in order for all content items that belong to that category, to change as well.

```
if ($context == 'com_categories.category')
{
    if (!$isNew && $this->old_cataccess != $row->access)
    {
        $this->categoryAccessChange($row);
    }
}
```

The Joomla CMS defines the relationship between content items and categories in such a way that when the category is inaccessible, its content items are inaccessible as well. It might be that you want to implement this differently. Perhaps all your content items should still be accessible even though the category that contains them has been unpublished. In that case, you might need to refactor the entire logic.

Finder events - onFinderAfterDelete

Last but not least, whenever we delete a content item, we also want its indexed content to be deleted. Here the `onContentDelete` event triggers the `onFinderAfterDelete` event, which looks like this:

```
public function onFinderAfterDelete($context, $table)
{
    if ($context == 'com_music.song')
    {
```

```
        $id = $table->id;
    }
    else
    {
        return true;
    }

    return $this->remove($id);
}
```

There is nothing fancy going on here. The context is checked and if it is the correct context, the parent method `remove()` is called.

9.4 Combining Smart Search with remote APIs

As you have seen in the previous section, creating a Smart Search plugin is quite a lengthy job, mainly because Smart Search is a complex mechanism that needs to guarantee the integrity of the index at all times. To make life a little bit easier, the parent class `FinderIndexerAdapter` contains lots of shortcuts to automate queries to the database. Checks for the `access` level, queries to list your content items, etc.

But what if your content is not stored in the Joomla database at all? What if your content is only accessible through a remote API using REST or SOAP? Obviously, methods like `getListQuery()` and `getStateQuery()` do not make sense, because SQL is not used to access the content.

It is still possible to integrate Smart Search though, and there is a great benefit to it as well. The remote system might be responding slowly, compared to a regular database. So, using a search index like Smart Search will increase the speed of search results. The downside is that the available examples for creating Finder Plugins (including the plugins that are part of the Joomla core and the samples in this book) will be of less interest to you. Studying the `FinderIndexerAdapter` code is a must.

Personally, I have created a Smart Search plugin for MageBridge (a bridge between Joomla and Magento), which offers an approach you might find interesting. It overrides the `getItems()` method to allow for a MageBridge call to the Magento API to fetch a list of products. Also the `getContentCount()` method is overridden to support running through all Magento products in batches.

 The code can be found in the GitHub repository **https://github.com/yireo/ MageBridgeCore**.

9.5 Using external search engines

Joomla offers you two search engines out of the box: regular search and Smart Search. However, there are many other search solutions that can be integrated with Joomla, such as ElasticSearch, Sphinx, Apache Solr (based on Apache Lucene). Using another search solution might give benefits. In the final sections of this chapter, we will discuss the various reasons for choosing an external search engine. We will also deal with some practical examples on how to integrate these engines into Joomla.

Joomla regular search is too basic

The Joomla regular search is basic. It allows you to enter a search query and that query is run, on the fly, to select data from various database tables. If you have a large number of articles, the query will take longer to run and puts a higher stress on the server. This happens every time a user (or robot) is using the Joomla search. Nothing is cached. From a performance angle, regular search gives problems.

Regular search allows you to choose whether any or all words are matched. However, it does not allow you to specify which field you want to search. You cannot find articles for which only the `title` and not the `text` matches. In other words, the additional filtering options are not very flexible.

One more drawback is that search results are grouped by the content type: For example, first all articles are shown, then all categories, then all weblinks - even if a certain category has the same relevance to the search phrase as a certain article. The ordering of Search Plugins determines which search results are shown first.

MySQL and text searching

Searching text in a database table always brings up performance issues. When a `SELECT` statement is used to search through a field of type `TEXT` (like the `introtext` and `fulltext` columns of the #__content table), using either `LIKE` combined with wildcards or `MATCH()`, MySQL needs to go through all the stored content to find a proper match.

Adding a `FULLTEXT` index on these columns improves things. However, this assumes there are enough server resources (mainly memory) available to make that index efficient. `FULLTEXT` indexes are fully supported with MyISAM. Before MySQL 5.6.4, InnoDB did not include support for `FULLTEXT` indexes. In other words, with older MySQL versions, it is best to use MyISAM for tables that need `FULLTEXT` searching. However, with MySQL 5.6.4 or later, the `FULLTEXT` search capabilities of InnoDB are better than MyISAM. So, with newer MySQL versions, switching the table #__content to InnoDB may improve search performance.

The main issue remains though: MySQL is troublesome when it comes to text searches with large tables. This is mostly because text search is not the main reason why MySQL exists. The same is true for other SQL databases like PostgreSQL and Microsoft SQL.

Smart Search takes you half way

Smart Search is a good step forward, when comparing it to the original search. The original text fields, that contain large chunks of data, are split up into a bunch of smaller fields, each containing a fragment of the original text. It is more efficient to search these fragments than it is to search through the original tables.

If you have a small site (say up to thousand articles) and the content is not updated daily, then Smart Search gives a good and fast way of searching this content. Additionally, the taxonomies that can be added to the index allow for better faceted search.

However, there are some downsides with Smart Search as well. When storing the indexed data on disk, `finder` uses quite a lot of rows spread out over multiple tables to make sure the correct results are found as quickly as possible. This requires more disk space. These days, disk space is not an issue. However, disk activity is. When the index is updated, all the `finder` tables need updating and this leads to more disk I/O. Additionally, it is recommended to clean up the entire `finder` index once in a while. If you have a lot of content, this will take a long time and increase disk I/O for that time. Make sure to test this thoroughly before going live.

Last but not least, Smart Search is Joomla based, so PHP based. The PHP / SQL combination is not the best choice when it comes to a high-performance search engine.

Searching PDF and Word documents

By default, Joomla search allows searching for content items in the database. Non-database content - like PDF documents or Office documents - is not included. There are third party extensions that allow you to extend Joomla search to the filesystem as well. However, searching files using PHP is relatively slow, especially in real time. Using Smart Search will cause only the indexing process to be slow, while returning search results is faster. However, with Smart Search, the amount of data stored in the database will be much larger. Search engines like Solr allow you to search files as well and are far more efficient than any Joomla based solution. There are even options to include searching of images.

Offloading search to external servers

It might be that your Joomla site is simply very busy. This puts a continuous stress on server resources. Of all page requests, search requests are the most dynamic and ask the most of performance. Offloading these requests to an external server (a standalone Solr or Sphinx server) allows you to save resources for handling the other requests. If you have a busy site with lots of searches, this is something you should look into.

Note that setting up an external search service requires quite some work and should be seen as a next possible step, when running Joomla on a dedicated server. If you have performance issues and are still running Joomla on a shared hosting environment, first consider migrating your site to a dedicated server with custom PHP and MySQL tuning.

9.6 Integration with Sphinx

Sphinx is an open source search engine, written in C++, that can be installed on your server to allow for more efficient full text searches. Sphinx runs as a daemon, which enables fast access to its indexed content. It allows various types of communication, of which two are definitely of interest to us. The first type that we will discuss thoroughly, involves the use of a PHP library, which offers a `SphinxClient` class. We can integrate the `SphinxClient` class easily in a Joomla search plugin.

Another communication method is to use a MySQL-like protocol (dubbed `SphinxQL`), which allows you to fetch Sphinx data using MySQL commands. Also, Sphinx is able to retrieve data from a MySQL table on its own. We will use this in our example: We will tell Sphinx where it can locate the Joomla articles. Sphinx will then fetch all relevant content from the Joomla database and index it.

Sphinx has many benefits compared to Smart Search. It is written in C++, so it is compiled instead of interpreted. Also, it integrates tightly with the operating system. In the Sphinx configuration, you can assign a specific amount of memory to the database. If you choose to run both MySQL and Sphinx on the same server, this means you can divide your RAM between MySQL and Sphinx. This allows you to tune things for the most optimal result.

Besides better performance, the Sphinx engine also allows for nifty features like ranking modes, dictionaries, spelling correction, autocompletion and much more. Most - if not all - features are also available through the PHP API.

The downside is that installing Sphinx is typically not an option on a shared host.

Installing and setting up Sphinx

To get up and running with Sphinx, we first need to install it. Here, we are assuming a CentOS Linux server, which allows us to install the needed packages using `yum`. If you are using Ubuntu or similar, there are similar `apt-get` commands available. Besides the main Sphinx package, we are also going to install the Sphinx PHP library, which comes as a PECL package.

```
yum install sphinx
yum install php-pecl-sphinx
```

Now that Sphinx is installed, the first thing we want to do is modify its configuration. The default configuration file is `/etc/sphinx/sphinx.conf`. We are going to add the following lines:

```
source joomla1_articles
{
   type                = mysql
   sql_host            = localhost
   sql_user            = joomla1
   sql_pass            = secret1
   sql_db              = joomla1
   sql_port            = 3306
   sql_query           = \
     SELECT `id`, UNIX_TIMESTAMP(`created`) AS `created`, \
     `title`, `introtext`, `fulltext` \
     FROM jos_content
   sql_attr_uint       = catid
   sql_attr_timestamp  = created
   sql_query_info      = SELECT `id` FROM skhiw_content WHERE id=$id
}


index joomla1_articles
{
   source       = joomla1_articles
   path         = /var/lib/sphinx/joomla1_articles
   docinfo      = extern
   charset_type = sbcs
}
```

First, we define a `source`. A `source` definition allows Sphinx to connect itself to the Joomla database and fetch a list of articles from it. There is one source per database table. We call our source `joomla1_articles`, naming it after the database and database table it connects to. The MySQL credentials are entered and the type is set to `mysql`. The value `sql_query` contains the actual query that we make to the database. We are only selecting those fields that are needed to allow Sphinx to be used for the `FULLTEXT` search.

Besides a `source` definition, we also need an `index` definition. The `source` itself does not store anything. It only allows Sphinx to fetch data from the Joomla database. Using the `index` definition, we tell Sphinx to store an optimized index of the data source defined as `source`. Later on, we will be querying the `index`, not the `source`.

You can find a copy of this Sphinx configuration in the GitHub repository: Browse to the folder **chapter09** and then **sphinx_conf** to find the sample configuration file.

We are done with a basic definition of the source and the index. However, before we can make use of them, we first need to create the index and start the Sphinx service. The index can be created with the Sphinx `indexer` command.

When Sphinx is installed, it also creates a Linux user `sphinx` and while common Sphinx tools may not yet be in the `$PATH` of other users, it is all setup properly for the user `sphinx`. Running Sphinx jobs manually is best done as user `sphinx`, to avoid issues with file permissions. The `--rotate` argument can be left out the first time that you run the command, though it needs to be added when an index has already been created:

```
sudo -u sphinx indexer joomla1_articles --rotate
```

This command creates an index `/var/lib/sphinx/joomla1_articles`. We can start using that index right away. Using the command `search`, we can search the index `joomla1_articles` for a keyword, in this case **joomla**:

```
sudo -u sphinx search -i joomla1_articles "joomla"
```

Once the command is run, the index is searched for the keyword. Make sure this runs ok, because if it does not, there is no point in attempting to access the same index from within Joomla.

Next, we are going to activate the Sphinx daemon and start it up. This allows us to contact Sphinx not only using command line tools, but also through the PHP library and SphinxQL.

```
chkconfig searchd on
service searchd start
```

We are done configuring Sphinx now.

Replacing the articles search with a Sphinx search

Now, we are ready to add Sphinx functionality to Joomla. We will be using a regular search plugin for this: There is no point in creating a Smart Search plugin, because Sphinx already does all the indexing for us. We start with a basic plugin structure. The class extends from `JPlugin`, we load its language files and we define a search area `sphinx`.

```
class PlgSearchSphinx extends JPlugin
{
    protected $autoloadLanguage = true;
```

```
public function onContentSearchAreas()
{
    static $areas = array(
        'sphinx' => 'PLG_SEARCH_SPHINX_SPHINX'
    );

    return $areas;
}

public function onContentSearch($text, $phrase, $ordering, $areas)
{
    // See below
}
}
```

 The source code for the following plugin can be found in the **chapter09/plg_search_sphinx** folder of the GitHub repository.

The onContentSearch() method starts by checking whether the search request was placed for a specific search area, and if so, the areas are matched. We have seen this before when we were creating a regular search plugin, at the beginning of this chapter.

```
if (is_array($areas))
{
    $array_keys = array_keys($this->onContentSearchAreas());

    if (!array_intersect($areas, $array_keys))
    {
        return array();
    }
}
```

To prevent the event method from becoming too complex, we place the calls to Sphinx in a separate method getSphinxResults(). This method returns a list of matches, which were found for the $text variable.

```
$text = trim($text);
$results = $this->getSphinxResults($text, $phrase, $ordering);

if (empty($results['matches']))
{
    return array();
}
```

Next, we loop through these search results and use the `getArticles()` method to fetch a list of the actual articles. These articles are returned as search results.

```
$ids = array();
foreach ($results['matches'] as $resultId => $result)
{
    $ids[] = $resultId;
}

$results = $this->getArticles($ids);

return $results;
```

This might seem odd: Both Sphinx and the original articles are loaded. Instead of indexing all article fields in Sphinx, we have only added a few of these article fields to Sphinx, assuming that searching these fields specifically is slow in Joomla, but fast in Sphinx. However, to return proper search results, we need much more information: the article ID, article alias, category ID and category alias. Also, the publication dates need to be matched properly as well as languages and access-levels.

While we can allow for that information to be indexed in Sphinx as well, there is a chance that this approach still requires additional queries to the Joomla database to guarantee the correct displaying of search results. For instance, checks for ACL rules. Instead, we are going to assume that replacing the FULLTEXT search with Sphinx was a good idea, but that selecting articles by ID from the Joomla database is still fast enough for us. So, we use Sphinx to determine which articles match the search query, then use Joomla to load the actual articles.

Fetching the Sphinx results

The Sphinx PHP client offers a class `SphinxClient`, which can be configured to connect with the Sphinx server. Initializing the `SphinxClient` object involves setting the host and port properly, for which we use plugin parameters.

Similar to the Joomla search flag `$phrase`, Sphinx has different modes that can be used for searching keywords. These modes are defined with constants starting with `SPH_MATCH`. In our code, we use a `switch` statement to match them with their Joomla equivalents:

```
protected function getSphinxResults(
    $text, $phrase = '', $ordering = ''
)
{
    $host = $this->params->get('host', 'localhost');
```

```php
    $port = $this->params->get('port', 9312);

    switch ($phrase)
    {
        case 'exact':
            $matchMode = SPH_MATCH_PHRASE;
            break;

        case 'all':
            $matchMode = SPH_MATCH_ALL;
            break;

        case 'any':
        default:
            $matchMode = SPH_MATCH_ANY;
            break;
    }


    $s = new SphinxClient();
    $s->setServer($host, $port);
    $s->setMatchMode($matchMode);

    $result = $s->query($text, 'joomla1_articles');

    return $result;
}
```

The first argument of the method `SphinxClient::query()` is the query string that is passed through to Sphinx, in our case `$text`. A second argument is, in our case, set to the name of the Sphinx index. It is hard coded, a little bit ugly. This second argument defaults to a star wildcard (*) matching all indexes. Matching all indexes is no problem, if you have only a few indexes. However, if you have more than one Joomla database table sourced through the same Sphinx instance, this will lead to conflicts.

Adding all article information

The `getSphinxResults()` method returns an array of matches, which is then converted into a list of article IDs. The `getArticles()` method then fetches the complete article objects using these IDs.

```php
protected function getArticles($ids)
{
    $db = JFactory::getDbo();
    $app = JFactory::getApplication();
    $user = JFactory::getUser();
```

```php
    $limit = $this->params->def('search_limit', 50);


    $fields = array('a.id, a.catid, a.title, a.alias, a.created');
    $concat = $query->concatenate(array('a.introtext', 'a.fulltext'));

    $query = $db->getQuery(true);
    $query
        ->select($db->quoteName($fields))
        ->select(array(
            $db->quoteName($concat, 'text'),
            $db->quoteName('c.title', 'section'),
            $db->quoteName('c.alias', 'catalias')
        ))
        ->from($db->quoteName('#__content', 'a'))
        ->join('INNER', $db->quoteName('#__categories', 'c')
            . ' ON ' . $db->quoteName('c.id')
            . ' = ' . $db->quoteName('a.catid'))
        ->where($db->quoteName('a.id')
            . ' IN (' . implode(',', $ids) . ') '
            . ' AND ' . $db->quoteName('a.state') . '=1'
            . ' AND ' . $db->quoteName('c.published') . '=1'
        )
    ;


    $db->setQuery($query, 0, $limit);

    $items = $db->loadObjectList();
```

The $query closely resembles the query of the default **Search – Articles** plugin, except that the WHERE statement is changed to simply select articles by their ID, instead of using a slower LIKE statement.

 The code above is a slimmed down version of the actual query needed. For readability, the checks for publication dates, access levels and languages are left out. See the GitHub source for the full code.

Finally, when the articles are collected from the database, they are prepared for display on the search results page:

```php
if (isset($items))
{
    $comPath = JPATH_SITE . '/components/com_content';
    require_once $comPath.'/helpers/route.php';
```

```
    foreach ($items as $key => $item)
    {
        $item->slug = $item->id . ':' . $item->alias;
        $item->catslug = $item->catid . ':' . $item->catalias;
        $item->href = ContentHelperRoute::getArticleRoute(
            $item->slug, $item->catslug);
        $items[$key] = $item;
    }
}

return $items;
```

Updating a specific article

Now, every time an article is updated, the Sphinx index needs to be reindexed manually. This can be done at set times through a cronjob. However, there is a real-time alternative to this.

The `SphinxClient` includes a method `updateAttributes()`, which allows updating of specific attributes for specific IDs. Ideally this is implemented using a Content Plugin, which hooks into `onContentBeforeSave` and `onContentAfterSave` events to see whether content changed. If a content item changed, a call can be made to update the values stored in Sphinx.

Let's assume an article `$row` was changed in the Joomla backend. In our `onContentAfterSave()` method, we can use the following code to update the corresponding values in Sphinx:

```
$index = 'joomla1_articles';
$attributes = array('title', 'introtext', 'fulltext');
$values = array(
    $row->id => array(
        $row->title,
        $row->introtext,
        $row->fulltext,
    )
);

$sphinx = new SphinxClient();
$sphinx->setServer($host, $port);
$sphinx->updateAttributes($index, $attributes, $values);
```

Deleting an article

There is no specific `SphinxClient` method to delete values from the index. This requires reindexing the entire index manually, which is why I would still recommend running a cronjob. However, as a temporary workaround, you can still use the `updateAttributes()` method for this, by simply updating the row with empty values.

```
$values = array(
    $row->id => array('', '', '')
);
```

With this approach, the indexed data for article will still exist. However, it will simply have no content and therefore, they will never match a search query.

Possible improvement: Running multiple queries

This example of a Sphinx plugin gets you going and gives you insight into how Sphinx works. Besides a Search Plugin, aContent Plugin also proves useful: It allows you to synchronize article updates and deletions to the Sphinx index.

As you have seen, the Search Plugin only supports one database table and one corresponding Sphinx `index`. Therefore, it also supports only one Joomla search area (`tags`, `content`, `categories`). This is something you can easily change though: When you create one Sphinx `source` and one Sphinx `index` per Joomla search area and stick to some kind of naming convention, you can create a single Search Plugin that still supports multiple search areas.

For instance, the name of the Sphinx index (`joomla1_tags`) can be defined by concatenating the Joomla database name (`joomla1`) and the name of the Joomla search area (`tags`). The chosen index can then be passed through as an argument to the `getSphinxResults()` method.

You can choose to run one `SphinxClient::query()` at a time for each index. However, this will open and close a connection to Sphinx for every query made. A better solution is to use `SphinxClient::addQuery()` to first add a query to a queue, and then send all the queued queries to Sphinx, using one single connection with the `SphinxClient::runQueries()` call.

9.7 Integration with other search engines

Sphinx is just one of many search engines out there. Here is a brief overview of some of the other options you have.

Integration with Apache Solr

Apache Solr is written in Java and based upon the Apache Lucene engine. While implementing Lucene is quite tough, getting Solr up and running is less work. Do not underestimate the work though. Implementing Solr still gives you far more work than Sphinx does.

On a Linux box, you will need to install Java, the Tomcat webserver, plus some other dependencies. As of yet, there is no simple `yum` command available to install it under CentOS easily. Still, installing Solr should not take you more than an hour or so. The real work goes into configuring Solr to do its job. Even though the Tomcat webserver gives you a slick looking GUI to work with, the setup still requires you to modify various XML files to get things going.

PHP can be extended with a `SolrClient` class, which includes a `query()` method similar to the `SphinxClient::query()` call. This is where the resemblance with the Sphinx client stops though. The Solr library is very object-oriented. The `query()` method receives a `SolrQuery` object as an argument. Parameters are handled by a `SolrParams` class. And the response from Solr comes in the form of a `SolrReponse` object.

While this may be overwhelming in the beginning, Solr has more to offer than Sphinx. The Solr PHP client allows for adding, updating and deleting articles. It is definitely more advanced than the Sphinx PHP client.

All content items are referred to as **Documents**. This concept also extends to other file formats like PDF and Word documents. Adding PDF documents to the Solr engine is not done through the PHP client directly. It is hard to decode PDF and Word into indexable content and it is even harder to do this in PHP.

Apache Solr itself relies for this on another tool called Apache Tika. There is no PHP client for Tika. However, a PDF document can be indexed through a different procedure. From within Joomla, the PDF document can be read into a string and this string can be POST-ed to a specific Solr URL using `CURL`. By creating a PHP mix of `SolrClient` calls and Apache Tika calls, you will be able to integrate Solr and Joomla in a solid way.

Integration with ElasticSearch

ElasticSearch is another popular search engine, similar to Sphinx and Solr. It offers a PHP client `elasticsearch-php`, which allows for communication with the ElasticSearch server. This client offers various methods (`search()`, `index()`, `delete()`, `create()`) with each method using an associative array as an argument:

```
$params['index'] = 'joomla1_index';
$params['type'] = 'joomla_article';
$params['body']['query']['match']['testField'] = 'test';
$return = $client->search($params);
```

In most cases, the array defines an `index` and a content type (`type`) and optionally an `id` (referring to a specific ElasticSearch document) or `body` (when creating a new content item in ElasticSearch).

Compared to Solr and Sphinx, ElasticSearch offers all the important features that the other two search engines do, plus it has some additional features, like importing data from external sources (Dropbox, Git, LDAP, Redis and RSS). It even includes the ability to import from Solr. However, these additional features are most likely not needed when you are simply looking for the replacement of Joomla search with an external search engine. The core functionality is sufficient in most cases.

More search engine options

We have now focused on Sphinx and have briefly touched upon Solr and ElasticSearch. However, there are many more search applications that offer better searching and better indexing. The main three (Solr, Sphinx and ElasticSearch) are nowadays accompanied by many other search engines: clucene (a C++ port of Apache Lucene), Whoosh (Python based), Indextank (open sourced Python engine created by the LinkedIn company), Xapian (C++ based), Haystack (for the Django crowd). The list goes on and on.

When you are new to the topic, the main three probably offer you a solution you can rely on. The question of which engine is best suited for the job, of course depends on the job itself. However, when you are looking for an alternative to regular MySQL search, all the engines listed above are fine.

One of the more important choices to make, depends on the language. For instance, Whoosh is written in Python and therefore focuses on Python developers. Even though interaction with Joomla is perfectly possible thanks to the Whoosh API, choosing Python seems less logical.

Solr (and its parent project Lucene) is based on Java. Running a Java application is best done on a dedicated machine. Running the search engine on the same server that runs MySQL and PHP, makes more sense if the memory footprint of the chosen search engine is as low as possible. For this, Java is less of an alternative. A C/C++ based search engine like clucene, Sphinx ElasticSearch or Xapian makes more sense.

There is no engine based on PHP.

Integrating Google Search?

Integrating Google Search and Joomla Search is not possible. What is possible is to replace the entire Joomla search with Google Custom Search Engine (CSE). The Joomla search module will need to be replaced with a custom HTML form and a simple Joomla article can be abused to load the search results through JavaScript. Things can be styled using CSS to get rid of the regular Google Search look and feel. However, there will always be some elements that will be recognizable as being from Google. It is a quick alternative though.

9.8 Summary

In this chapter, you have learned the difference between three types of search: regular search using Search Plugins; Smart Search using Finder plugins; and external search using engines like Solr and Sphinx. By discussing the backgrounds but also dealing with the practical code, it is more clear what the pros and cons are of each type.

So far, we have discussed one or two plugin types per chapter. The next chapters – chapter 10 and chapter 11 – deal with all plugin types that we have not yet discussed: editors, buttons, quick icons, CAPTCHA, installer events and more.

Editors, buttons, icons, CAPTCHA

When editing content, an editor is used.
The editor itself is implemented by using an Editor
Plugin, plus various buttons created with Button
Plugins. This chapter gives you insight into how
you can build your own editor or editor buttons.
The chapter also discusses the quick icons shown
on the Joomla Administrator dashboard, and the
implementation of CAPTCHA.

10.1 **Editor plugins**

In both the Joomla frontend and the Joomla backend, a textbox can be turned into a complete WYSIWYG editor by using the field type `editor`. Everybody knows this, because this textbox is where you enter the main text while editing an article. When this field type editor is shown, the Joomla Editor Plugin is called to display the chosen WYSIWYG editor on screen. Common WYSIWYG editors are TinyMCE, JCE, JCK Editor and ACE.

It is important to differentiate between the Editor Plugin and the WYSIWYG editor. Most - if not all - WYSIWYG editors are JavaScript based, providing an editing toolbar to content managers like Joomla. To make the WYSIWYG editor functional, additional code is used. It is the Editor Plugin that loads the relevant content into the WYSIWYG editor. It is the Editor Plugin that inserts the modified WYSIWYG content back into Joomla when saving an article.

For instance, the **Editor - TinyMCE** plugin is an Editor Plugin that integrates the third party software TinyMCE into Joomla. The **Editor - JCE** plugin is another Joomla plugin that loads the same TinyMCE into Joomla, but now with additional features. There are also Editor Plugins that do not load a WYSIWYG environment at all. For instance, the **Editor - None** plugin simply adds autofocus to a textarea and the **Editor - CoreMirror** plugin adds syntax highlighting to a basic textarea.

Plugins events for editor plugins

This book will not cover writing a complete WYSIWYG editor, which has much to do with JavaScript and little to with Joomla. However, it is interesting to discuss the various plugin events that allow you to integrate an existing WYSIWYG editor into Joomla.

An Editor Plugin should have the following structure:

```
class PlgEditorExample extends JPlugin
{
    public function onInit() {}
    public function onSave($id) {}
    public function onGetContent($id) {}
    public function onSetContent($id, $content) {}
    public function onGetInsertMethod() {}
    public function onDisplay($name, $content, $width, $height, $col,
$row, $buttons = true, $id = null, $asset = null, $author = null,
$params = array()) {}
}
```

As you can see,the event methods do not have a proper prefix.

onInit() and onDisplay()

Of all methods, the `onInit()` and `onDisplay()` method are the most important. When the `editor` field is initialized, Joomla loads the `JEditor` class from the file `editor.php` in the folder `libraries/cms/editor/`.

Next, the `JEditor::_loadEditor()` method is called once, even if there are more editors on the same page, and this method calls upon the plugin's `onInit()` event method. Because the `onInit()` method is called only once per page, the method is ideal for all things that are needed for the editor to load properly, but are needed only once. A good example of this is the loading of JavaScript and CSS. A shortcut also exists: Any return value of the `onInit()` event method is added as custom JavaScript to the Joomla header.

The `onDisplay()` method is used to display the editor's output. For instance, the **Editor - None** plugin uses this method to simply return a textarea with its own unique DOM ID. WYSIWYG editors add JavaScript code that allow for the WYSIWYG effects for that unique textarea. The method has a ridiculous amount of parameters (eleven). They are used to pass `JForm` variables to the editor itself.

Other editor events

All other event methods contain JavaScript. This might sound a little bit odd. It is important to note that the WYSIWYG editor only lives within the browser. It has no connections with the PHP based Joomla application. It can work in a static HTML page as well.

To make the WYSIWYG editor work for Joomla, its functionality is connected to generic Joomla bindings. For instance, the `onSave()` event method is used to copy content from the WYSIWYG area to a plain old textarea, which is then posted back to Joomla. The`onSave()` method should therefore contain JavaScript code that does this copying. As an example, the TinyMCE editor implements this as follows:

```
public function onSave($editor)
{
    return 'if (tinyMCE.get("' . $editor . '").isHidden()) {tinyMCE.
get("' . $editor . '").show()}; tinyMCE.get("' . $editor . '").
save();';
}
```

The remaining three methods contain additional hooks for **Editor Buttons**: When an Editor Button is used to insert text into the editor (like an image), the Editor Button calls upon a dynamic JavaScript method, which in turn will call the `onGetInsertMethod()` event method.

Similarly, the `onGetContent()` event method returns the entire text of the editor, while `onSetContent()` again replaces the entire editor text with new content.

10.2 **Button plugins**

Originally called **Editor-Xtd** Plugins - where the **Xtd** stands for **Extended -,** these plugins are mainly meant for one thing: to display a button. I will refer to these plugins as **Button Plugins** or **Editor Buttons**. Another reason for naming them Button Plugins instead, is that the plugin class starts with `PlgButton`. Note that these plugins are still placed in the folder `plugins/editors-xtd`.

Whenever an editor is initialized, the editor will initialize all Editor Buttons, which are then displayed below the editor itself. An Editor Button has only one event method: `onDisplay($name)` with its argument being the `$name` of the editor. The Editor Plugin fills in the value of the `$name` variable: Typically, it contains the DOM ID of the editor.

A basic Button Plugin looks as follows. Note that we also include the `$autoloadLanguage` flag, because a button most definitely always needs a label and this label should always be made translatable using a language file.

```php
class PlgButtonExample extends JPlugin
{
    protected $autoloadLanguage = true;

    public function onDisplay($name)
    {
        JHtml::_('script', 'plg_example/button.js');

        $button = new JObject;
        $button->modal = false;
        $button->class = 'btn';
        $button->onclick = "return doExample('".$name."');";
        $button->text = JText::_('PLG_EDITOR-XTD_EXAMPLE_BUTTON');
        $button->name = 'arrow-down';
        $button->link = '#';

        return $button;
    }
}
```

When the editor is being rendered, the object that is returned is displayed using the JLayout file `layouts/joomla/editors/buttons/button.php`. When writing your own button, it is best to have a quick peek at this file, to see which object property is doing what.

Adding JavaScript

The example plugin class loads an additional script `button.js`. The `onclick` property of the $button object allows for a JavaScript function doExample() to be contained in this script file. Such a JavaScript method may do something like this:

```
function doExample(editor)
{
    var example = 'Hello World';
    jInsertEditorText(example, editor);
}
```

The Joomla core includes a JavaScript function jInsertEditorText, which in turn calls upon the JavaScript code that was defined by the Editor Plugin through its event methodonGetInsertMethod(). Thanks to this mechanism, the Editor Button is able to insert any value in any editor generated by any other Editor Plugin. It is quite flexible, once you get the hang of the mix of JavaScript and PHP.

The button is also styled a little bit. The class property is used as HTML attribute class, while the name property is used to refer to a specific **IcoMoon** image. The class property can be seen as the old Joomla 2.5 approach, while the IcoMoon approach is used in Joomla 3. To see which class names are supported, check out the IcoMoon website (**http://icomoon.io/**) and the Joomla CSS file media/jui/css/icomoon.css. Note that the original IcoMoon set is slightly modified for the usage in Joomla.

Using modal windows

A button is also able to popup a modal window. In this case, the modal behavior is first initialized and the button property modal is set to true. Also, the link property now points to the URL that is opened in the modal window, while the options define the proportions of this modal window.

```
JHtml::_('behavior.modal');

$link = 'index.php?option=com_content'
    .'&amp;view=articles'
    .'&amp;layout=modal'
    .'&amp;tmpl=component'
    .'&amp;'.JSession::getFormToken().'=1'
;

$button = new JObject;
$button->modal = true;
$button->class = 'btn';
$button->link = $link;
$button->text = JText::_('PLG_EDITORS-XTD_EXAMPLE_BUTTON');
$button->name = 'file-add';
$button->options = "{handler: 'iframe', size: {x: 800, y: 500}}";
```

Within your modal window, you can allow for items to be browsed and eventually selected: To select an item and return its value to the editor, the click on the item link should be caught and trigger a JavaScript function instead:

```
<a href="#" onclick="doClickItem('Item'); return false;">Item</a>
```

Next the JavaScript file that we include with our Button Plugin needs to define this JavaScript function:

```
function doClickItem(itemValue)
{
    jInsertEditorText(itemValue, editor);
    SqueezeBox.close();
}
```

We close the modal window using `SqueezeBox.close()`.

10.3 Quick Icon plugins

In the Joomla CMS, there are two **Quick Icon** plugins installed by default: one for Joomla core updates and one for Joomla extension updates. When enabled, they both display in the **Control Panel** of the Joomla Administrator in the module position `icon`.

The plugins themselves do not deliver output. Instead, they are called upon by the `mod_quickicon` module. This module outputs a predefined array of icon definitions, including various icons that lead to manager pages. This array can be extended through the `onGetIcons` event, which is where our plugin comes into play.

```
class PlgQuickiconExample extends JPlugin
{
    public function onGetIcons ($context)
    {
        if ($context != $this->params->get('context', 'mod_quickicon')
        {
            return;
        }

        $iconPath = '../../../../media/plg_quickicon_example/images/';
        $icon = $iconPath . 'icon-48-items.png';
        $link = 'index.php?option=com_example&view=items';

        $return = array(
            'link' => JRoute::_($link),
            'text' => JText::_('PLG_QUICKICON_EXAMPLE_VIEW_ITEMS'),
            'group' => 'MOD_QUICKICON_CONTENT' ,
            'image' => 'stack',
            'icon' => $icon,
        );

        return $return;
    }
}
```

In it's basic form, the onGetIcons() event method returns either an associative array describing the icon or it returns nothing (return null). The associative array needs to include the following elements:

o link: A backend URL.

o text: A text to be displayed in the button.

o group: One of the groups defined by the mod_quickicon module. To see which groups are available, it is best to inspect the file helper.php in the folder administrator/modules/mod_quickicon/. Common group names are MOD_QUICKICON_CONTENT and MOD_QUICKICON_CONFIGURATION.

o image: The class name refers to a specific IcoMoon image. To see which class names are supported, check out the IcoMoon website (http://icomoon.io/) and/or the Joomla CSS file media/jui/css/icomoon.css.

o icon: A PNG image of 48 by 48 pixels.

o The values for image and icon do the same thing. They both pimp up the button with a graphical element. However, IcoMoon is only included in Joomla since the coming of Bootstrap, so Joomla 3. The `icon` allows for backwards compatibility with Joomla 2.5.

If your extension is only meant for Joomla 3 or later, you can skip the `icon` value.

Dynamically load the button text

Both of the core plugins are more advanced than the example above. Instead of returning just a static array, they also add jQuery scripts to make an AJAX call that automatically updates the text of the button. The jQuery framework is initialized first. Next, a custom script is added to the HTML document.

To make sure that JavaScript strings are properly translated, we define these strings first in a custom script declaration, which outputs `JText` strings directly in the HTML `head` section. The JavaScript variables, that now contain translated text, are then used in the separate JavaScript files:

```
JHtml::_('jquery.framework');
JHtml::_('script', 'plg_quickicon_example/ajax.js', false, true);

$example_notice = JText::_('PLG_QUICKICON_EXAMPLE_NOTICE');
$script = "var example_notice = '$example_notice';";

JFactory::getDocument()->addScriptDeclaration($script);
```

To make sure the jQuery scripts can reference our specific icon through the DOM, we need to ensure the button is referenced with a unique ID. We can add this ID to the associative array:

```
'id' => 'plg_quickicon_example',
```

The ID now allows you to reference the button through jQuery within the `ajax.js` script that was previously added:

```
jQuery('#plg_quickicon_example').find('span').html(example_notice);
```

Regulating access

The return array can be enhanced even more by adding an `access` key. This access key contains an array of value pairs (so, sets of two values), where each set defines a specific ACL rule. The following defines two sets of two values. Each set refers to a specific ACL rule for the com_example component.

```
'access' => array(
    'core.manage',
    'com_example',
    'core.create',
    'com_example',
),
```

The code may be a little bit confusing. Let's illustrate the usage of this `access` array by showing you an alternative way of making ACL calls that can check for the same privileges. If both `$allowContentManage` and `$allowContentCreate` are `true`, the admin would be allowed to manage and create content. Therefore, the button will be shown. If either is `false`, no button is shown:

```
$user = JFactory::getUser();
$allowContentManage = $user->authorise('core.manage','com_example');
$allowContentCreate = $user->authorise('core.create','com_example');

if ($allowContentManage == false || $allowContentCreate == false)
{
    return;
}
```

Both the `access` key and our custom `$allowContentManage/$allowContentCreate` flags do the same thing and you can use both as you prefer. The `access` key allows you to accomplish the same thing. It is just a little bit confusing that it is using a flat array instead of a multidimensional array for this.

10.4 CAPTCHA plugins

CAPTCHA is one of those abbreviations that only geeks can come up with. It stands for **Completely Automated Public Turing Test to Tell Computers and Humans Apart**. A CAPTCHA check attempts to validate whether the user agent (browser) that accesses a form, is controlled by a human or by some kind of robot. The test itself can be anything from a simple sum or some garbled text to a puzzle that needs to be solved by the user by moving the puzzle pieces to the correct places.

```
Is the following sum correct? 1 + 1 = 3
```

Coming up with a new CAPTCHA mechanism requires inspiration. It can be some kind of technical wonder. However, it can also include a simple set of questions that are specific to your website. For instance, you can ask your visitors "Which is the best CMS? Joomla or WordPress?", where - obviously - the correct answer is Joomla. The main challenge when creating a new and effective CAPTCHA technique is that, if you make the test too simple, it will be easy for robots to break it. However, if the test is too difficult, robots will be stopped, but so will your human visitors. It is a battle between usability and security. Supporting multiple languages and accessibility complicate things even more.

Not user friendly

While the original Turing Test written by Alan Turing himself dates back to around 1950, CAPTCHA tests are still very common on the web today. The main reason for this is that spam is a serious issue and site owners want to protect their website from spam robots. CAPTCHA offers a nice solution for this.

However, one thing is often forgotten about CAPTCHA: It is always annoying. Always. If you are visiting a website and that website tells you to do something more difficult, simply because they do not trust you by default, it is annoying. It downgrades the user experience.

Therefore, the best solution for your visitors is to have no CAPTCHA at all.

Not using CAPTCHA

While CAPTCHA offers one approach to stop spambots, there are more approaches. Each Joomla form should include a session token, in order for basic robots to be stopped right away. More advanced robots that are specifically targeting Joomla, will have no problem bypassing this security. It is nonetheless useful to stop the majority of attacks and is therefore considered a must:

```php
<?php echo JHtml::_( 'form.token' ); ?>
```

Parsing the incoming HTTP request also offers you some options. Most robots identify themselves as being robots through the HTTP_USER_AGENT variable. Blocking by IP is a good alternative as well. There are some spam lists like the ones of Spamhaus (**http://www.spamhaus.org/**) that you can use to block IPs from sending forms.Some of these lists also include IP-addresses that are used from people at home, getting paid for manual form submissions – not computer-based. You can even block people by country – for instance Italy if you do not like Italian food.

Honeypot

One nicer approach is the honeypot technique. Instead of preventing robots from entering certain form values, thus making it harder for your visitors as well, you can simply add a field tothe form that is intentionally left blank. By hiding this field from your visitors (by setting the `visibility` to `hidden` or moving it 10,000 pixels to the left), no human visitor will ever enter a value. If a value is entered anyway, you can assume it is a robot and not a real visitor.

The honeypot technique is not covered with Joomla CAPTCHA plugins. Instead, you can create a **System Plugin** that modifies the `JForm` form to add a dummy field, use CSS to hide it from your visitors and then use the **System Plugin** again to make sure the posted value of that field is always empty. If it is filled in anyway, you can assume you are dealing with a robot. To make things even more tempting, you can name the field in such a way that is more tempting for a robot to fill (`email`, `comment`, `body`). Note this might give issues with autocompletion extensions in some browsers, like address completers and autologin mechanisms.

Example: Writing your own Captcha

Enough of bashing CAPTCHA. Joomla offers a flexible way of creating your own CAPTCHA plugins. Each plugin can be enabled in the **Global Configuration** options as **Default Captcha**. Optionally, each plugin can be configured to load for a specific component if that component offers this as a component option.

Let's work on an example plugin that requires the user to do some counting. Every time the form is loaded, the plugin will generate a new random string and the user will be asked to provide the number of vowels, consonants or capital letters in the string. To freshen up your grammatical skills, let's take the phrase **Joomla Plugins Book**. It contains 3 capitals, 7 vowels and 10 consonants.

 You can find a copy of this code in the GitHub repository: Browse to the folder **chapter10/ plg_captcha_example** to view the sources.

The basic structure of a CAPTCHA plugin looks like this:

```
class PlgCaptchaExample extends JPlugin
{
    protected $autoloadLanguage = true;

    public function onInit($id)
    {}

    public function onDisplay($name, $id, $class)
    {}

    public function onCheckAnswer($answer)
    {}
}
```

As you can see, there are three methods to implement. The `onInit()` method and `onDisplay()` method are both called when CAPTCHA is enabled for a specific page, like the contact page. The `onCheckAnswer()` is called when the form is submitted and the CAPTCHA needs to be validated.

The onInit() method

The `onInit()` method and `onDisplay()` method are called almost simultaneously - first the `onInit()` method, then the `onDisplay()` method. However, the reason why there are two methods instead of one, is that the `onInit()` method can be called only once per page. The `onDisplay()` method can be called multiple times if there are multiple forms on the page that require CAPTCHA.

The CAPTCHA that we are going to create, has two elements that are randomly generated per page. A question type and a random string to which the question applies. The question is always the same. The user is asked to count how many characters of a specific type there are in the random string. The question type determines this type: consonants, vowels or capitals. We put them in a class variable `$question_types`, so we can select them from any of the plugin methods:

```
protected $question_types = array(
    'vowels' => 'PLG_CAPTCHA_EXAMPLE_FIELD_QUESTION_VOWELS',
    'consonants' => 'PLG_CAPTCHA_EXAMPLE_FIELD_QUESTION_CONSONANTS',
    'capitals' => 'PLG_CAPTCHA_EXAMPLE_FIELD_QUESTION_CAPITALS',
);
```

The `onInit()` method uses this array right away: It picks a random value from the question types, in order for the question type to become either `consonants`, `vowels` or `capitals`. It also generates a random string through the `generateRandomString()` method.

```
public function onInit($id)
{
    $this->question_word = $this->generateRandomString();
    $this->question_type = array_rand($this->question_types, 1);

    $session = JFactory::getSession();
    $session->set('captcha.example.word', $this->question_word);
    $session->set('captcha.example.type', $this->question_type);
}
```

Both this random string and the question type are stored in the Joomla session. So, when the user input needs to be validated, these variables are readily available. Each session variable has a prefix `captcha.example`, to prevent conflicts with variables stored by other extensions.

The `onInit()` method also has an argument `$id`, which we do not use. If your CAPTCHA requires some JavaScript and this JavaScript needs to create some unique variables, the `$id` (which refers to the DOM ID of the field that displays the CAPTCHA) can be used for generating the unique name. We do not need this in our example.

Generating a random string

Using the method `generateRandomString()`, random characters are being generated. When you look at the Joomla core, there is already such a method available: The class `JUserHelper` contains a method `genRandomPassword()`, which is normally used to generate passwords. We can use this method in our own plugin:

```
protected function generateRandomString()
{
    jimport('joomla.user.helper');

    return JUserHelper::genRandomPassword();
}
```

There is one downside though. The entire string that `JUserHelper` generates is random. It might contain a combination of letters and numbers. It might also contain only numbers. Let's take the following random string:

```
39354019355398
```

When we apply our CAPTCHA technique on this string and ask the user how many uppercase letters it contains, the answer will always be zero. The default would also be zero, so spambots always have the answer right.

Therefore, when generating a random string, we want to guarantee a few things. For every one of the question types (vowels, consonants, capitals) we will guarantee there are at least two or more characters matching. Otherwise, our CAPTCHA will be too easy to defeat.

To do this, we are going to create some ranges - for instance, a list of vowels - and generate a random string based upon that range. Two methods help us with this: `generateRandomStringFromRange()`, which creates a random string per range and `generateRandomString()`, which defines the range, calls upon the other method and outputs the total as one string:

```
protected function generateRandomString()
{
    $characters = array();
    $ranges = array(
        'abcdefghijklmnopqrstuvwxyz', // lowercase
```

```
        'ABCDEFGHIJKLMNOPQRSTUVWXYZ', // uppercase
        'aAeEiIoOuU', // vowels
        'bBcCdDfFgGhHjJkKlLmMnNpPqQrRsStTvVwWxXyYzZ', // consonants
        '0123456789', // numbers
    );

    foreach ($ranges as $range)
    {
        $length = rand(2, 5);
        $rangeChars = $this->generateRandomStringFromRange(
            $length, $range);
        $characters = array_merge($characters, $rangeChars);
    }

    shuffle($characters);

    return implode('', $characters);
}


protected function generateRandomStringFromRange($length, $range)
{
    $base = strlen($range);
    $randomChars = array();
    $random = JCrypt::genRandomBytes($length + 1);
    $shift = ord($random[0]);

    for ($i = 1; $i <= $length; ++$i)
    {
        $randomChars[] = $range[($shift + ord($random[$i])) % $base];
        $shift += ord($random[$i]);
    }

    return $randomChars;
}
```

Showing the CAPTCHA question

Now that the session contains both a question type and a question word, we can display
a little form based upon this. This is done using the onDisplay() method. It simply
outputs whatever HTML needs to be displayed within the form to let our CAPTCHA work.

In our case, we fetch the question type and question word from where they are set by
the onInit() method. Next, we display them. The question type can be conveniently
matched in the $this->question_types array to output the actual question,
translated and all.

```php
public function onDisplay($name, $id, $class)
{
    $html = JText::_($this->question_types[$this->question_type]);
    $html .= '<pre>' . $this->question_word . '</pre>';
    $html .= '<hr/>';
    $html .= JText::_('PLG_CAPTCHA_EXAMPLE_FIELD_ANSWER') . ': ';
    $html .= '<input type="text" name="' . $name . '" id="'
        . $id . '" class="' . $class . '" />';

    return $html;
}
```

The method provides us with a field ID, field name and field class, so we are just adding that information to the input element as well. As you can see, the question word is visible in plain text. To make this more secure, you can draw the letters in a PNG image using the PHP GD library. Note that most spambots are capable of OCR (the ability to convert text in images into computer text).

Validating the answer

The plugin method onCheckAnswer() is called as soon as the form is submitted. If we used the onDisplay() method argument $name to define our input field, the variable $answer now contains our answer. If we did not follow this $name standard, we would have needed to retrieve our answer from the POST ourselves using JFactory::getApplication()->input.

The code validates whether the $answer is a number and higher than 0. If not, the method sets an error and returns `false`. Next, the answer is validated using a custom method `matchAnswer()`. If this validation succeeds, no error is set and we return `true`.

```php
public function onCheckAnswer($answer)
{
    $answer = (int)trim($answer);

    if (!$response > 0)
    {
        $error = JText::_('PLG_CAPTCHA_EXAMPLE_ERROR_NO_RESPONSE');
        $this->_subject->setError($error);
        return false;
    }

    $session = JFactory::getSession();
    $qtype = $session->get('captcha.example.type');
    $qword = $session->get('captcha.example.word');

    $answer = $this->matchAnswer($response, $qtype, $qword);

    if ($answer == false)
    {
        $errorMsg = 'PLG_CAPTCHA_EXAMPLE_ERROR_INCORRECT';
        $error = JText::sprintf($errorMsg, $response);
        $this->_subject->setError($error);
        return false;
    }

    return true;
}
```

Last but not least, we deal with the actual validation method `matchAnswer()`. In this method we focus on the user's input `$answer` and check whether it matches with the question we initially asked:

```php
protected function matchAnswer(
    $answer, $question_type, $question_word
)
{
    $validAnswer = 0;
    switch($question_type)
    {
        case 'capitals':
            $regex = '/[ABCDEFGHIJKLMNOPQRSTUVWXYZ]/';
```

```
            preg_match_all($regex, $question_word, $matches);
            $validAnswer = count($matches[0]);
            break;

        case 'vowels':
            $regex = '/[aouie]/i';
            preg_match_all($regex, $question_word, $matches);
            $validAnswer = count($matches[0]);
            break;

        case 'consonants':
            $range = '/[bcdfghjklmnpqrstvwxyz]/i';
            preg_match_all($regex, $question_word, $matches);
            $validAnswer = count($matches[0]);
            break;
    }

    if ($answer == $validAnswer)
    {
        return true;
    }

    return false;
}
```

No CAPTCHA prefix in the methods

You have learned in the previous chapters that a plugin method is not strictly bound to a plugin group. For instance, you can intercept any event by including the event method in aSystem Plugin. In other words, you can implement CAPTCHA using a System Plugin.

The standard in Joomla is to include the group's name in the event itself. For example, Content Plugins deal with events like onContentBeforeDisplay or onUserAfterDelete. The CAPTCHA events defy this standard with names like onInit, onDisplay and onCheckAnswer. Maybe one day these methods will be renamed to include a prefix onCaptcha.

Including CAPTCHA in your own component

Even though this book does not cover component development, it is nice to know how your CAPTCHA plugin is going to be implemented in components anyway. There is no PHP code involved here, only XML code.

Any CAPTCHA plugin can be used for any component, as long as that component has a

CAPTCHA-enabled form available. The setup of CAPTCHA is flexible: You can use the core's **Recaptcha** plugin for the user creation form and our example CAPTCHA plugin for the contact form. The component is configured with a specific CAPTCHA plugin.

To allow for this flexibility, the following XML code needs to be added to the component's `config.xml` file, located in the folder `administrator/components/com_example`:

```
<field name="captcha" type="plugins"
    folder="captcha" default="" filter="cmd"
    label="COM_EXAMPLE_FIELD_CAPTCHA_LABEL"
    description="COM_EXAMPLE_FIELD_CAPTCHA_DESC"
    >
    <option value="">JOPTION_USE_DEFAULT</option>
    <option value="0">JOPTION_DO_NOT_USE</option>
</field>
```

This XML code allows an administrator to configure a CAPTCHA plugin for this component, when opening up the component **Options** in the Joomla backend.

In the frontend the `JForm` based form of the component needs to define a fieldset `captcha` and a field `captcha`. This field is automatically filled by the configured CAPTCHA plugin:

```
<fieldset name="captcha">
    <field name="captcha" type="captcha"
        validate="captcha" namespace="foobar"
        label="COM_EXAMPLE_CAPTCHA_LABEL"
        description="COM_EXAMPLE_CAPTCHA_DESC"
    />
</fieldset>
```

In the XML code the `namespace` refers to the component name.

10.5 Summary

This chapter has given you examples of creating plugins for various purposes: Editors, editor buttons, quick icons and CAPTCHA. With this chapter, we have almost accomplished one of the main goals of this book: To explain each and every one of the plugin types that are included in the Joomla core. The next chapter will complete this goal. However, after that, there is still a lot more interesting stuff to tell: Best practices, architectural design, tips and tricks – all can be found at the end of this book.

(11) Other plugins and events

We have almost covered all plugin types. This chapter will give you insight into the remaining core plugins that we have not yet discussed. The extension events and installer events will definitely be interesting for extension developers. We will also discuss some third party extensions to see how plugin events can be applied there.

11.1 Extension plugins

The plugin group `extension` allows you to influence the behavior of Joomla when it is handling extensions (plugins, components, templates, libraries and modules). The Joomla core offers only one plugin in this group: The **Extension – Joomla** plugin. The plugin handles the update URL entries for every extension, in case the extension XML manifest is indeed listing an update site (see chapter 3 for details).

It is a little bit hard to come up with good use cases, when it comes to this plugin group. In most cases where you want to do something specific for an extension, that extension is already yours and you can add these tasks to the extension XML manifest itself. Because the plugin group is setup to be generic for all extensions and not just for one specific extension, the plugin group may allow for scenarios where sites are managed in batches or there needs to be a generic solution for a specific hosting environment. For instance, the extension installation can be logged somewhere, or a message can be displayed to remind the Joomla admin to create a proper backup. Let's play with it a little bit to see where this brings us.

Base plugin

We start off with a base class again, which extends from `JPlugin`. The event methods can be added to this base class as we go along:

```
class PlgExtensionExample extends JPlugin
{
}
```

Installing extensions

Within the Joomla CMS, extensions are installed using the **Installation Manager** and this backend component calls again for the `JInstaller` class within the CMS library. Whenever an extension is installed, the event `onExtensionBeforeInstall` is called before installing the extension and the event`onExtensionAfterInstall` is called afterwards.

The event method `onExtensionBeforeInstall` has four arguments:

o `$method`
o `$type`
o `$manifest`
o `$extension`

The $method is a string being either `install` or `discover_install`. When updating an extension, different events are being used – we will discuss them later. With the value `install`, the package is either being uploaded through a package archive (ZIP file) or downloaded through a package URL (**Install From URL**). In both cases, the extension arrives in Joomla as a ZIP file, of which the contents need to be extracted and copied to the right place. After this, the extension is registered in the Joomla database. When the $method has the value discover_install, the extension files already exist at their final destination and the extension only needs to be registered properly in the Joomla database.

The $type argument refers to the extension type as it is defined in the XML manifest. Its value is set to component, plugin, template, library, file or module.

The $manifest variable contains the extensions XML manifest file as a SimpleXML object. This can prove very useful, if you want to parse XML attributes that are not handled by the core installer but are present in the XML manifest nonetheless.

Last but not least, the $extension flag is always 0. It is there for future purposes. However, it needs to be included anyway, if you want your plugin method to be PHP E_ STRICT compliant.

```
public function onExtensionBeforeInstall(
    $method, $type, $manifest, $extension
)
{}
```

Let's come up with a practical example of using this event: Many hosting providers offer some kind of method to automatically install Joomla. In some of these cases, the **Global Configuration** is left half-broken. The variables tmp_path and log_path are wrong, making it impossible to write logs or use the temporary folder properly. When you try to install an extension, the temporary folder needs to be accessible and when it is not accessible, the installation fails.

The installation manager has a workaround for when the tmp_path folder is empty or when it does not exist. So, that is already covered by the Joomla core. However, when the tmp_path folder does exist but is simply not writable, the warning **Failed to move file** appears without further clues why.

We can create a plugin to improve this. Whenever an extension is being installed, the plugin checks whether the tmp_path is writable or not. If the path is not writable, the plugin generates a friendly warning.

```
public function onExtensionBeforeInstall(
    $method, $type, $manifest, $extension
)
{
    $app = JFactory::getApplication();
```

```
$tmp_path = JFactory::getConfig()->get('tmp_path');

if (empty($tmp_path))
{
    $warning = 'PLG_EXTENSION_EXAMPLE_WARNING_TMP_PATH_EMPTY';
    $app->enqueueMessage(JText::_($warning), 'warning');
}
elseif (is_writable($tmp_path) === false)
{
    $warning = 'PLG_EXTENSION_EXAMPLE_WARNING_TMP_PATH_NOWRITE';
    $app->enqueueMessage(JText::_($warning), 'warning');
}
}
```

Unfortunately, the return value of the event method is disregarded. If you want your plugin to stop the Joomla installer from installing extensions under a certain circumstance - for instance, because extensions are not allowed to be installed on Sundays - the only way to deal with this is to redirect the administrator to another location:

```
$app = JFactory::getApplication();
$app->redirect(JRoute::_('index.php'));
$app->close();
```

Just as there is an event before the extension is installed, there is also an event for after the extension is installed: `onExtensionAfterInstall`.

```
public function onExtensionAfterInstall($installer, $eid)
{
}
```

Here, the `$installer` variable contains an instance of the `JInstaller` class used during installation. The `$eid` either contains the numerical ID of the newly installed extension, or it is `false` when the installation has failed. The ID can be used for instance to look up the extension in the `#__extensions` table for further processing.

 You can find a sample **plg_extension_custom** plugin in the book's GitHub repository. Using this plugin, you can log what extension is installed or saved at what point.

Uninstalling extensions

For uninstalling extensions, the events are very similar to the installation events. There is an event before removal (`onExtensionBeforeUninstall`) and after removal (`onExtensionAfterUninstall`):

```
public function onExtensionBeforeUninstall($installer, $eid)
{
}
```

```
public function onExtensionAfterUninstall($installer, $eid, $result)
{
}
```

The return value of the event methods is ignored. It is not possible for a plugin to stop the uninstall process, except for redirecting the administrator to another page. The $installer variable contains an instance of the JInstaller class. The $eid variable contains the extension ID. Note that having the $eid in case of the onExtensionAfterUninstall event is probably not very useful, because the core database table have been cleaned up already and any reference to this $eid is gone.

Updating extensions

The events for updating extensions are similar to the ones for installing or uninstalling extensions. Whenever an extension is updated using the **Extension Manager**, the events onExtensionBeforeUpdate and onExtensionAfterUpdate are called.

Note that uploading an updated version of an already installed extension through the **Install** pages of the **Extension Manager** does not count as an update. Instead, it is considered to be a fresh install that simply overwrites existing files. These update events are only triggered when the **Extension Manager** installs the new versions through the **Update** pages.

The update events can be caught using your plugin as follows:

```
public function onExtensionBeforeUpdate($type, $manifest)
{
}
```

```
public function onExtensionAfterUpdate($installer, $eid)
{
}
```

Again, it is unfortunate that the return value is ignored. You cannot properly stop the update from happening.

Saving extensions

The last set of events in the extension group deals with saving extensions. The events onExtensionBeforeSave and onExtensionAfterSave allow you to hook into the event when an extension is saved to the database.

```
public function onExtensionBeforeSave($context, $table, $isNew)
{
    return true;
}
```

When does this event happen? It depends a little bit on the extension type.

Whenever a module is being saved, the events are thrown with the first argument $context set to com_modules.module and the second argument being an instance of the JTableModule class.

The fact that this event is being thrown while saving a module is a little bit strange. There is a major difference between a module (an extension) and a module instance (settings for that extension that you save to the database). The extension already exists in the filesystem and it cannot be saved again. However, within the **Module Manager** you can create a new module instance that uses the extension files to function. You can also create multiple module instances of the same module – for example, multiple menu modules that all use the same code of the mod_menu extension. Saving the module instance triggers the event.

You can modify the behavior of the save action by returning false and setting a relevant error in the $table instance:

```
public function onExtensionBeforeSave($context, $table, $isNew)
{
    $table->setError(JText::_('SOME_ERROR'));

    return true;
}
```

Similar to the onExtensionBeforeSave event, there is also the onExtensionAfterSave event:

```
public function onExtensionAfterSave($context, $table, $isNew)
{
}
```

The return value of the event onExtensionAfterSave is discarded.

Just as you can save module instances, you can also save plugins (context com_plugins. plugin), languages (contextcom_languages.language) and template styles (context com_templates.style). Note that a template style (your customized set of template parameters) is not the same as the template (which is an extension). The difference is similar to the difference between a module and a module instance.

There is no event being triggered for components. It might be that this is going to change in future Joomla versions: Saving component parameters is similar to saving a template style or a module instance.

11.2 Installer events

There is also a set of `installer` events that can be used to modify the behavior of the **Installation Manager**. However, there is no specific plugin group `installer` that is initialized at the moment these events are being thrown, so these events are best caught by using a System Plugin.

The following events are currently present in the Joomla core:

```
onInstallerViewBeforeFirstTab
onInstallerViewAfterLastTab
onInstallerBeforeInstallation
onInstallerBeforeInstaller
onInstallerAfterInstaller
onInstallerBeforeDisplay
onInstallerBeforePackageDownload
```

These events are not commonly used though, except for the `onInstallerBeforePackageDownload` event, which is discussed below.

Allowing for software subscriptions

The `onInstallerBeforePackageDownload` event allows you to modify the package URL used by the Joomla **Update Manager**. The event has become popular among extension developers, to allow commercial extensions to be updated using the Joomla **Update Manager**.

The most popular way of making money with Joomla extensions is to sell subscriptions. During the subscription period, the customer is able to download extension updates. However, once the subscription expires, updates become unavailable. The challenge with this business model is to restrict downloads in such a way that the **Update Manager** still works.

With free extensions, the extension's update URL is normally hard-coded in XML code. We have discussed this in chapter 3. Whoever has access to the XML code, is able to access this update URL, and use it to download and install that extension. If the same mechanism is used with subscription-based extensions, this will make the extension freely available, instead of being only available during a paid subscription.

To overcome this, the update URL needs to be made more dynamic. A possible scenario is to have an update key available, which is valid as long as the subscription is valid. The customer is able to use this update key and this update key is appended to the update URL.

Let's see how we can put this into practice.

Adding your own update key to download URLs

To allow for adding an update key to download URLs, we create a System Plugin that implements the event method `onInstallerBeforePackageDownload()`. The return value of the method is of no importance.

The method has two parameters: `$url`, which is a string holding the actual download URL and an array of headers, `$headers`, which is empty by default. Both parameters are references, so we can modify them directly. In this case, we will be modifying the `$url` to authorize this download request. You might also consider using the `$headers` array instead. Any name-value pair set in this array will be added as HTTP header to the outgoing request for the actual download. Instead of adding an update key to the URL, you can use an `X-Authenticate` header to set the update key instead.

```
public function onInstallerBeforePackageDownload(&$url, &$headers)
{
    if (preg_match('/example.com\//', $url) == false)
    {
        return false;
    }
```

The first thing we do is to check whether the given URL is ours. The event method is called for any update request of any extension. To make sure the update key is only appended to update requests for our own extensions, we can simply check for the domain name in the URL. If the domain name does not match our own update server (`example.com`), we exit.

As mentioned, the return value is of no importance: It can be anything (`null`, `true`, `false`). However, it seems nicer to return `false`, when this method does not fulfill its purpose.

Another preflight check we have to make, is to see whether the update key has already been added or not. It depends a little bit on your extension architecture whether this is the case or not. Perhaps the update key is added by default but with a wrong value? Or perhaps the update key is added by another extension? Anyway, in this case we simply check whether the key is there and when it is, we exit.

```
if (preg_match('/(\?|\&)key=/', $url) == true)
{
    return false;
}
```

If we have only one extension that we need to update with this mechanism, we can simply look up the value of the update key as it is stored in Joomla and apply that update key to the URL. Most commonly, you will add a field for this update key to the component parameters, the plugin parameters or the module parameters – depending on the extension type. The user is then able to use this field to store his personal update key in Joomla. Next, the stored parameters can be used in your plugin to fetch the update key. For instance, if you want this update key to be appended to your own component `com_example`, you may use the following code to extract the key:

```
JLoader::import('joomla.application.component.helper');
$key = JComponentHelper::getParams('com_example')->get('key');
```

Things become more difficult when we are using the same **System Plugin** to manage update keys for multiple extensions. Let's say we have three components that all require an update key to retrieve extension updates. Our new `System Plugin` can be made to work for all three components. We only need to inspect the URL to see which component the update URL is meant for. In this case, we are assuming an update URL like the following for a dummy component `com_example`:

```
http://updates.example.com/com_example/com_example.zip
```

Now, to get the proper update key, we need to fetch the component parameters and to do that, we need the component name. The following code simply takes the URL and extracts the component name from it:

```
$filename = basename($url);
$filename = preg_replace('/\.(zip|tgz|tar.gz)$/', '', $filename);
$extensionName = $filename;
```

```
if (preg_match('/^com_/', $extensionName) == false)
{
    return false;
}
```

The next example uses the `JComponentHelper` to get the updater key from the parameters. If the current extension is not a component, the plugin exits. This does not mean this mechanism does not work for modules or plugins. Similar code can be added to include supporting modules (starting with `mod_`) and plugins (starting with `plg_`).

Let's continue with our component example `com_example`. With this name, we can call upon the `JComponentHelper` to get an instance of the component with which we can access the component parameters to fetch the updater key:

```
JLoader::import('joomla.application.component.helper');
```

```php
$component = JComponentHelper::getComponent($extensionName);

if (empty($component))
{
    return false;
}


$key = $component->params->get('key', '');

if (empty($key))
{
    return false;
}
```

Finally, we have an updater key and we can now add it to the URL:

```php
$separator = strpos($url, '?') !== false ? '&' : '?';
$url .= $separator . 'key=' . $key;

return true;
```

Setting up an update server that validates update keys

Whenever the Joomla **Update Manager** is used to install new updates, our plugin will be called into action. When the update URL matches our update server, the plugin will try to find out for which Joomla extension the update request was made and add the corresponding updater key to the URL. This URL is then used to fetch the extension file (such as a ZIP file) from the update server, with the URL containing a reference to the key for the extension's subscription. This means that we need to modify our update server as well, in order for it to be able to validate the given update key. When the validation fails, the download will also fail.

You can use a custom PHP script plus `htaccess` rules to make this happen. Instead of allowing direct access to the actual ZIP files, all requests are handled by an `index.php` file:

```
http://updates.example.com/index.php
```

To make sure direct file requests are ignored, we add some rewrite rules to the webserver configuration. When you are using Apache, you can add the following to a `.htaccess` file in the root folder, which also contains `index.php`:

```
RewriteEngine on
RewriteRule ^(.*)$ index.php [QSA,L]
```

This routes all requests to `index.php`. In other words, a request like the following will be routed to our `index.php` file instead:

```
http://updates.example.com/com_example/com_example.zip?key=1234
```

In that PHP script you can refer to the `$_SERVER['REQUEST_URI']` to get the extension name and use `$_GET['key']` to get the updater key. From there, you can work your way to complete validation of these input values. If validation is successful, you can simply stream the content of the ZIP file back to the browser. If validation is not successful, you can simply return nothing. The Joomla installer is able to pick up on the HTTP status, so it is best practice to also set an HTTP status `403 Forbidden` in this case.

Reporting expired subscriptions

When the update URL leads to an unsuccessful validation – in other words, the updater key is not correct – there is no clean way of reporting back to the Joomla admin that the validation failed. When the Joomla installer encounters an HTTP status other than `200`, this status is reported back to the Joomla backend with a text like **Error connecting to the server: 403**. Unfortunately, the actual reason why the download failed is not shown. This leads to questions from your users.

The event method `onInstallerBeforePackageDownload` only modifies the URL (or headers) and there is no additional event method to check the content ofthe downloaded ZIP to see whether it is a ZIP or whether it is empty.

A workaround for this would be to first validate the key before using it to change the URL. This way a remote call is made to the update server, not to download the ZIP but to validate the key instead. The response of the update server may be a plain text value,describing the status of that key (`active`, `blocked`, `pending`, `expired`). In the case of the status `expired` we can set a session message to inform the admin about this status:

```
if ($validation == 'expired')
{
    $message = 'PLG_SYSTEM_EXAMPLE_ERROR_SUBSCRIPTION_EXPIRED';
    JFactory::getApplication()->enqueueMessage($message, 'warning');

    return false;
}
```

If the validation of the key succeeds, so the `$validation` key holds the value `active`, you can proceed with downloading the actual extension file.

11.3 Contact plugins

There are two events that work specifically with the com_contact component. This component offers a frontend form that allows visitors to send a mail to a specific contact. Whenever a contact form is submitted within the frontend, these events are triggered. When the POST request is received by the com_contact component, it initializes the contact controller, which triggers the first event onValidateContact:

```
public function onValidateContact($contact, $data)
{
    return true;
}
```

The first argument $contact contains the stored data of the contact to be contacted. The $data array contains all data that was submitted by the visitor. The purpose of this event method is to validate whether the posted data can indeed be used to contact the person identified by the contact entry. If this is the case - if the $data has been validated - the method should return true. If the $data is invalid, the method should return false.

When the validation succeeds, the second event is fired. The event onSubmitContact is triggered right before the actual email is sent. This allows for integration with other applications, like a CRM or ERP database, which can be used to log all contact requests.

```
public function onSubmitContact($contact, $data)
{
}
```

The return value of the onSubmitContact() event method is of no importance.

11.4 Other events

onCategoryChangeState

The event onCategoryChangeState stands on its own: It is implemented in the com_categories component to allow other extensions to hook into the event when a category is enabled or disabled. We have seen this event before, while discussing Smart Search in chapter 9.

Right before the event onCategoryChangeState is triggered, the com_categories component initializes Content Plugins, which seems to suggest that this event is part of the content plugin group. However, its name does not start with onContent but with onCategory. This seems to suggest the existence of a group of Category Plugins. However, there is no such group. To cut it short, consider this event as a strange incidental event that can be caught using System Plugins and Content Plugins.

The first argument $extension indicates for which extension the category is used. Categories are commonly used for com_content articles. However, they can also be used for other extensions like com_weblinks or com_contacts or third party components. The second argument $pks contains an array of primary keys, the IDs of categories that are changed state. The third argument, $state, is either 0 (disabled) or 1 (enabled).

```
public function onCategoryChangeState($extension, $pks, $state)
{
}
```

11.5 Third party plugins

There are numerous extensions of various types available for Joomla - components, modules, plugins, templates, etc. The more complex components often include the ability to be extended themselves using plugins. There are plugins to extend CCKs with additional fields. For example, there are plugins to add new payment methods to shop components. Not to forget, there are numerous components that call upon generic content events, so that any Content Plugin may be used to extend its behavior.

There are so many plugins. Documenting all of them is a difficult, almost pointless task. It makes more sense to pick out a few of the most popular extensions that allow for additional plugins to extend them, and learn from them. In chapter 5, we have already dealt with a couple of content components like K2 and ZOO. Now, we will continue with one of the best known Joomla extensions: VirtueMart.

VirtueMart plugins

Like it or hate it, VirtueMart is still one of the most popular extensions for Joomla and while somep parts of its architecture date back to the Mambo days, VirtueMart 2 brings a lot of improvements. The VirtueMart 2 API documentation is still a work in progress. However, when you are serious about developing VirtueMart plugins, reading the source code of VirtueMart itself will provide the necessary clues.

There are numerous plugins and events that allow VirtueMart to be extended. The VirtueMart plugins are based upon parent classes that predefine a lot of the required functionality. For instance, a plugin in the vmcustom group extends from the class vmCustomPlugin.

It is good practice to manually check for the parent class and load it if does not exist yet, as the VirtueMart classes are not picked up by the Joomla autoloader.

```
if (!class_exists('vmCustomPlugin'))
{
    require(JPATH_VM_PLUGINS . '/vmcustomplugin.php');
}

class PlgVmCustomSpecification extends vmCustomPlugin
{
}
```

Currently, these are the plugin groups available with VirtueMart:

- vmcalculation – Allowing you to change price calculations, based on various parameters like pricing rules, product quantities and customer profiles.
- vmpayment – Of course, no cart solution would be complete without a proper way of adding new payment methods. The plugin type vmpayment offers various methods that allow a plugin to add a new payment gateway to VirtueMart. This involves modifying payment method displays, currency conversions, payment notifications, order confirmation and the actual payment handling of course. One of the more noticeable things about VirtueMart payment plugins is that you can have one plugin serve more than one payment method.
- vmshipment – Similar to payment methods, you can also write plugins to add shipment methods. A shipment method can add shipment charges. It also allows for integration of remote shipping APIs.
- vmuserfield – Plugins belonging to this group can extend the VirtueMart customer profile, similar to how a Joomla **User Plugin** can extend a Joomla user profile.
- vmextended – A plugin group that allows you to extend the VirtueMart pages through events like onVmAdminController and onVmSiteController. Instead of just inserting new output into existing pages, this allow you to add new pages as well.
- vmcustom – A plugin group for everything that does not fit in other plugin groups. This includes modifying various views like cart pages and product views, extending backend forms and reacting on stock updates.

When extending VirtueMart with a plugin, you may also have a need to add a new database table. When a VirtueMart plugin is installed, the methodgetVmPluginCreateTableSQL() allows for running SQL commands. Technically, this method does not count as an event, because it is not called through the Joomla event dispatcher. Instead, the VirtueMart code simply instantiates the plugin class and calls upon the method if it exists.

Some of the events used in VirtueMart adhere to the Joomla coding standards. Their names start with on followed with the VirtueMart prefix Vm followed by the actual event name. For instance, onVmSqlRemove. Unfortunately, most of the events follow a legacy naming instead, which seems to refer to a plugin class instead of to an event method. An example of this is `PlgVmSelectSearchableCustom`, which is actually used as an event name and not as a plugin class name. It is confusing.

Writing a VirtueMart plugin involves becoming a VirtueMart expert. At the time of writing, the code was still messy, with various coding standards and mixes of new MVC implementations and archaic phpShop structures. That said, there is quite a bunch of events that definitely allow for extending VirtueMart in a flexible way.

Akeeba Subscription plugins

Akeeba - best most known for its **Akeeba Backup** solution and **FOF** – offers the **Akeeba Subscription** extension to create membership plans in your Joomla site. It is a great example of how plugins can be applied to extend an extension's functionality.

AkeebaSubs is based on **Framework on Framework**, which already offers its own set of plugin events. On top of this, there are various other events more specific to subscriptions. Most of the Akeeba events start with a prefix onAK like `onAKPaymentNew`. It is a more generic prefix that applies to all Akeeba extensions. Some other events are more entity based, like `onSubscriptionFormRender`.

The plugins available for AkeebaSubs are divided into two groups:

o akeebasubs – AkeebaSubs specific plugins, which vary a lot in functionality. For instance, there is a plugin to add custom fields to a subscription plan. There is a plugin to deal with invoices. There is a reCAPTCHA plugin. Put simply: Any event that deals with AkeebaSubs specifically belongs to this group.

o akpayment – Payment plugins reusable by other extensions that use the same payment API.

AkeebaSubs is based on the **FOF** libraries (not to be confused with the **FoF** libraries) and its classes extend from generic classes like `FOFModel` and `FOFTable`. This multiplies the number of events that are available for AkeebaSubs, because with FOF, events are all over the place.

A model based on `FOFModel` automatically triggers various content related events. If the model does not serve content, it should not extend from this class. These `FOFModel` events resemble the events used by Content Plugins: `onContentBeforeSave`, `onContentChangeState`, `onContentAfterDelete`, etc. Every `FOFTable` also generates its own set of events: `onBeforeBind`, `onAfterBind`, `onAfterLoad`, `onBeforeStore`, etc.

It is even more flexible. Events are also generated per entity. For instance, AkeebaSubs defines a model `AkeebasubsTableSubscription`, which extends from `FOFTable`. An event `onAfterLoad` would fetch the load of any table. However, the event `onAfterLoadSubscription` is fired specifically for the subscription table. You can imagine this is very useful and flexible.

As you can see a `F0F` specific prefix is missing. This seems to make sense, because the events are meant to be more for general purposes anyway.

My own Yireo plugins

Personally, I have developed many components over the years. For the more complex components, I often found it useful to add plugin events to the code as well. Plugins allowed me to extend my own components in an easy and flexible way. It also allowed me to keep my own code clean. By showing you some of the extensions I created, I can perhaps inspire you to build even greater extensions for Joomla.

Yireo Dynamic404 plugins

Dynamic404 is a component that allows for 404 errors to be handled in a flexible way. When a SEF URL is encountered, Joomla will translate this SEF URL into a system URL. Take the following example:

```
http://example.com/blog/12-my-example-article
```

Here, the URL refers to a page served by the `com_content` component. That component will then look for an article with ID 12 and when that article is not found, a **404 Not Found** error is generated.

Let's assume the article still exists in the Joomla database, but under a different ID 68 due to a Joomla migration. Instead of displaying an error page with **HTTP Status 404**, it would be friendlier to redirect to the correct page with article ID 68 using an **HTTP Status 302**.

```
http://example.com/blog/68-my-example-article
```

This is exactly what Dynamic404 does. The **System - Dynamic404** plugin replaces the core Joomla **System – Redirect** plugin and it replaces the default Joomla error handling with its own by adding the following code to its constructor:

```
JError::setErrorHandling(E_ERROR, 'callback',
    array('PlgSystemDynamic404', 'handleError'));
```

```
set_exception_handler(array('PlgSystemDynamic404', 'handleError'));
```

This was explained in chapter 6. Thanks to this code, whenever Joomla encounters a 404 error, it calls upon the plugins method `handleError`, which in turn calls upon the Dynamic404 component. The Dynamic404 component then extracts the article alias from the URL and uses it to search the Joomla database for possible matches:

```
my-example-article
```

When a direct match is found (like in our example the article with ID 68), a redirect to that match is made. Dynamic404 goes even a step further by allowing for fuzzy matches: In its basic form, the alias is exploded into segments (my, example and article), which are then used to search the database. Articles with aliases like my-article or article-my-example will still be found using this fuzzy matching, and each match gets a rating, indicating the accuracy of that match.

Searching for Joomla articles and Menu-Items is possible right out of the box. When you are using a third party content component (K2, ZOO, Kunena, EasyBlog), the content of these components can also be searched by using either a normal **Search Plugin** or a Dynamic404 Plugin. A Dynamic404 Plugin allows for fine-graining the matches. It has the following structure:

```php
class PlgDynamic404Example extends JPlugin
{
    public function getMatches ($urilast = null)
    {
        $matches = array ();
        $match = (object) null;
        $match->type = 'component';
        $match->name = 'Example title';
        $match->rating = $this->params->get ('rating', 85);
        $match->url = JRoute:: _ ('index.php');
        $matches [] = $match;

        return $matches;
    }
}
```

To standardize the matches returned by Dynamic404 Plugins, the Dynamic404 architecture expects each match to have a specific set of fields. To allow for the Joomla admin user to prefer certain matches above others, each match defines a rating (for instance the number 85), which is used as a base number upon which further calculations are made by the Dynamic404 component.

By using Joomla plugins, the Dynamic404 component is able to search for any content in any Joomla database table, as long as there is either a Search Plugin or a Dynamic404 Plugin available. By extending from a Dynamic404 plugin parent class, it is also fairly easy to write a new Dynamic404 Plugin, without the need to modify the architecture of the component.

Yireo SimpleLists Link plugins

SimpleLists is a component that allows you to quickly create listings of **Content Items**. Well, so does Joomla itself with articles. What makes SimpleLists special is the way these listings are configured. Each content item can have a title, a text, an image and a link. For each of these elements you can configure whether you want to display them or not.

Let me give you some examples to show how this works in practice: Enabling title, text, image and link will resemble something like a blog listing. Enabling title and image, pointing the link to a larger image and disabling the text, will give you an image gallery. Pointing the link to a ZIP file, will give you a basic download page. With predefined **Layouts**, you can tune things even quicker. The layout adds basic styling through HTML and CSS, to allow you to accomplish a certain task even quicker, without the need for a template override.

With SimpleLists, you can quickly create FAQs, teaser pages (similar to blog listings but with the blog teaser being different from the articles introtext), directories, image galleries and so on. I personally use SimpleLists most of the time for FAQs and download pages. You can even create mashups of different types of content in a single SimpleLists page.

While the concept behind SimpleLists is a little bit tricky, its usage is definitely simple. When youcreate a SimpleLists item, you can enter a title and text. This is the same for Joomla articles. What makes SimpleLists really different is the link.

Each item can have a link. And SimpleLists makes it very easy to configure this link. When you want to link the item to a Menu-Item, you can pick that Menu-Item from a dropdown. When you link the item to an article, a modal window allows you to pick the article. In other words, for every link type (article, file, image) there is a separate input field available. This is made possible through **SimpleLists Link** plugins.

The structure of a **SimpleLists Link** plugin is as follows:

```
class PlgSimpleListsLinkExample extends SimplelistsPluginLink
{
    public function getTitle() {}
    public function getName($link) {}
    public function getUrl($item = null) {}
    public function getInput($current = null) {}
}
```

To briefly cover this: The `getTitle()` method identifies the plugin's field within the backend. The `getInput()` should return HTML code that allows the Joomla admin user to input whatever needs to be inputted. For instance, this can be a dropdown of items from a `com_example` component. In the SimpleLists backend, when editing an item, you will see the title and input field of each enabled SimpleLists Link Plugin, so you can easily choose what kind of link to create.

The input field delivers a POST variable `example`, named after the plugin, and its value is stored in the `link` field for each SimpleLists item. Typically, this will be a numerical ID referring to your own content. For instance, the article's ID in case of an article. This ID is then used to display the content's name within the SimpleLists backend (`getName()`). For example, in order for the article title to be displayed, the `getName()` method should perform a query to look up the article by its ID (stored in the `link` field). Also, the ID is used to construct either a system URL or a SEF URL through the method `getUrl()`.

There is more to SimpleLists. **SimpleLists Content Plugins** allow other content to be used for filling up the item's title and text. For instance, instead of generating listings of SimpleLists items, you can also generate listings of regular Joomla articles.

Yireo MageBridge event forwarding

MageBridge allows you to integrate Magento into Joomla (and vice versa). With MageBridge, plugins are everywhere. While the basic API allows you to bridge various data like output blocks and user profiles, the integration between Joomla and Magento is much more than just a visual integration.

Joomla uses plugin events to allow you to hook into core behavior. So does Magento. Magento allows you to catch events by defining an observer in the XML code of your extension. The event is then picked up by a specific method in your own observer class. MageBridge picks up on this concept by forwarding Magento events through the bridge and transforming them into Joomla events. This allows you to catch the Magento event `catalog_product_save_after` with the Joomla plugin method `mageCatalogProductSaveAfter()`. On both sides, this mechanism is easily extended, thanks to the MageBridge API.

11.6 Calling plugin events from within components

Now that you have seen how powerful Joomla plugins can make your component, it is time to learn how to invoke plugins from within your component. Let's assume you have a component `com_example` and a plugin group `example` that allows for plugins to hook into the `com_example` component with events like `onExampleItemDisplayBefore` and `onExampleItemDisplayAfter`. The code to call these plugins might look like this:

```
JPluginHelper::importPlugin('example');
$dispatcher = JEventDispatcher::getInstance();

$arguments = array();
$results = $dispatcher->trigger(
    'onExampleContentDisplayBefore', $arguments
);
```

```
$arguments = array();
$results = $dispatcher->trigger(
    'onExampleContentDisplayBefore', $arguments
);
```

What can you do with your plugins?

The code above does not do anything yet. The `$arguments` array is empty and there is no code parsing the `$results`. How these two variables should behave, depends entirely on what you want to do with these plugins. Or actually, in what way you want plugins to change the behavior of components.

Let's take the example of `onContent` events: With a Content Plugin, you can either implement the `onContentBeforeSave()` method or the `onContentAfterSave()` method or both. Each has its own purpose. The plugin method `onContentAfterSave()` is not meant to change the original content and its results are also not blocking the saving process either. To change content, we would use the `onContentBeforeSave()` method. For the method `onContentAfterSave()`, the `$arguments` and `$results` can be left out.

With the `onContentBeforeSave()` method however, the `$arguments` are important. The event is meant to allow another developer to change the content before it is being saved. Therefore, the `$arguments` include a reference to the original content, in order for the plugin to modify this content.

This can be applied to our example events: It is logical to pass the content item as an argument to the event `onExampleItemDisplayBefore`. To allow easy modification of this `$item`, it is also a good idea to pass it as a reference:

```
$arguments = array(&$item);
```

We can also take the return value of each plugin and let a single plugin disrupt the workflow. If the plugin returns `false`, it can be picked up by the component, which can give an error, effectively stopping the content from being displayed.

```
$results = $dispatcher->trigger(
    'onExampleContentDisplayBefore', $arguments
);

if (in_array(false, $results, true))
{
    die('No data');
}
```

In the component code, you need to make various decisions on which kind of arguments to pass to the events and what to do with the return values of these events.

Where to do things with your plugins?

Another good question: Where in your component code should the dispatcher be called? Or in other words: Where do you allow developers to modify the logic of your component? Assuming our `com_example` component is based on the MVC principles of Joomla, we have various places where we can add events to: models, views, controllers, tables, helpers. The event code definitely does not belong in layout templates, because when someone would want to change something there, an output override is the correct approach. The correct answer to where the code should go, depends on the type of event.

When you are allowing plugins to modify data before or after it is being saved into the database, the model class is the correct place. Triggering the event within the table class is also an option. Keep in mind though that the table is primarily meant as an objected oriented way of accessing a specific database table, while the model class is a more generic container for your item. If a plugin is allowed to modify the item (the data), the model class should be used. If a plugin is allowed to modify the way specific fields are stored into the database, the table class should be used.

When plugins enable modifying the way data is moved around between the various parts of the MVC model, adding the dispatcher to the controllers is preferred. When modifying the item to allow it to be displayed properly (extending `JForm` forms, HTML encoding, transforming text for readability), the view is best used. Helpers should only contain dispatcher code, when it is the only way to keep your code **DRY**.

Calling plugins from within plugins

To make things more exotic, you can also call plugins from within a plugin. When events are being picked up by plugins, there might be multiple plugins repeating the same tasks. Instead of just duplicating the code, you can either move that common functionality into a parent class or – if the logic is more complex – create a new set of plugins for this.

I personally created such a scenario for MageBridge. Earlier in this chapter, I explained the concept of **event forwarding**: The MageBridge architecture allows you to forward a Magento event to the Joomla plugin system, thereby allowing you to create a Joomla plugin within the plugin group `magento` that is triggered whenever Magento fires an event. One great application of this is to allow for post-sales actions in Joomla whenever a Magento product is sold. When a pack of stroopwafels (a Dutch waffle) is sold in Magento, a Joomla plugin can be used to send a customer download-instructions to get a PDF with the secret recipe. Similarly, customers who buy another Magento product can be added to a specific Joomla mailing list.

To allow for all this magic to take place, a Joomla plugin of type `magento` needs to implement the plugin method `mageSalesOrderSaveAfter`, check the order status, loop through the ordered products to find the product, extract the Magento customer data, look up the equivalent Joomla user record, load it and perform the relevant post-sales action. Quite a lot of actions for one plugin. Worse, each MageBridge plugin that wants to do a post-sales action for a specific Joomla user, needs to have the same code. Instead of duplicating all this code, a single plugin of type `magento` was created instead, which calls upon a new plugin type `magebridgeproduct`, which uses a method `onMageBridgeProductPurchase` with the Joomla user as an argument. Even better, MageBridge offers an entire interface to configure specific post-sales actions for each selection of Magento products. All in all, introducing a new plugin type allowed for a lot more flexibility.

Naming your event methods

Besides determining where to put which code to dispatch events to plugins, it is also highly important to pay attention to the correct naming of your events. The standard with Joomla is to start an event name with the keyword on, followed by the name of the plugin group, followed by the action:

```
on + [group] + [action]
```

The event name should be in camel case. An action like `do_something` within a component `com_example` should result into an event `onExampleDoSomething`. Preferably, the event should also define the object to which the action is applied: An event `onExampleDisplay` is not useful, because the action does not describe what is being displayed. An event `onExampleItemDisplay` explicitly tells you the thing that is being displayed is an item.

The action `onExampleItemDisplay` is not stating whether the plugin method is run before or after the item is being displayed. A more useful name would be `onExampleItemDisplayBefore`. Whether you put the preposition `Before` at the end of the name or in the middle (like `onExampleItemBeforeDisplay`) is a matter of taste.

Unfortunately, this naming convention is not applied everywhere. This can lead to confusing situations. For instance, let's take a component `com_example` that generates an event called `getHandles()` to allow plugins in the group `examplePayment` to deliver payment methods. If, by coincidence, a System Plugin uses the same method `getHandles()` to simply return a listing of handles included in this plugin, this plugin's method will be called by the `com_example` component with unexpected results.

Any public method of any plugin can be used to fetch an event thrown by some other extension. To prevent a non-event method (so, a task method or helper method) from being called upon as if it was an event method, conventions are used: An event should always have a prefix `on`. If an event does not have this prefix, the extension generating this event has a serious bug.

Note that the Joomla core itself does not always stick to these standards. In this chapter, we have come across the event `onGetIcons`, which does not state to which plugin group this event belongs (Quick Icons). Similarly, the event `onDisplay` is used by multiple plugin types for different reasons (editors, editor buttons, CAPTCHA). It would be better to have prefixes like `onEditor`, `onCaptcha` or `onQuickIcon`.

In short, think what your event will be doing in real-life, when other developers make use of it. Make sure its name is descriptive enough. Make sure it is unique. Make sure it sticks with conventions.

11.7 Summary

This chapter covered various events that do not long belong to the plugin types of the previous chapters. Now, all of the Joomla core events are covered. This chapter also dealt with examples of third party plugin events and it has shown you how to implement events in your own component.

With this chapter, we have covered all plugin events. What is left is deepening your understanding of how plugins work (chapter 12) and discussing some best practices while developing plugins (chapter 14).

(12) Joomla Architecture

Joomla plugins are a vital part of the Joomla CMS architecture. But how do they fit into this architecture? What are their strengths and weaknesses? This chapter gives you background information on how Joomla fits together: It covers basic design patterns. It gives you insight into the internal workings of Joomla, to help you better understand the functioning of plugins.

12.1 Platform or framework?

There were days that Joomla was just Joomla. Those days are long gone. Nowadays, we use terms like **platform** and **framework**, with the aim of making it easier for developers to create applications inside and outside the Joomla CMS. Unfortunately, all this renaming has led to confusion.

Originally, Joomla (or actually Mambo, Joomla's predecessor) was designed for one purpose. To be a CMS. In that regard, the architecture of Joomla was monolithic. Code was only added to allow for CMS functionality and everything functioned as one application. Yes, there was the option to build extensions. However, Joomla was not designed to be as extendable as it is today.

Since the Mambo fork produced the Joomla project, the right approach to building Joomla has been the subject of debate. Should Joomla be just simple and friendly? Should it be highly extendable? Should parts of Joomla even be reusable in other non-Joomla applications? Joomla has always been community driven, and because communities change over time, the architecture has changed as well.

CMS and framework

Joomla is a CMS. No doubt about this, although there can be discussions as to which functionalities should be included in a CMS. With Joomla 1.5, one of the goals was to get rid of all legacy Mambo code. This also gave the way for the opportunity to reconsider the purpose of a CMS. The core was split into the CMS itself and the **Joomla Framework** – a set of library classes in the folder `/libraries/joomla`, meant to resemble other frameworks like **Zend Framework**.

From framework to platform and back

In 2011 the **Joomla Framework** was renamed to **Joomla Platform**. One of the reasons being that it would be clearer to developers that it is possible to create non-Joomla applications based on the Joomla classes. The idea behind the Joomla Platform was to allow for the option to create a custom application with the platform as its base. You could even use platform classes for the creation of another CMS.

To differentiate between the classes themselves, the classes to be reused elsewhere (the **Platform** classes) were still placed in the `/libraries/joomla` folder, while classes that only existed to support the **CMS** were moved to the `/libraries/cms` folder. Additionally, a folder `/libraries/legacy` was created as a placeholder for classes that would be phased out sooner or later. To enable non-Joomla developers to contribute non-CMS code, it was decided to create a separate **CMS** repository and **Platform** repository on GitHub.

In 2013, it was decided that this approach was too limiting. The classes of a platform can only be used to build an application based entirely on that platform, while it is much harder to reuse a single Joomla class in - for instance - a Laravel application. To allow for more flexibility, the **Platform** was merged back into the **CMS** and a new project – the **Joomla Framework** – was started. Death to the Joomla Framework, death to the Joomla Platform, long live the Joomla Framework.

Though it might give you the impression that the work of going from **Framework** to **Platform** to **Framework** has been a waste of time, it really is not. While the original framework was already setup with flexibility in mind, the Joomla project as a whole was focused on getting the Joomla CMS to the next level. With Joomla 3, so much has been improved that we can safely say we have reached that level. And when reaching that level, it is a good step forward to take all the good stuff from Joomla and present it to non-Joomla developers as the **Joomla Framework**. The renaming and redefining of projects has just been part of this learning curve.

12.2 **API**

Today, there is the **Joomla CMS**, which we use daily of course. There is also the **Joomla Framework**, which can be seen as a collection of classes that can be used outside of the CMS. Finally, there is also a vague word **API**, which does not really fit with this talk on frameworks. However, it is used so often that it demands a better explanation. The abbreviation stands for **Application Programming Interface** – a way of saying that the application (Joomla) offers a way for third party developers to extend it.

Each class with public methods can serve as an API, because it can be used within your own code. A Joomla extension reuses various classes of Joomla and is therefore based upon the API of Joomla. Some of the classes are preferred – using them as API is considered best practice - and some are not recommended for use at all - applying them is bad practice. The API itself is less clear about what to use and what not – except for some classes and methods that are marked as deprecated. Of more importance are the Joomla coding guidelines and the API documentation that provide explanation of what to do and what not.

Remote APIs

Do not confuse this type of **coding API** with **remote APIs** like **XML-RPC** and **SOAP**. Those APIs allow for third party developers to call upon Joomla resources (articles, users, etc) remotely and require a service to handle those calls. For instance, a Joomla component could be created to offer such an API. Joomla 1.5 used to include XML-RPC support and even included the ability to extend the XML-RPC API through XML-RPC plugins. However, this was removed from the core since Joomla 1.6. Nowadays, remote APIs are not part of the core itself, though work is in progress to add **REST** support to the core.

12.3 Common design patterns

What is a design pattern?

When we create code, we often reflect on our code in one way or another. Often, we as developers think alike. As we become better programmers - starting with a **Hello World** program, becoming more familiar with object oriented programming - we encounter the same issues, face the same challenges. However, often we do not know about this shared experience, for instance because we are not working on the same codebase. So we keep on reinventing the wheel.

Working together in an open source project is one way to share our solutions, in order for other developers to benefit from them. For instance, by checking out the PHP code of other developers, you can often learn how you can improve your own work. Others can give you feedback on the code you have written. Together, we learn.

Unfortunately, looking at C++ code is not particularly useful to the average PHP developer. Similarly, Python code is less meaningful to a Java programmer. This is unfortunate, because it may be that the same challenges were encountered and the same solutions were constructed. It was just written in another language, while the problem and the type of solution could have been the same.

To overcome the boundaries of a specific programming language, these challenges and solutions can be described in a more generic way. This is where design patterns come in. Design patterns describe reusable solutions for common problems. Often, they are described in such a way that they can be applied with different code structures and even different languages. And because of this normalization, many programmers can use them to improve their coding.

The design patterns discussed in these sections are used (fully or partially) in the Joomla project. It offers you a good starting point in case you want to get your programming skills to a higher level. It is less meant for the purist who is able to spot code smells, but more for the intermediate programmer who wants to know how Joomla works.

Model-View-Controller

The most commonly discussed design pattern in Joomla is **MVC**, which stands for **Model-View-Controller**. A properly built component is based upon this pattern. Some of the better Joomla features, like database abstraction (`JTable`) and template overrides, depend on it. The pattern splits up the features of a regular application into three parts: the part that does all the data handling (**Model**), the presentation part (**View**) and the logic that mediates between the two parts (**Controller**).

MVC can be applied in many different ways. For example, a browser/webserver interaction can be seen as partly MVC. The browser acts as Controller, requesting data from the webserver - so the webserver acts as Model. The received output is then displayed by the browser (View). As for Joomla components, the entire MVC pattern takes place within the Joomla application and only in the timeframe that Joomla calls upon the component (from dispatching until rendering).

One way to differentiate types of MVC is by looking at the workflow between the three parts. When the browser sends a request to Joomla, the request will be dispatched to the `JController` instance of the current component. The main task of this controller is to either deal with the request and redirect to a new page, or to render the view (an instance of `JView`). When the view is rendered, the view (and not the controller) is responsible for fetching data from the model (an instance of `JModel`). It is designed in such a way that only the controller writes to the model and the view only reads from the model.

However, because all methods that are accessible through the controller are defined as public, there is no way to stop a view from actually writing to a model. To write to a model from within a view would be a sign of bad coding, even though it would still work. The workflow of Joomla relies more on conventions. In other MVC implementations like CakePHP, the data from the model is pushed into the view by the controller and the view is not able to access the model at all. The controller is used as mediator between model and view. This is not the case in Joomla.

In its basic form, one component has one set of MVC classes: one view, one model and one controller. There are a lot more variations possible though. While the MVC pattern itself is meant to have one model, one view and one controller, it does not mean these variations are wrong. Multiple controllers can call upon a single model. A controller may also depend on multiple models. Different views can share the same model. Models can even include other models. There are many more variations to think of.

Singleton

A **Singleton** is a design pattern guaranteeing that a single class instance is used throughout the application. In other words, once this class is instanced into an object, every time the Singleton is used to fetch an instance of that class, the exact same object is returned. These days, Singletons are often called evil. The design pattern is often called an anti-pattern. Personally, I think Singletons still serve a purpose. Let's take a look at both the good parts and the bad parts of a Singleton.

Singletons proved their value to PHP developers when they found out that global variables (`$_GLOBAL`) were not a very good approach. One of the challenges a developer faces is to have access from within scope A to a specific object, which is instantiated in scope B. By defining the object as a global variable, the problem was simply overcome. However, this meant that the space where the object was first instantiated (scope B), had to be on a global level. Also, that space was in control of whether the object was to be called globally, whereas it sounds more logical to let the object decide in what way it should be called upon.

These issues are solved by creating a Singleton, of which the following is a basic example in PHP:

```
class Example
{
    private static $instance;

    public static function getSingleton()
    {
        if (!isset(self::$instance))
        {
            self::$instance = new __CLASS__;
        }

        return self::$instance;
    }
}
```

This code can be put to use with lines like these:

```
$example1 = Example::getSingleton();
$example2 = Example::getSingleton();
```

The important thing here is that $example1 and $example2 are referring to the exact same object. This can be very useful. For instance, if your class holds a connection to a database and you want to guarantee the same connection is used throughout your application. Singletons are easy to create and offer a quick solution to various problems. Also, Singletons can be used anywhere in your application.

Nonetheless, Singletons are considered bad practice these days. While globals are bad, the Singleton pattern offers a new way of creating globals anyway. Some of the reasons for calling Singletons a bad thing are directly related to the nature of PHP. While the Singleton pattern states that it is designed to prevent the creation of multiple instances of the class, it does not really fly with PHP. PHP will fire up a new instance per request anyway. Some other objections are related to the fact that PHP - as a language - has evolved over time as well. Although previously, creating a copy of an object ($b = $a) would give you two separate copies, with PHP 5 the copy ($b) is by default a reference to the original ($a) unless you change it.

One of the most important arguments against Singletons, is that its usage is often overkill.

Using Singletons is not necessarily bad. It is just that they have been applied too easily in many situations where other patterns should have been applied. It is often overlooked that there is a difference between a Singleton and the concept of a single instance. Having a single instance of a class X is often very desirable, especially in cases where performance is important. A Singleton is one way to achieve this. However, a Singleton also means giving access to that object from anywhere in the application.

Take the MVC pattern for instance. The controller should initiate both the model and the view. However, you might want to prevent the view from messing with the controller again. If the controller was a Singleton, there would be nothing stopping the view from accessing the controller. Using Singletons too frequently leads to architectural flaws. However, if an application does make use of Singletons, it does not necessarily mean it is badly written.

When working with Joomla plugins, using Singletons should not be a big deal. As an extension developer, you are limited by the architecture of the existing Joomla application. If there is no alternative to fetching a certain object in your plugin than using a Singleton - because the underlying Joomla architecture does not offer this as functionality - using a Singleton is what you should do. It is important though that you as a plugin developer know about the discussions on Singletons. It may determine the direction Joomla is heading in the future.

Factory

When you are programming with Joomla, you will without doubt come across the `JFactory` class, which evidently implements the **Factory** pattern. A Factory allows for the creation of certain kinds of objects, without the need to know how those objects were created.

A good example is the `JFactory::getUser()` call. It returns a `JUser` object without the need to know how the `JUser` object has been constructed. Zooming in on the actual code of the `JFactory::getUser()` method, you can see that the `JUser` object is instantiated using a Singleton call `JUser::getInstance()`. Additionally, it also initializes the Joomla session, which is a requirement when handling users in Joomla. The benefit of using `JFactory::getUser()` is that the user session is dealt with automatically - it is taken care of. Another benefit is that if Joomla decides to refactor the way that the `JUser` object is instantiated, your code will be based upon the `JFactory::getUser()` method and will not require any updates.

There are various types of Factory patterns and of all of these, the **Factory Method** pattern comes closest to the `JFactory` implementation. Instead of having a `JUserFactory` (connected to `JUser`) or a `JDocumentFactory` (connected to `JDocument`), the `JFactory` offers various method to get instances of unrelated classes. Each method of `JFactory` is a **Factory Method**.

In most cases, the Factory method that returns the desired class, calls upon a `getInstance()` method of that class -a Singleton. In other words, the Factory pattern often uses a Singleton to return the right object instance. Earlier, we learned that Singletons are regarded (by some people) as completely evil practice. Is the Factory then also bad practice? No, the Factory is a perfect example of how Singletons should be applied. Not scattered all over the place, but nicely listed in a single Factory class.

Observer-Observable & Publish-Subscribe

The architecture of Joomla plugins is often referred to as an **Observer** pattern, which may not be entirely correct. An Observer pattern (also known as an **Observer-Observable** pattern) allows for an object (for example, a component's model) to become observable by other objects (the observers), while the object itself maintains a list of all those observers. It implies that the observable object is in charge of who is allowed to observe it. Common practice is to pass the observable object itself as an argument to the observers.

With Joomla plugins however, the component is never in charge of the plugins that may modify its behavior. Also, the component model never contacts the plugins directly. Instead, a third party - the event dispatcher - is called into action and this dispatcher notifies the plugins. Joomla implements the **Publish-Subscribe** pattern instead. An event is published by the component model (in the pattern called the publisher or the communicator). Plugins can subscribe to this event. The dispatcher sits in between the component and the plugins, serving as a broker. Not the model object itself but data (like an `$item`, `$context` array or some kind of flag) is passed as an argument. The mechanism allows a message to be passed through, instead of the original object (like with the Observer-Observable pattern).

Nonetheless, the Observer-Observable pattern and Publish-Subscribe pattern are very similar. The Publish-Subscribe pattern describes the purpose of the class `JEventDispatcher`, which sits between the plugins (derived from the `JPlugin` class) and the place where the event was triggered (most commonly an MVC component). The Observer-Observable pattern is known to a wider public. It offers an easier explanation of how events can be triggered by one extension and caught by another.

Chain of command

The concept of events is great when it comes to notifying other parts of the application when something is changing. For instance, when a user record changes in Joomla, the `onUserSaveAfter` event allows for a remote CRM to be updated as well. The relation between the original data and the event is read-only.

However, with Joomla plugins, the event can also be used to modify the original data. This is not covered by the Publish-Subscribe pattern, but a side effect of passing the data as reference to the event method.

Additionally, there is the **Chain of Command** pattern. With this pattern, a chain of objects (for example: all plugins in a certain group) is responsible of moving the pointer (data) from one object to the other, while every object could choose to break this chain. With Joomla, there is only one example of this: the `onUserAuthenticate` event. Each plugin in the chain is called for proper authentication. When authentication fails, the user credentials are moved to the next plugin in line. The chain is stopped as soon as one of the plugins returns a successful authentication.

O, patterns

One of the downsides of the current approach of events in the Joomla core is that the events are not shared directly between all components. If the CMS offered a framework for all types of content, and if this framework dealt with dispatching the right events, components would automatically implement cool features as soon as they were added to the framework.

Currently, when you build your own component, you need to dispatch events manually, therefore a lot of logic is duplicated. Initiatives like **Nooku** and **FoF** were developed to overcome this shortcoming. Now that Joomla is slowly moving into a more generic approach, things may gradually change to make the framework more responsible for dispatching events.

As you can see, when it comes to design patterns, Joomla plugins implement different design patterns - Observer/Observable, Publish-Subscribe, Chain of Command. However, it labels them all in the same way: plugins. From an architectural point of view, this is confusing or perhaps simply incorrect. From a pragmatic point of view, this is less important: Plugins do their job in a way that many developers understand them to work. Which patterns are implemented to make this magic happen, is something that belongs under the hood.

12.4 Joomla boot procedure (or bootstrap)

When Joomla is used to generate a webpage, there are various steps to be taken to get to the end result: sending the HTML page to the browser. These steps are commonly referred to as bootstrap. To avoid confusion with the **Twitter Bootstrap** framework (which only deals with output through HTML, CSS and JavaScript), in this book we refer to this as the **boot procedure**.

The flow chart at the end of this book (appendix 1) gives you an insight as to where system events occur in the Joomla application. However, it still leaves some room for explanation. We will discuss the startup of Joomla step by step here.

Initializing Joomla

The first step that Joomla takes to get the CMS up and running is to define the location of the required PHP files by including a `defines.php` file. After these definitions, Joomla is able to loadvarious libraries. The `configuration.php` file is loaded as well. Only with this file will Joomla know how to connect to the Joomla database. As soon as all the necessary files are loaded, the Joomla application class(`JApplicationSite` or `JApplicationAdministrator`) is instantiated and its `execute()` method is called. Once the application is instantiated, a database connection is setup and a session is started, which also brings alive the `JFactory::getUser()` method.

At this moment, plugins are loaded. The database is accessible, so all necessary plugin records canbe fetched from the `#__extensions` database table. Because the user session is started, plugins which do not match the ACL rules are skipped. With one single query, all plugin records belonging to any given plugin group may be loaded. This list of plugin records is stored within the Joomla application.

Next, System Plugins are loaded through the call `JPluginHelper::importPlugin('system')`. At this point, the list of plugin records is used to locate and include the plugin file of each System Plugin. The plugin class is instantiated and then stored in an internal list in the event dispatcher. After this, the `onAfterInitalise` event is called, so that the `onAfterInitialise()` method of each System Plugin is called, if it is defined.

Routing the request

Now that the Joomla core is initialized and up and running, Joomla needs to interpret the URL and handle the request as needed. For this, the `JRouter` class is called to parse the current URL (`$_SERVER['REQUEST_URI']`). This URL is most commonly a SEF URL, which needs to be matched with a **Menu-Item**'s alias. In most cases, a **Menu-Item** will point to a component and this component is called upon when the request is dispatched. If a **Menu-Item**'s alias offers a complete match with the requested URL, `JRouter` will be able to fetch all the URL parameters from the **Menu-Item**.

For example, a **Menu-Item** with alias `blog` and ID 3 will be a perfect match for the URL `/blog`. However, if the URL is `/blog/23-example-article`, the remainder of the URL `23-example-article` still needs to be parsed. At this point, `JRouter` will call for the component's `router.php` file for further processing. This has been discussed in chapter 6 in more detail. For the example above, this leads to the following input variables, which are inserted into the `JApplication->input` object.

```
Itemid = 3
option = com_content
view = article
id = 23
```

Once `JRouter` has done its job and the input variables have been parsed, the SEF URL has effectively been turned into a system request, the request has been routed and the event `onAfterRoute` is triggered.

After the `onAfterRoute` event, a call to the application's `authorise()` method is made to make sure the current user has access to the page.

Dispatching to the component

The next step is to dispatch the request to the component. The input variables contain clues about what type of page has been requested – RSS, HTML, etc. Depending on this type, a specific child class of `JDocument` is instantiated, for instance the `JDocumentHtml` class. Some basic information like a page title and description is inserted into the document right away. However, the most important task here is to call upon the component for further processing. In other words, dispatching the request to the component.

The component is asked for output through the call `JComponentHelper::renderC omponent()`. The component's entry file is called. For the component `com_content`, this entry file is `components/com_content/content.php`. For a component `com_ example`, this entry file would be `components/com_example/example.php`.

What happens next is completely up to the component. Output can be delivered directly by the component's entry file, or the component can use the MVC architecture to let a controller call on a view that then delivers output through layout files. Alternatively, the controller can redirect to another URL instead.

When the component chooses to deliver output, it is not sent directly to the browser. Instead, the output is placed in a buffer in the `JDocument` object. After this, the event `onAfterDispatch` is triggered. The next step in the Joomla boot procedure is to render the entire page. While dispatching the request to the component, the component itself has already been rendered. Joomla now only needs to render additional extensions, like the template and modules.

Rendering the page

Even though the component output has already been buffered in `JDocument`, the template and modules have not been called into existence yet. When the component delivers output (even though it might be empty output), the next step in the boot procedure is to call upon the template to see which module positions are defined and so which modules need to be instantiated.

This template rendering is preceded by the event `onBeforeRender`. All placeholders are replaced with actual content, generated by the Joomla document or Joomla modules:

```
<jdoc:include type="head" />
<jdoc:include type="modules" name="position-0" />
<jdoc:include type="message" />
```

The component placeholder is replaced with the rendered output of the component:

```
<jdoc:include type="component />
```

The rendering process is now complete, so the event `onAfterRender` is fired. While the rendered output at the time of the event `onAfterDispatch` only included the component output, the rendered output at this stage also includes the output of the template and all modules.

Sending output to the browser

Last but not least, all rendered output is sent to the browser. Right before this happens, the compression flag of the **Global Configuration** determines whether the page needs to be compressed. If enabled, the buffered HTML is compressed and the event `onAfterCompress` is triggered. Next, all buffers are flushed, effectively sending output back to the browser. After all output is sent, the event `onAfterRespond` is called allowing System Plugins to do some cleaning up.

Variations on the boot procedure

There are some variations on this boot procedure. For instance, if the current page is an RSS document, the rendering of the template and modules is skipped. When the CMS is asked to deliver only component output (`?tmpl=component`), the entire workflow still applies, except that the component is rendered in a template file `component.php` that (normally) does not contain any module positions.

It is also important to realize that, when the component decides to redirect the page to another location, the rest of the boot procedure is skipped. The events `onAfterRender`, `onAfterCompress` and `onAfterRespond` will not be called.

When a component or plugin decides to stop the application – using either an `exit()`, `die()` or `JApplication::close()`, the application really stops. No Joomla code is executed after this.

12.5 How plugins work internally

JPlugin and JEvent parent classes

Every plugin class has the `JPlugin` class as its parent. This class is not large and as its name suggests, offers functionality that comes in handy when creating plugins. The JSON encoded parameters are converted into a `JRegistry` object (`$this->params`). Also, some handy variables are defined, like `$this->app` and `$this->db`. The class defines a `loadLanguage()` method, which can either be called directly or automatically using the `$autoloadLanguage` flag.

The `JPlugin` class extends from the `JEvent` class, which extends from the very generic `JObject` class. The `JEvent` class registers the plugin as an observer with the object that needs observing (the observable). This mechanism can be rather difficult to grasp the first time you encounter it. To fully understand it, we need to discuss how plugins are instantiated and called upon.

Importing plugins

When Joomla triggers an event, it usually boils down to code like the following:

```
JPluginHelper::importPlugin('somegroup');
$dispatcher = JEventDispatcher::getInstance();
$dispatcher->trigger('onSomeEvent');
```

Let's break this down line by line. The `JPluginHelper` loads all available plugins of the specified group: It instantiates the class of each plugin, thereby automatically calling upon the constructor of the plugin. Loading the plugins into memory allows Joomla to quickly refer to the list of plugins with every event, preventing additional database queries from being made. One of the features of the `JPluginHelper::importPlugin()` method is therefore to guarantee best performance.

Attaching the event dispatcher

When zooming in on the plugin's constructor, we can see something interesting happening, which explains how plugins fit into the Joomla application. We have learned before that a plugin is always based upon the `JPlugin` parent class, which is again based upon the `JEvent` plugin class.

To make sure a plugin functions properly, it always needs to call the parent constructor in some way or another. Not calling the parent constructor will give you a plugin that does nothing.

```
class PlgSystemExample extends JPlugin
{
    public function __construct(&$subject, $config = array())
    {
        parent::__construct($subject, $config);
    }
}
```

The plugin's constructor is called with two arguments: a $subject, which contains the JEventDispatcher object and a $config, which contains an optional list of configuration settings. The $config array is mainly used by the JPlugin class itself and is not that exciting.

The $subject variable is much more interesting though. A plugin's constructor usually does not do anything special with the $subject. However, the JEvent constructor does. It allows for the plugin to attach itself to the dispatcher as a means for the plugin to contact the dispatcher at a later stage. You can see what is being done in the JEvent parent class, located in the file libraries/joomla/event/event.php.

```
abstract class JEvent extends JObject
{
    public function __construct(&$subject)
    {
        $subject->attach($this);
        $this->_subject = &$subject;
    }
}
```

When the $subject->attach($this) method is called, the plugin is added to an internal array $_observers of the dispatcher (the $subject variable). This way, the dispatcher knows which plugins are available. There are various checks done within the attach() method that guarantee that the plugin behaves in such a way that it does not kill Joomla.

Additionally, each plugin method is mapped to an internal array $_methods in the dispatcher. A System Plugin is able to implement a large list of event methods. If the dispatcher needed to check for the existence of an event method every time an event is thrown, it would result in additional overhead. The $_methods array allows the dispatcher to know which tasks a plugin can perform as soon as it is attached to the dispatcher.

Using the dispatcher in your plugin

One usage of the $subject variable, which is referencing the dispatcher, is to send a message back to the dispatcher in the event that the plugin encounters some kind of error:

```
public function onSomeEvent()
{
    if ($somethingGoesWrong)
    {
        $this->_subject->setError('SOMETHING_WENT_WRONG');

        return false;
```

```
        }
    return true;
}
```

The dispatcher error is not printed automatically as a session error though. It is the responsibility of the code that calls upon the dispatcher to do that. Your component, for instance, can include the following code to check whether one of the plugins did something stupid:

```
$results = $dispatcher->trigger('onSomeEvent', array(&$item));

if (in_array(false, $results))
{
    throw new Exception($dispatcher->getError(), 500);
}
```

The JEventDispatcher class extends from the JObject class and this generic class has magic methods that allow you to use getters (methods like getSomething()) and setters (methods like setSomething()) without an actual definition of these methods. This means that anything can be set from within a plugin into the $subject. For instance, the following code inserts a value foobar into the dispatcher's property anything, without the setAnything() method being actually defined in the class:

```
$this->_subject->setAnything('foobar');
```

In the component code, the value can be read again from the dispatcher and used to set a dummy session message:

```
$foobar = $dispatcher->getAnything();
JFactory::getApplication()->enqueueMessage($foobar);
```

12.6 Summary

In this chapter, we discussed the architecture of the Joomla core, while focusing on the various plugin events that occur during the startup. We have also discussed some common design patterns like the Factory pattern and MVC. Additionally, we have discussed how Joomla can be used to write a completely different application and how plugins can still exist in such an application.

The next chapters serve as the finishing touch on this book: They will give you useful tips and tricks, help you with best practices and give you some ins and outs for releasing your plugin to the public.

Tips and tricks

This chapter contains various subjects (that do not fit in other chapters) to make your programming life easier: It includes some very neat tricks like creating layout templates in a plugin, overriding core classes and debugging your code.

13.1 Using Joomla plugins without the Joomla CMS

Over the years, Joomla has become more than just a CMS. It has become a framework for building software. This software can be either part of the Joomla CMS (extensions) or an application that is completely separate from the CMS. It is possible to use the Joomla classes to build your own custom web application, command-line scripts and even daemon-like services (based on the `JApplicationDaemon` class).

With all of these non-CMS scenarios, the question comes up as to whether plugins are still of use or not. The correct answer, of course, is that it depends. It depends on how the application was written and whether that code included support for plugins or not. Can you use plugins? Yes.

Cloning the Joomla boot procedure

It is important to realize that most Joomla plugins have been written specifically for the CMS and the best way to integrate these plugins into your own application is to mimic the CMS. When you are running the CMS frontend, the boot procedure instantiates the `JApplicationSite` class, which then routes, dispatches and renders. You can build an application that extends from this class, skips things you do not need (for instance component handling), but reuses handy things (for instance plugin events). Every time you encounter a plugin event that you want to reuse, you can simply use the dispatcher to call upon the events, just like you would within a component.

This approach might sound like a solid way to build your own application – getting rid of the bad parts of Joomla and only keeping the good parts. However, be prepared to hit a lot of walls. Most of the Joomla CMS boot procedure simply assumes that the CMS is there and in the end you might end up with an application that is 99% the same as Joomla. What is the purpose of that?

Building a Joomla app from scratch

By starting from scratch, you will be able to keep only the code that you really need. As you can see in the section on PHPUnit testing (chapter 12), you can initialize the Joomla framework with a few constants and a couple of includes. With the PHPUnit example, the site application is also started and the `JEventDispatcher` is called. These are the parts that you most likely want to rewrite completely, because they are too tightly connected to the CMS.

Writing your own event dispatcher allows you to implement an **Observer/Observable** pattern based upon your own rules, while still reusing plugins.

Joomla as a daemon

If you are using Linux or some other UNIX-like operating system, the word **daemon** should not be unfamiliar. A daemon is a service that runs continuously in the background, waiting for something to do. It may seem a little bit similar to a cronjob or scheduled task, but it is not. A cronjob is run only for a specific task and it exits once that task is complete. However, a service or daemon will keep on running until the next task needs to be performed. Actually, the program that checks whether a cronjob should be executed is a daemon itself (the cron daemon).

You can create your own Joomla daemon by creating a class that extends from the JApplicationDaemon class. The class should have a doExecute() method, which is executed every second. Within that method, you can for instance check for the existence of some flag (a specific file, or a condition on the webserver) that then allows for execution of another task.

```php
<?php
define('_JEXEC', 1);
define('JPATH_BASE', dirname(__DIR__));
require_once JPATH_BASE . '/includes/defines.php';
require_once JPATH_LIBRARIES . '/import.legacy.php';
require_once JPATH_LIBRARIES . '/cms.php';
require_once JPATH_CONFIGURATION . '/configuration.php';

class Mydaemon extends JApplicationDaemon
{
    public function doExecute()
    {
        // Check for a flag
        $flag = false;

        if ($flag == true)
        {
            // Do stuff
        }
    }
}

$app = JApplicationCli::getInstance('Mydaemon');
$app->execute();
```

The cli/ folder of the Joomla CMS contains some sample command line scripts that resemble something similar. The daemon is executed as follows:

```
php ./mydaemon.php
```

To make sure the script runs at all times, it can be wrapped in a shell script that can be integrated in the Linux initd or SystemV startup system.

The `JApplicationDaemon` class contains some events that allow us to extend our dae mon:`onBeforeExecuteonAfterExecuteonReceiveSignalonFork`

By default, the application is instantiated with the `JEventDispatcher` class as dispatcher. This mainly has a benefit when the daemon is started in the same environment that serves the CMS. In that case, all plugins of the CMS can be used in your daemon as well. However, they are not instantiated right away. To make use of them, your script needs to import the plugins as part of the `doExecute()` method or import the right plugins before executing the application:

```
$app = JApplicationDaemon::getInstance('Mydaemon');
JPluginHelper::import('cli'); // initialize plugins

$app->execute();
```

Next, the `doExecute()` method can instantiate the event dispatcher again and trigger an event, or we can use the shortcut that all children of `JApplicationBase` have:

```
$this->triggerEvent('onContentBeforeRender');
```

If the environment does not include the CMS, but only the Joomla framework, the `JEventDispatcher` can still be used. However, there are no plugins registered with it. You can reuse parts of the `JPlugin` architecture to allow for your kind of event handling, or you can base your work on the `JObserver` class instead.

13.2 Adding templates to your plugin

While components and modules are based on MVC, plugins are not. With components and modules, you can include a layout template that offers a clean way of adding HTML output. There is no such mechanism in place for Joomla plugins however. The reason for this is of course that plugins are not designed to be MVC and they do not always deal with output. Having a template for an Authentication Plugin does not make sense.

You can easily create your own templating mechanism though. The procedure is simple. Start output buffering, include the layout file and end output buffering:

```
$file = dirname(__FILE__).'/tmpl/default.php';
@ob_start();
include_once $file;
$html = @ob_get_clean();
```

Even though this works, it has some shortcomings in design. First of all, the $file variable (and other variables in the method scope that includes this code) will be included in the template itself, whereas it has no purpose there: The template file will be polluted with pointless variables.

Secondly, with Joomla, we love the ability of template overrides and our current code does not support this. We need to add a little bit more code here.

Template override the FoF way

Let's deal with the template override first:

```
$file = 'default.php';
@ob_start();
$overridePath = FOFPlatform::getInstance()
    ->getTemplateOverridePath('plg_system_example', true);

JLoader::import('joomla.filesystem.file');

if (JFile::exists($overridePath . $file))
{
    include_once $overridePath . $file;
}
else
{
    include_once __DIR__ . '/tmpl/' . $file;
}

$html = @ob_get_clean();
```

Now, we use the FoF function `getTemplateOverridePath()` to return the path for overrides (`/templates/TEMPLATE/html/plg_system_example`) and use the override file if it exists there, otherwise we just use the default location.

Template override the non-FoF way

We can also skip FoF and simply create our own `if-else` check for a template override. It is dead-easy. Catch the current Joomla template and construct the path:

```
$template = JFactory::getApplication()->getTemplate();
$overridePath = JPATH_THEMES . '/' . $template
    . '/html/plg_system_example';
```

Separate loadTemplate method()

As a final step, we want to strip all variables that are not needed. Because this involves extra code, and because these variables will be limited to a method scope, we are using a separate method for this: `loadTemplate()`.

This method can be called upon from any other plugin method:

```
$template = 'default.php';
$variables = array('foo' => 'bar');
$this->loadTemplate($template, $variables);
```

Let's create the function itself:

```
private function loadTemplate($file = null, $variables = true)
{
    $template = JFactory::getApplication()->getTemplate();
    $overridePath = JPATH_THEMES . '/' . $template
        . '/html/plg_system_example';

    if (is_file($overridePath . '/' . $file))
    {
        $file = $overridePath . '/' . $file;
    }
    else
    {
        $file = __DIR__ . '/tmpl/' . $file;
    }

    // Unset variables
    unset($template);
    unset($overridePath);

    // Include the variables here
    if (!empty($variables))
    {
        foreach ($variables as $name => $value)
        {
            $$name = $value;
        }
    }

    // Unset remaining variables
    unset($variables);
    unset($name);
    unset($value);

    if (isset($this->this))
```

```
    {
        unset($this->this);
    }

    @ob_start();
    include $file;
    $html = ob_get_contents();
    @ob_end_clean();
    return $html;
}
```

13.3 Loading class files

Using jimport()

In Joomla 1.5, the `jimport()` function was introduced to allow for Joomla framework classes to be easily included in your extension, without using native PHP functions like `include()` and `require()`. For instance, all plugins use the same parent class `JPlugin`. To make sure this class is loaded by Joomla, the following `jimport()` call can be used:

```
jimport('joomla.plugin.plugin');
```

This effectively includes the file `libraries/joomla/plugin/plugin.php`, which again contains the class `JPlugin`.

Since the introduction of Joomla 1.5, a lot of things have changed. One of the major changes was to separate the CMS from code that can be reused in other non-Joomla classes: this lead to the creation of the Joomla Platform. The platform was located in the folder `/libraries/joomla`. All files related to the Joomla CMS were moved to `/libraries/cms`. There was some outdated stuff as well, which was moved to a folder `/libraries/legacy`.

This change posed a problem. When a file was relocated from the `/libraries/joomla` folder to the `/libraries/cms` folder, all `jimport()` calls that referred to that class also needed to be updated. Of course, this could easily be hacked into the `jimport()` function itself - look for the location A to see if the class is there, or else use location B, and if that fails, use location C. Nonetheless, it showed a design flaw. When the location of a class was changed, suddenly all dependent code that was using that class also needed to be updated. Good design would be to make sure such a change would have no effect at all on dependent code.

Implementing spl_autoload_register()

PHP 5 includes a cool solution for this. Instead of letting the dependent code find the required class - for instance, let the plugin itself have a `jimport()` call that determines the location of the parent class `JPlugin` - you can also make the Joomla core responsible for determining this. Instead of creating long listings of which class is to be found in which PHP file, this can be done using some kind of naming convention automatically: autoloading.

PHP 5 includes an autoloading feature, which allows the PHP engine to encounter an undefined class in runtime, which again triggers PHP to call upon a custom function, which contains the logic to locate the correct file that contains the required class. While this feature already existed in PHP 4 in the form of the `__autoload()` function, this PHP 4 function could only be added once – in other words, there could only be one autoloader for finding classes and not multiple autoloaders. With PHP 5, the `spl_autoload_register()` allows for registering a second autoloader, or a third, and so on.

Using a System Plugin to implement an autoloader

To allow for your autoloader to be used as well, you can simply call upon the PHP function `spl_autoload_register()` in a System Plugin:

```php
<?php
class PlgSystemCustomloader extends JPlugin
{
    public function __construct(&$subject, $config)
    {
        spl_autoload_register(array('CustomLoader', 'load'));

        parent::__construct($subject, $config);
    }
}
```

In the same plugin file, we define an additional class `CustomLoader`, which will be used by the PHP autoloading mechanism:

```php
class CustomLoader
{
    static public function load($class)
    {
        if (preg_match('/^custom/i', $class) == false)
        {
            return false;
        }
```

```
    $class = strtolower($class);
    $class = preg_replace('/^custom/', '', $class);

    $path = JPATH_PLUGINS.'/system/customloader/libraries/';
    $filename = $path.$class.'.php';

    if (file_exists($filename))
    {
        include_once($filename);
    }
  }
}
```

As you can see, the plugin's constructor contains a call to `spl_autoload_register()`, which registers our `CustomLoader::load()` method as a new autoloader method. When a class is not found by PHP, the Joomla autoloader will be called. When the class is still not found by Joomla, our autoloader will be called.

Let's take an example: Say we have a Joomla module which relies on some helper class `CustomFormat`, which contains all kinds of useful formatting methods (currency formatting, HTML output, etc). Within the module's layout file, we call upon this helper as follows:

```
<?php echo CustomFormat::currency($money); ?>
```

Now, when the class is not found, normally a PHP Fatal Error is generated, stopping all PHP execution. However, when our System Plugin is enabled, the autoloader is triggered instead. The `CustomLoader::load()` has the `$class` set to `CustomFormat` and first makes sure - with `preg_match()` - that the class name is starting with either `custom` or `Custom` (either uppercase or lowercase). Next, the classname is transformed into lowercase (`customformat`), the prefix `custom` is stripped and a filename based upon this stripped down version of the classname is located.

Schematically the name goes through the following stages:

```
CustomFormat
customformat
format
/plugins/system/customloader/libraries/format.php
```

Our new autoloader will only be loaded when our plugin is loaded and our plugin is only loaded when it is enabled in the **Plugin Manager**. Also note that the ordering of autoloaders cannot be changed. When a class is not found, PHP will first call upon the Joomla default autoloader and then upon our own autoloader. There is no good approach that allows you to reverse this order, so that you can prefer your own classes over the Joomla originals.

Using the JLoader instead

With Joomla 3, the `jimport()` function has become deprecated. In case of Joomla core classes, a replacement is not even needed, because Joomla implements the `spl_autoload_register()` function. If Joomla sees that the class you are using in your own script is not loaded into the PHP runtime environment, it will use the Joomla autoloader class `JLoader` to locate this class by naming convention in the Joomla filesystem and load it automatically. It even gives you the ability to define new prefixes (like the prefix `Custom` in the example above), to add a specific class in a specific location or to add Joomla classes (beginning with the `J` prefix) from a different location instead. In the next pages, we will discuss these options.

Some examples: Let's say we want to place our `CustomFormat` class in a file named `format.php` placed in the plugin's subfolder `libraries`, which is the same path as used in our previous example above. We can do this by adding the following call to the plugin's constructor:

```php
<?php
class PlgSystemCustomloader extends JPlugin
{
    public function __construct(&$subject, $config)
    {
        $path = JPATH_PLUGINS.'/system/customloader/libraries/';
        JLoader::register('CustomFormat', $path.'format.php');

        return parent::__construct($subject, $config);
    }
}
```

This new example accomplishes the same thing as the previous example: As soon as we call a class like `CustomFormat`, the autoloader will locate this file in our plugin's subfolder. This time no custom autoloader class is needed. We simply reuse the autoloader of Joomla.

Loading a whole library of classes

With the call `JLoader::register()`, you can tell Joomla where to locate a single class. Of course, this still looks pretty good when you only have a few classes. But what if our `libraries` folder contains numerous classes with the `Custom` prefix (`CustomHtml`, `CustomPluginHelper`, etc), which we want to include in our plugin?

For this, we can use a statement like the following instead:

```php
JLoader::registerPrefix('Custom', $libraryPath);
```

Any class starting with `Custom` will now lead to Joomla searching the `$path` folder for a matching file. This easily allows you to create your own library and ship it with your own plugin.

Files and subfolders with JLoader

By using the `JLoader` approach, the location of our class `CustomFormat` is a little bit different though. It is no longer located directly in the folder `$path`, but in a subfolder `$path/format/` instead. The entire path to the class looks as follows:

```
/plugins/system/customloader/libraries/format/format.php
```

The rule here is that class files should never be placed in the root of your library (`$path`). The library contains class packages and each package has its own subfolder. To put it differently: Joomla will remove the prefix from the classname and chop the remaining name into segments, following the **camelCase** standard. If there are multiple segments, the last segment will form the filename, the segments before that will be subfolders. If there is only one segment, that segment will be used as both the first subfolder and the class file within that subfolder.

Let's show an example: We create a second class `CustomFormatHtml`, that contains specific formatting tricks for HTML documents as opposed to other output like JSON, XML, emails or PDFs. The location of this class will be `libraries/format/html.php`: The classname has two segments (excluding the prefix `Custom` itself). Our files and folders now look like this:

```
/plugins/system/customloader/libraries/format/
/plugins/system/customloader/libraries/format/format.php
/plugins/system/customloader/libraries/format/html.php
```

Adding more Joomla classes

The `JLoader` also allows you to write classes with the `J` prefix - the same prefix that Joomla normally uses. This allows you to comply more to the Joomla standards. For instance, if you have a class that really helps other developers as well, using the prefix `J` is good practice. Instead of enforcing your own `Custom` namespace, you are simply extending the `J` namespace, which makes your class feel more like a real core class. Perhaps, when the code is good enough, you can even request the class to be included in either the CMS or the platform?

We can add our own library to the Joomla autoloader like this:

```
JLoader::registerPrefix('J', $libraryPath);
```

Now, if we call upon a class `JFormatHtml`, it will look in our plugins libraries folder as well, provided the class has not been found in the regular Joomla libraries first.

The following helps you to better understand how the prefix behaves: When you look through the Joomla code itself, it may strike you that sometimes a class belongs to the

Joomla CMS (located in the /libraries/cms folder) and sometimes to the Joomla Platform (located in the /libraries/joomla folder). In either case, the JLoader class magically loads the correct class. How this works is simple. The J prefix is first registered to point to /libraries/joomla and later the /libraries/cms is added as an alternative to the same prefix. The code looks a little bit like the following (but spread over more than one file):

```
JLoader::registerPrefix('J', JPATH_PLATFORM.'/joomla');
JLoader::registerPrefix('J', JPATH_PLATFORM.'/cms');
```

Overriding classes

When you want to replace a core class with your own duplicate class, you can do so by using the JLoader::register() call. Previously, we have seen how we can use this call to register a new class and path. By adding a third argument $force and setting it to true, we can overwrite any previous class declaration as well:

```
JLoader::register($class, $path, true);
```

A real life example of this would be:

```php
<?php
class PlgSystemCustomloader extends JPlugin
{
    public function __construct(&$subject, $config)
    {
        $path = JPATH_PLUGINS.'/system/customloader/overrides/';
        $file = $path.'module/helper.php';
        JLoader::register('JModuleHelper', $file, true);

        return parent::__construct($subject, $config);
    }
}
```

We then copy the original class file to our new overrides/ subfolder and start modifying things there. Joomla will now use your class override, instead of the original.

There is one thing to be aware of, which has to do with the boot procedure of Joomla. When the Joomla application is started up and our plugin is being initialized, a bunch of core classes are already loaded and therefore, we definitely cannot override them. Some examples are JApplication, JApplicationHelper and JPlugin. There is no way to override these files in a clean Joomla way. Once a class is declared in the PHP runtime, you cannot declare it twice.

Overriding classes one at the time, works nicely though. Unfortunately, you cannot just override the entire J prefix with your own library path. What you can do, is register your own path with the J prefix as well (JLoader::registerPrefix, see above). However, this will add your own path at the end of the search list, so after /libraries/joomla and /libraries/cms. There is no option to reverse this order.

Storing your library in /libraries

When you want to add a bigger set of classes to Joomla, it is best to add them to the /libraries folder, instead of to a subfolder of your plugin. Libraries can be treated as an extension as well. You can define an XML manifest file and create a ZIP-file to easily install your library in a Joomla site. You can even create a parent package (with XML manifest) that contains both your plugin and your library.

13.4 Using a plugin to add new JFormFields

When a component, module or plugin defines parameters, they are defined in JForm XML files. When a **Menu-Item** gets specific parameters, they are defined in JForm XML files. If you encounter a form in either frontend or backend, chances are the form is again created using JForm XML files. JForm is all over the place. It allows developers to easily create forms, complete with validation and output formatting. Even better: A JForm form is based upon fields that are reusable in any other form.

Creating new form fields

Joomla includes various useful field types, ranging from generic input fields and dropdowns to calendars and modal windows. However, it may be that you need to develop some fields that do not exist in the CMS yet. You may want to add custom select boxes with values from an external SOAP service; you may want to implement cool fields based on jQuery Tools; or you may just want to add non-existing attributes to plain input fields.

Thanks to the flexible architecture of JForm, creating new field types is perfectly possible. You can define a new class like JFormFieldExample, that extends from JFormField and that implements the getInput() method along side with some class variables. In this case, the class file is placed somewhere in a subfolder of your extension. For instance, a subfolder fields of a component com_example:

```
components/com_example/fields/example.php
```

Adding new field classes through XML

Once the field class is defined, it can be used within a JForm XML file. Because the form will not be aware that there is a new file example.php that defines a field example, we need to tell JForm to include a new path when searching for field classes. This is done by adding an `addincludepath` attribute to either the `<fields>` or the `<fieldset>` element:

```
<fields>
    <fieldset addincludepath="/components/com_example/fields/">
        <field type="example" name="field2" />
    </fieldset>
</fields>
```

There are a couple of downsides to the approach of this XML argument. When you have many XML files that all make use of the field type `example`, you need to apply the `addincludepath` attribute again and again. Also, when you want to use the `addincludepath` statement multiple times, it is limiting. Adding the `addincludepath` attribute multiple times to the same element does not make sense:

```
<fieldset addincludepath="path1" addincludepath="path2">
```

This is not how XML works – parsing the XML will only apply the second statement, not both.

You can add the `addincludepath` attribute to multiple elements though. However, at the count of three, you are stuck. The first attribute can be added to the `<fields>` element, the second can be added to the `<fieldset>` element. However, there is no place for the third one. There is still the workaround of adding in new fieldsets, each with their own `addincludepath`. This is just trying to fix something that is ugly anyway. There is a better solution though: plugins.

Adding new field classes through a plugin

New field paths can also be added using the `JFormHelper::addFieldPath()` call. The method receives a path as an argument, which can be relative to the current PHP file or an absolute path starting with `JPATH_SITE`. When using the call, your own path is added to an internal array of the JForm library. Once a new path is added, you can remove the `addincludepath` attribute in the XML file and still use the field class that lives within that path. This can really clean up your XML forms.

When you build only one component, the `JFormHelper::addFieldPath()` call can be placed somewhere in your component, right before it starts dealing with forms. Once the field type is used in multiple extensions, it is smarter to place the call in a plugin. Preferably, as early as possible in the boot procedure, in order for the new field classes to become available as soon as the extensions need them. This can be done by placing it in the `onAfterInitalise()` method of a System Plugin or even including it in the constructor of a System Plugin:

```php
public function __construct(& $subject, $config)
{
    parent::__construct($subject, $config);

    JFormHelper::addFieldPath(__DIR__ . '/fields');
}
```

Adding rule paths

Besides field types, `JForm` also has the ability to add validation rules to the form. These rules are checked upon when the field in the XML defines an attribute like `filter`, `unique` or `validate`.

```xml
<field type="email" validate="email" unique="true" />
```

New rules can be added in a similar way as field types, using the call `JFormHelper::addRulePath()`:

```php
public function __construct(& $subject, $config)
{
    parent::__construct($subject, $config);

    JFormHelper::addRulePath(__DIR__ . '/rule');
}
```

13.5 Customizing the constructor

In the previous chapter, you have learned how plugins are triggered. Every plugin class extends from the `JPlugin` class, which extends from the `JEvent` class. Without this extend, the plugin does not function. When overriding the constructor, it is therefore important to call upon the parent constructor explicitly:

```php
public function __construct(&$subject, $config)
{
    parent::__construct($subject, $config);
}
```

Note that you do not need to override the constructor at all. A plugin behaves perfectly fine when having only a class with event methods. It is good practice not to override the constructor at all when you do not really need to.

In your constructor you can do various things. When you want to trigger certain behavior a little bit earlier than the event `onAfterInitalise`, you can use the constructor for this. This guarantees your code is being executed, as soon as the plugin class is instantiated.

More commonly, the constructor is used to load the language, although the $autoloadLanguage flag can also be used for this:

```
$this->loadLanguage();
```

13.6 Creating a custom plugin per project

With the help of this book, you should be able to create plugins more easily. One reason for creating a plugin, is to put together reusable features that can be shared with others through Github or the **Joomla Extension Directory**.

Another reason to create a plugin is when you have specific needs for a specific project. You can create a plugin per project, with project specific hacks. It contains code that can be modified directly at will. Most likely, it is not going to be reused anywhere else. This opens up some great ways of enhancing your project. Let's see what is possible.

Creating a base plugin

We are going to create a plugin called `Custom` and this plugin will be used to do numerous things in our Joomla environment. Our plugin will be able to support all possible events and therefore is created as a System Plugin.

```
jimport( 'joomla.plugin.plugin' );
class PlgSystemCustom extends JPlugin
{
}
```

Create an equivalent XML file, discover the plugin using the **Extension Manager** and you are done. The plugin can be enabled using the **Plugin Manager**. And that is it. It is not doing anything. It serves as a placeholder for whatever code we have yet to create - not highly advanced stuff but just some handy code that we can quickly create. This skeleton can then be implemented for any of your projects.

Blocking access by IP

Let's say we are still developing a site and we want to make sure access to this site is only allowed from specific development IPs. All other IPs will receive an **Access Denied** message. To do this, we add a `onAfterInitalise()` method that refers to a method `checkIp()`, which checks whether the `REMOTE_ADDR` variable matches or not.

```
public function onAfterInitialise()
{
    $this->checkIp();
}


protected function checkIp()
{
    $currentIp = $_SERVER['REMOTE_ADDR'];
    $allowIps = array('127.0.0.1', '192.168.1.1');

    if (in_array($currentIp, $allowIps) == false)
    {
        die('Access denied');
    }
}
```

Of course, IP-based access rules can also be added to your `.htaccess` file, however that is Apache specific and will not work on other webservers like Nginx or IIS. By using a plugin, the functionality is part of the Joomla environment - wherever our Joomla site goes, so does this functionality.

Redirecting to specific domains

Another example: When the Joomla site is served under various domain names (`example.com`, `www.example.com`, `example.info`, `example.co.uk`), search engines may start indexing your site under the various domain names, leading to the problem of duplicate content. To prevent this, it is best to redirect all requests to a single domain instead, for example `www.example.com`.

The problem is, however, that we are developing from `dev.example.com`, so requests to `dev.example.com` need to be accepted as well, without redirecting. Again, we use the `onAfterInitalise` event to make this happen:

```
public function onAfterInitialise()
{
    $this->checkDomain();
}


protected function checkDomain()
{
```

```php
$app = JFactory::getApplication();
$url = JURI::root();


$primaryDomain = 'www.example.com';
$domains = array('www.example.com', 'dev.example.com');


$domainMatch = false;
foreach ($domains as $domain)
{
    if (stristr($url, $domain) == true)
    {
        $domainMatch = true;
    }
}

if ($domainMatch == false)
{
    $primaryUrl = 'http://' . $primaryDomain;
    $newUrl = str_replace($url, $primaryUrl, JURI::current());

    $app->redirect($newUrl);
    $app->close();
}
}
```

Without doubt, there is a third party Joomla plugin available that does the same thing. However, by implementing small hacks like this in your own custom plugin, you can keep the number of extensions within a Joomla site limited. Plus, you are in complete of control of these hacks.

13.7 Debugging your own code

When writing plugins, you may sometimes make small mistakes. The code is not functioning as expected. Debugging is needed. Here are some debugging tips that you may want to include in your plugin (or custom parent class) by default.

Debugging to a log

One common task you will have when working with plugins is to debug the variables you are working with. Because plugins act a lot of times under the hood, a simple `print_r()` is often not sufficient. The output may never appear on screen, when the user redirects to another page. A `die()` statement is not preferred either, because it may interrupt the application flow too much. Dumping variables into a custom log offers a much cleaner way of debugging things. Here is an example debug function:

```php
private function writeLog($message, $variable = null)
{
    $file = JPATH_SITE . '/logs/plg_system_example.log';

    if (!empty($variable))
    {
        $message .= var_export($variable, true);
    }

    $message .= "\n";

    file_put_contents($file, $message, FILE_APPEND);
}
```

In our plugin methods we can implement this method as follows:

```php
$this->writeLog('Debug arguments', $someArguments);
```

Instead of using our own code to write to a log, we can also use the Joomla framework for this:

```php
private function writeLog($message, $variable = null)
{
    jimport('joomla.log.log');

    JLog::addLogger(
        array('text_file' => 'plg_system_example.php'),
        JLog::ALL,
        array('plg_system_example')
    );

    if (!empty($variable))
    {
        $message .= var_export($variable, true);
    }

    JLog::add($message, JLog::WARNING, 'plg_system_example');
}
```

As you can see, more lines of code are needed when doing it the Joomla way. The benefit here is that you are writing your logs to a PHP file, which is never accessible from a browser. Also, your logs can be categorized and formatted with better syntax.

Additionally, each log gets a specific priority, which behaves similar to the `error_reporting` settings of PHP itself:

- o   JLog::WARNING
- o   JLog::CRITICAL
- o   JLog::EMERGENCY
- o   JLog::DEBUG
- o   JLog::ALL

Just as with normal PHP error reporting, the second argument to the `JLog::addLogger` method allows for bit-wise operations. The `JLog` constants contain integers that allow calculations and with that, fine tuning of what to log. For instance, the following will include all logs (`JLog::ALL`) except for debugging messages:

```
JLog::ALL & ~JLog::DEBUG
```

The following will include only critical and emergency messages:

```
JLog::CRITICAL + JLog::EMERGENCY
```

Debugging database queries

Just like writing debugging information to a log, printing out queries is a thing you will do frequently when coding in Joomla. A query is usually created by using the `JDatabaseQuery` object as follows:

```
$db = JFactory::getDbo();
$query = $db->getQuery(true);
$query->select($db->quoteName('user_id'));
$query->from($db->quoteName('#__users'));
$db->setQuery($query);


$results = $db->loadObjectList();
```

This query will fail though, because the Joomla table #__users (Joomla will automatically replace the dummy prefix #_ with the actual table prefix) does not contain a field `user_id` (the primary key is actually `id`). This query will throw an exception so we need a catch statement to properly catch it:

```
try
{
    $results = $db->loadObjectList();
}
catch(Exception $e)
{
    $log = 'Query failed';
```

```
    $this->writeLog($log, $e->getMessage());
}
```

Thanks to this approach, our plugin will not crash and hopefully still leave the CMS intact, while the actual SQL statement that caused the error is logged to our custom log file. This is excellent.

However, we may want to do this for every database query – inserts, deletions, updates and all the other `JDatabase` methods available. For this, we will create a helper method `doQuery()`, which dynamically calls the right method of the `JDatabase` class with as an argument the `$query` object.

```
public function doQuery($method, $query)
{
    try
    {
        $results = $db->$method();
    }
    catch(Exception $e)
    {
        $failedQuery = $db->getQuery()->dump();
        $log = "Query [$failedQuery] failed";
        $this->writeLog($log, $e->getMessage());
    }

    return $results;
}
```

Instead of using the `$db->loadObjectList()` call, we can now replace it with the following, which guarantees that any SQL exceptions are logged, while the CMS continues to work:

```
$results = $this->doQuery('loadObjectList', $query);
```

13.8 Manipulating plugins in the #__extensions table

When an extension is installed in Joomla, its files are being copied to the right places and a new entry in the databasetable #__extensions is created. Sometimes, modifying the #__extensions table may prove handy. For instance, when the Joomla Administrator is not available to you or when you want to quickly want to update things without requiring too many clicks.

The #__extensions table is used not just for plugins, but for any Joomla extension –

components, modules, language packs. Plugins can always be identified by the `type` field being set to `plugin`. The `folder` field is used to identify the plugin group.

Disabling a plugin

Of all fields in the `#__extensions` table, the `enabled` field is the most commonly used. When a plugin is causing issues, it can be disabled with one SQL statement that toggles this `enabled` field:

```
UPDATE `#__extensions` SET `enabled`=0
  WHERE `type`="plugin"
  AND `element`="example"
  AND `folder`="system"
```

You can copy and post this SQL statement into your database manager (like phpMyAdmin or the SQL command-line).

Renaming a plugin

Another good example is the `name` field. The value of the `<name>` tag inside the XML manifest is copied to this `name` field in the database. When you change the name in the XML manifest, the database will still contain the original value, so it will need to be updated through a database query.

Normally, this should not be necessary though. When you stick to the standards, you will be using a system name like `PLG_SYSTEM_EXAMPLE`, which will be stored in the field `name`. Next, you can translate this `name` using the plugins language file. This way, the name can always change by editing the language file, while the XML manifest (and therefore the corresponding entry in `#__extensions`) stays the same.

```
<name>PLG_SYSTEM_EXAMPLE</name>
```

Removing extensions

Theoretically, you can also uninstall a plugin by simply removing its files and removing its entry from the database table `#__extensions`. This works but is not recommended. Plugins may change in future Joomla versions in such a way that a plugin's information is spread out over more tables than just the `#__extensions` table. For instance, for components this is already the case: The `#__assets` also contains various entries, which would need to be removed as well. If you want to get rid of a plugin that is causing problems, it should be sufficient to disable the plugin through the database and then remove it by using the `Extension Manager`.

13.9 Finding out about plugin events

Finding out where and when an event is fired can be hard and time consuming. This book is meant to give you a good coverage of all core events. However, each third party extension may bring along its own set of events. Quite often, proper documentation is needed but lacking. So, be prepared to read through the source code to see which events are there.

 The Yireo site contains a mapping of which events exist in which Joomla version. This allows you to easily look up which event method can be implemented under a certain Joomla version. This compatibility matrix can be found on the following link: **http://yireo.com/ joomla-events-matrix**

Scanning the source code

One way to find out about plugin events is to scan the Joomla source. The best thing to search for is the `trigger()` call of the dispatcher. Use the following phrases in your code search:

```
JEventDispatcher::getInstance()->trigger
dispatcher->trigger
```

It may also be that the `triggerEvent` method of the `JApplication` class is used as a shortcut:

```
triggerEvent
```

In most cases, the method will include the event name as first argument. Sometimes a variable is used instead, so be prepared to poke around a little bit in the code to find the actual event name. Or ask for a fine manual.

Beware of unused events

There are some events that appear in the Joomla source, but are never used. For instance, at the time of writing, the Joomla core contained an event `onAfterSessionStart`, which appeared to be triggered when the `loadSession()` method in the application was executed. However, when debugging this, the `loadSession()` method was never executed and therefore, the event was never triggered.

If you want to know for sure whether an event is thrown, it is best to write a plugin, install it and use it to intercept the event with some debugging function. In the GitHub repository in the folder **chapter12**, you will find a **plg_system_eventlog** package that contains code to log every event to a logfile, once it is triggered. You can keep the plugin running for some time, and inspect the logfile afterwards to see if it contains the event you need.

Hacking the dispatcher

Another way of finding out about events is to hack the dispatcher class. The event dispatcher is located in the file `libraries/joomla/event/dispatcher.php`. Its `trigger()` method is used every time an event is fired. By adding custom code to this method, you can write the event name to a log file or do some profiling with it. For this development purpose, making a temporary core hack is not that bad. Just remember that all core hacks are evil.

Writing a plugin for all events

You can also attempt to write a plugin that listens to all possible events. This sounds great. However, the event dispatcher requires a plugin to have an event method in place for each event it listens to. Using magic methods to fetch any event is not possible. Therefore, this approach works well when you want to write a plugin to listen to all events that you already know about. However, this approach will not work for events that you do not know about.

13.10 Summary

In this chapter, you have learned a bunch of tips and tricks: Ranging from loading different library classes, to debugging your code easily. With these tips and tricks, you can add even more features to your plugin. The next chapter – chapter 14 – will focus on adding these features properly: It discusses code compliance, testing and other best practices.

14) Best practices

This chapter deals with writing code properly. This involves code compliance. It also involves testing with PHPUnit. By sticking to the standards, you make the life of other developers easier when they get to look at your code. This chapter gives you some hints on how to write beautiful plugins.

14.1 Letting your plugin grow and grow

Once your plugin contains more and more functionality, it is good practice to make sure your code does not get too complex. A single `onAfterInitalise()` method with over 500 lines of code is hard to read and hard to maintain – both for you and for other developers. Here are some tips and tricks to make sure your code remains as clean as possible.

Keep your event methods clean

Try to keep your event methods as clean as possible. A plugin may perform various tasks at a single event. However, do not implement all these tasks in the same event method. Instead, place these tasks in a separate task method and refer to that task method from within the event method.

```
public function onAfterRender()
{
    $body = JResponse::getBody();
    $body = $this->replaceSomeTags($body); // dummy task 1
    $body = $this->replaceSomeMoreTags($body); // dummy task 2

    JResponse::setBody($body);
}
```

Place the event methods at the top of your class, so that it becomes easy to determine which events are used by your plugin. Your task methods should come after your event methods. If you have any helper methods (that aid in performing a certain task) place them at the bottom of the class. Make them protected, because helper methods do not offer an API to your plugin.

```
class PlgSystemCustom extends JPlugin
{
    public function onAfterDispatch() {} // event method
    protected function doSomething() {} // task method
    protected function arrayToString() {} // helper method
}
```

Keep your own methods meaningful

The names of the methods that you create, should describe what they are doing. For instance, if you create a User Plugin that allows you to sync profile changes to an external CRM (in the examples below we will use the dummy name **Mycrm**), it is best to use the `onUserAfterSave()` event method to refer to a `syncUserRecordToMycrm()` task method. By simply looking at the task method's name, everybody knows its purpose. Do not care too much about the length of that name. The method's length is not an issue. Be as descriptive as possible.

```
class PlgUserMycrm extends JPlugin
{
    public function onUserAfterSave($user, $isnew, $success, $msg) {}
    protected function syncUserRecordToMycrm($user, $isnew) {}
}
```

Using plugin helpers

If a plugin class has only two or three methods - one of them being an event method and the others being task methods – the code's logic will be easy to understand. However, if your plugin class contains multiple event methods and dozens of task methods, the structure of the plugin class is already overwhelming on its own. Most likely, you can group task methods together - methods that serve the same purpose or methods that are working on the same event method.

To make the code more readable, consider the usage of a separate file that contains a separate class - a **helper class** or **plugin helper**. Such a helper can have the obvious name helper (with a file helper.php and a classname derived from the plugin class, plus a suffix Helper):

```
// File: mycrm.php
class PlgUserMycrm extends JPlugin
{
    public function onUserAfterSave($user, $isnew, $success, $msg)
    {
        PlgUserMyCrmHelper:: syncUserRecordToMyCrm($user, $isnew);
    }
}
```

```
// File: helper.php
class PlgUserMyCrmHelper
{
    static public function syncUserRecordToMyCrm($user, $isnew) {}
}
```

Typically, a helper class stands on its own and also includes task methods that are called upon statically. However, there are no rules here. You can also make your helper methods non-static, instantiate the helper from within your plugin and use it like that:

```
$helper = new PlgUserMyCrmHelper();
$helper->syncUserRecordToMyCrm($user, $isnew);
```

Code is considered of better quality once it complies to specific quality principles. One such a principle is the concept of **DRY - Do not Repeat Yourself**. As soon as code is reused, it should be implemented in such a way that as little code as possible is duplicated. This also means that code is easily identified as performing a certain task. Putting this code in methods and classes that describe that task is therefore logical.

Custom parent classes and your own library

When you are writing multiple plugins and implementing the same features in these plugins, creating your own parent class might be a good option to prevent copying the same code over and over again. Normally, plugins extend from `JPlugin`. However, we can introduce a new parent class that extends again from `JPlugin`, so that we can add in methods and properties that will be shared among our plugins.

 The Joomla framework allows you to easily introduce your own classes using the `JLoader` class. Once a class has been added, it can be reused from anywhere in the Joomla application. More on using `JLoader` is explained in chapter 13.

When our plugins are based on a new parent class, we have to make sure this parent class is available as soon as the first plugin is loaded. There are two approaches for adding our new class, so that plugins can extend from it. In both cases, we are using a System Plugin, because this will allow us to add the class as early as possible. In the first case, we will add the class through the constructor of the plugin class.

```
public function PlgSystemExample extends JPlugin
{
    public function __construct(&$subject, $config)
    {
        $path = JPATH_PLUGINS.'/system/example/libraries/';
        JLoader::register('ExamplePlugin', $path.'plugin.php');

        parent::__construct($subject, $config);
    }
}
```

The class `ExamplePlugin` is now being loaded from the file `system/example/libraries/plugin.php` and from now on any other plugin can extend from it as follows:

```
public function PlgContentExample extends ExamplePlugin
{
}
```

This works perfectly. However, the downside is that the **System Plugin** class `PlgSystemExample` itself is not based upon this parent. To allow for this, we can use the second approach: loading the class outside of the plugin class. This is considered less beautiful though, because the file `plugins/system/example.php` is meant to contain only one code structure: the plugin class. With this approach, it suddenly contains two purposes. To initialize another class and to define the plugin class. Of course, the first purpose is there to fulfill the second purpose, so consider it an evil that does no harm.

```
$path = JPATH_PLUGINS.'/system/example/libraries/';
JLoader::register('ExamplePlugin', $path.'plugin.php');

public function PlgSystemExample extends ExamplePlugin
{
}
```

Now that the `ExamplePlugin` is added, we can use it to define all kind of handy things. For instance, we can make sure it is autoloading language strings for every plugin that extends from it. Or we can automatically add parameters to the plugin class, based upon some other conditions.

```
class ExamplePlugin extends JPlugin
{
    protected $autoloadLanguage = true;

    public function __construct(&$subject, $config = array())
    {
        parent::__construct($subject, $config);

        $this->params->set('example', 'test');
    }
}
```

14.2 How to write a bad plugin

When you are writing a plugin, this book gives you all the examples of how to do this correctly. Sometimes, seeing bad examples is also helpful. It tells you what not to do. Here are some examples of bad code that definitely should not be in your plugin.

Bad: Including $_GET and $_POST directly

When you are familiar with PHP but new to Joomla, nothing is more tempting than to fetch an input variable using either $_GET or $_POST. For instance, if you would want to fetch a variable `id`, the following can be used:

```
$id = (isset($_GET['id'])) ? $_GET['id'] : 0;
```

Assuming that the `id` should be a number, you can also cast this to an integer:

```
$id = (int)$id;
```

This works perfectly fine in Joomla as well. However, there is a very suitable Joomla class that you should use instead: `JInput`. The following line fetches the input variable `id` from either `$_GET` or `$_POST` and makes sure it is an integer:

```
$id = JFactory::getApplication()->input->getInt('id');
```

It can be debated which method is better. However, with Joomla code, the Joomla way should always be preferred above the regular PHP way. Choosing the Joomla way makes sure the Joomla framework is implemented properly. When a change is introduced to enhance input filtering, your plugin will automatically profit from this.

Of course, this also counts for other global variables. If you want to refer to the session, do not use `$_SESSION`: Use the object-oriented `JSession` instead:

```
$session = JFactory::getSession();
$session->set('name1', 'value1');
$session->get('name2');
```

The `JInput` class also allows you to fetch data from globals by using a subclass. The following fetches a `monster` cookie from the `$_COOKIE` array:

```
$input = JFactory::getApplication()->input;
$cookieMonster = $input->cookie->getCmd('monster');
```

As a general rule, whenever a Joomla class is available for a certain task, use the Joomla class, even though you could also perform that task in simple PHP code.

Bad: Including classes in your main PHP file

If your plugin requires additional classes, you can put these classes anywhere, including in the main PHP file. For instance, if you have a System Plugin called `example` and a helper class `ExampleHelper`, it is possible to include both the plugin class `PlgSystemExample` and the helper class `ExampleHelper` in one and the same file `example.php`.

Do not do this though. When somebody opens up your class file and sees this helper class is being used, it is not obvious to scroll all the way down to see the definition of that class. Joomla itself places each class in its own file, in order for classes to be located easily by their file name. A class `ExampleHelper` should be contained in a separate file `helper.php`.

Bad: Not calling the parent constructor

It is possible to override the plugin's constructor and not call the parent constructor. This is not so much a bad habit. It will simply give you a plugin that does not work. Every plugin needs to make a call to its parent constructor (the constructor of the class `JPlugin`), which again calls the constructor of its parent class `JEvent`. If this not done, the plugin will not work.

Bad: Having more than 10 indents in one method

When you write any control structure like `if`, `for` or `while`, the code will be indented. Having more than 10 indents will make your code very complex to read and maintain. Instead, helper functions should be applied. If there are too many helper methods in the plugin class, create a helper class instead. If your code does contain 10 indents or more, make sure you have a good reason for this.

Good: Learn by reading good code

There are many more ways to write a plugin of low quality. Of course, the actual goal is to write a plugin of high quality instead. It is best to read through the source code of Joomla itself – especially the code in the folders `libraries/joomla` and `libraries/cms` – to get used to the coding standards and syntax of Joomla. When you apply the same standards to your own code, you can guarantee your code fits in with the existing code in the best possible way.

14.3 Validating code compliance

 The Joomla coding standards can be found online at: **http://joomla.github.io/coding-standards/**

When writing code to extend a certain application, it is good practice to stick to the coding standards of that application. Some of the rules of the Joomla standard may be different from what you are used to. They are slightly different from more common standards like the Zend Framework coding standard or the PEAR coding standard.

Some examples: Tabs should be placed as real tabs and not spaces. However, these tabs should be displayed using four spaces, not eight. Also, curly brackets - used to create structures like classes, functions, `if-else` checks and so on – are always placed on a new line:

```
if ($something)
{
}
```

The standards may vary a little bit from time to time. Changing it in your code should give you little work though, especially when you use an IDE like **PhpStorm** or **Zend Studio** with features like code refactoring.

To make sure your code always validates correctly, you should use **PHP CodeSniffer**. The URL **http://docs.joomla.org/Joomla_CodeSniffer** gives you steps to help you add the Joomla Coding Standards to CodeSniffer. Make sure you install CodeSniffer version 1.5 or higher, because older versions have issues with imported standards like the one from Joomla. As soon as CodeSniffer is installed, you can use the command-line script `phpcs` to validate your own code as follows:

```
shell$ phpcs -standard=Joomla plugins/system/example/
```

The `phpcs` tool contains various other handy features, like a reporting mode that produces XML or CSV code (allowing you to reuse the report in other applications). Also, the `-i` flag tells you which coding standards are available in CodeSniffer. This allows you to quickly see whether the Joomla standard is installed or not:

```
shell$ phpcs -i
```

14.4 Testing your plugin with PHPUnit

To make sure that your plugin code behaves correctly in all situations, testing is key. What kind of tests are needed depends entirely on the functionality of the plugin. For instance, when you have created a System Plugin that replaces a specific tag, its class might have the following structure:

```
class PlgSystemExample extends JPlugin
{
    public function onAfterRender()
    {
        $body = JResponse::getBody();
        $body = $this->replaceTagsInBody($body);

        JResponse::setBody($body);
    }

    public function replaceTagsInBody($body)
    {
        return str_replace('<foo>', '<bar>', $body);
    }
}
```

In this case, the `onAfterRender()` event method hooks deeply into the Joomla application, making it hard to test its behavior. However, its sole purpose is to fetch the current document buffer and pass it (in the form of the variable `$body`) through to the function `replaceTagsInBody()`. The `replaceTagsInBody()` function is ideal for unit testing and allows us to quickly use different values for `$body` to see how our function deals with different use cases. Creating a unit test with PHPUnit is therefore a good testing option.

A completely different use case involves logging into Joomla using credentials of some remote application. The Joomla **Authentication Plugin** that needs to be tested relies on a POST (possibly including form token stored in the session), remote calls to the remote application, redirects and COOKIE values being set afterwards. This functionality is best tested using a tool like Selenium instead, focusing on frontend behavior instead of the behavior of class methods.

As you can see, choosing the best testing scenario depends entirely on the functionality offered by the plugin. This book is about coding and therefore, we will focus on getting PHPUnit ready to test our plugin methods.

Getting started with PHPUnit

To get started with PHPUnit, create a temporary folder – for instance a folder `plugin-tests` – and install `composer` to this directory:

```
curl -sS https://getcomposer.org/installer | php
```

This will create a file `composer.phar`. Next, create a file named `composer.json` with the following contents:

```
{"require-dev": {"phpunit/phpunit": "4.1.*"}}
```

This tells composer that you want to initialize a project that depends on PHPUnit. Next, use the `composer.json` definition to let composer find the PHPUnit requirement and install it. Note that this will install the 4.1 branch of PHPUnit, while (at the time of writing) most unit tests of the Joomla core have been written with 3.7 branch of PHPUnit. For creating our own unit tests, the 4.1 branch is fine.

```
php composer.phar install
```

Starting our unit test

We have now added PHPUnit to our folder `plugin-tests` and it is time to perform an actual test. We are going to test our System Plugin `example`. Its plugin class is `PlgSystemExample`. To follow the PHPUnit standards we are going to add a test

classPlgSystemExampleTest in a file PlgSystemExampleTest.php. The file has
this content:

```php
<?php
class PlgSystemExampleTest extends PHPUnit_Framework_TestCase
{
    public function testReplaceTagsInBody($body)
    {
        $testBefore = 'test before';
        $testAfter = 'test after';
        $this->assertNotEquals($testBefore, $textAfter);
    }
}
```

This only creates a dummy test. The values of $testBefore and $testAfter
are never equal. When we perform a test on this, we are going to use $this-
>assertNotEquals() to check whether these values are not matching. If they do not
match, it is ok. If they do match, it is not ok. This may read as some kind of twisted logic, but
it should show you how tests are working with PHPUnit.

To run this dummy test, we call upon the phpunit command with our file as an argument.
Composer has tucked away phpunit in a subfolder.

```
php ./vendor/phpunit/phpunit/phpunit PlgSystemArticletext.php
```

This will give some output including a line like the following:

```
Tests: 1, Assertions: 1
```

It tells us there was one test encountered and it was run successfully. The entire class
forms our unit test. Each method with a prefix test counts as a test. Within a test method,
we can add multiple assertions (PHPUnit methods starting with assert).

Initializing Joomla

To turn our dummy test into an actual plugin test, we need to instantiate our plugin class.
That plugin class again depends on JPlugin and JEvent, which again depend on the
event dispatcher, which depends on ... well, the rest of Joomla. Sometimes, a plugin method
can be tested with a standalone PHP script. However, in most cases, we will need to
startup the entire Joomla application, allowing us to access all parts of Joomla including the
database.

To initialize Joomla, we create a new method initJoomla(), which will contain all the
code needed to startup the Joomla application, including our plugin.

```php
public function initJoomla()
{
}
```

First we define several constants that are required by Joomla. We set the _JEXEC security flag. Assuming our `plugin-tests` folder is a subfolder of the Joomla root folder, we set the Joomla root to be the parent folder of the current folder. Once the Joomla root is set, we change the working directory to be this Joomla root.

```php
define('_JEXEC', 1);
define('DOCUMENT_ROOT', dirname(dirname(__FILE__)).'/');
define('JPATH_BASE', DOCUMENT_ROOT);
chdir(JPATH_BASE);
```

Having these constants in place, allows us to load the definitions of the Joomla environment. Next, the framework is loaded.

```php
require_once(JPATH_BASE.'/includes/defines.php');
require_once(JPATH_BASE.'/includes/framework.php');

jimport('joomla.environment.request');
jimport('joomla.database.database');
```

Now the Joomla framework is fully available, we want to simulate the Joomla CMS frontend as best as we can. For this, the `JApplicationSite` is instantiated. Last but not least, we import all System Plugins, just like we would in a component.

```php
$app = JFactory::getApplication('site');
$app->initialise();


jimport('joomla.plugin.helper');
JPluginHelper::importPlugin('system');
```

We can now use the `initJoomla()` in our previous test method `testReplaceTagsInBody()` and access the plugin class. The constructor of our plugin requires two arguments: the dispatcher and an array describing the plugin. The dispatcher is fetched easily and for the second argument we are just using an empty array.

```php
public function testReplaceTagsInBody()
{
    $this->initJoomla();
    $dispatcher = JEventDispatcher::getInstance();
    $plugin = new PlgSystemArticletext($dispatcher, array());
}
```

Running a test

We are ready to add tests. Having an instance of our System Plugin class available in the variable `$plugin`, allows us to call upon any public method within that class. Our `testReplaceTagsInBody()` method was meant to test the workings of our plugin method `replaceTagsInBody()`. It receives a text, replaces the tags within and returns the modified text.

One thing we can test is whether a text that contains the correct tag is modified. Hence, a text that does not contain the correct tag will not be modified. We will add these conditions into an array `$checks`. Each check has a `body` and a flag `has_tag` indicating whether that body contains the relevant tag or not.

```
$checks = array();
$checks[] = array(
    'body' => 'body without tags',
    'has_tag' => false,
);


$checks[] = array(
    'body' => 'body with tag: {tag id=2}',
    'has_tag' => true,
);


$checks[] = array(
    'body' => 'body with tag: {tag id=2',
    'has_tag' => false,
);
```

The third check is intentionally broken. It seems to contain a tag, however the tag is not ending with an ending curly bracket and therefore does not classify as a valid tag. We assume that this tag is therefore left alone.

Next we loop through the `$checks` to pass the body value to the `replaceTagsInBody()` method. Based upon the output, we either assert that the modified text should be the same (`assertEquals()`) or not the same as the original text (`assertNotEquals()`).

```
foreach ($checks as $check)
{
    $textBefore = $check['body'];
    $textAfter = $plugin->replaceTagsInBody($textBefore);

    if ($check['has_tag'] == true)
```

```
    {
        $this->assertNotEquals($textBefore, $textAfter);
    }
    else
    {
        $this->assertEquals($textBefore, $textAfter);
    }
}
```

Running the updated unit test should reveal there is one test with three assertions, while none of them fails. If one or more assertion fails, we should fix this in the plugin code. For instance, our third check contained a broken tag. If assertion fails, it means that the plugins method `replaceTagsInBody()` replaced the broken tag with something, whereas this was not the expected result. The test allows us to anticipate working behavior as well as broken behavior. As long as we anticipate things correctly, the test succeeds.

Tips for testing

As you can see, the test class `PlgSystemExampleTest` that we created, contains quite some code to initialize Joomla properly. When running multiple unit tests, it is a good idea to create either an include file or a parent class to let each test extend from. This way you can easily initialize Joomla in each test. You can for instance create your own `Joomla_Plugin_TestCase` parent class.

When you are testing plugin classes, best practice is to create a test for every method included in your plugin. However, this requires that these methods have their access set to `public` and not `protected`. Earlier, I explained that task methods and helper methods are best set to `protected`. However, the unit testing requires otherwise.

The Joomla CMS is written for the web. While there are other applications of Joomla available (daemon, command line), our plugin lives within the CMS and we therefore need to base our tests upon the CMS. Frequently, this will generate some warnings about $_SERVER variables that are not available. For instance, running PHP from the command line will not set the `HTTP_HOST` variable and any code that depends on that variable might throw a **PHP Warning**. This is easily fixed by defining a dummy value in our `initJoomla()` method:

```
$_SERVER['HTTP_HOST'] = null;
```

The same is true for $_POST and $_GET variables. While it is a little bit hackish, we can fake input variables by setting them in the beginning of the `initJoomla()` method.

14.5 Summary

This chapter dealt with code beautification and validation. It also gave you advice on the things not to do in your own code. Last but not least, it gave some hints on how to setup unit tests to see if your plugin works in various circumstances. If everything went alright, your plugin is now fully tested and written in a clean manner. Nothing is stopping you now from sharing your work with the rest of the world: This is what the next chapter will cover.

Releasing your plugin

When you are writing a plugin, you can either keep the code for yourself or share it with the rest of the world. If you choose to share the plugin, this chapter helps you with some additional best practices for releasing your plugin to the public.

15.1 Testing in actual Joomla environments

In chapter 3, we discussed many things that can be included in the XML manifest. When releasing your package, make sure to test the plugin installation in various Joomla environments. Unit testing – discussed in chapter 14 – will help you test the PHP functionality of your plugin. However, the only good way of testing the XML manifest, is by actually trying to install the plugin in actual Joomla sites: Make sure to test things in different Joomla versions (Joomla 2.5, Joomla 3.1, Joomla 3.3) and if possible in different hosting environments (Linux and Windows, different PHP handlers like **mod_php** and **FastCGI**). The more you can test things before releasing your plugin, the better.

15.2 Semantic versioning

In chapter 3 we mentioned that your first plugin should logically have version 0.0.1, while your first stable release should have version number 1.0.0. Good developers think everything through, quite extensively, so obviously the concept of versioning has received some good thought as well.

It now has become common practice to apply a versioning standard that is called **semantic versioning**, which is documented on the website **http://semver.org/**. By using semantic versioning, other developers will know more or less which kind of changes are made available in your new release, simply by looking at the version number.

Semantic versioning uses three digits with dots separating the digits:

```
MAJOR.MINOR.PATCH
```

The MAJOR number represents the main version. It only changes when things are no longer backwards compatible. When you have a component that offers plugin events and these events change name, this would break the API for plugins implementing these events. Therefore, a change in the MAJOR number would be required.

The MINOR number represents changes that are still backwards compatible. The PATCH number represents bugfixes. Whenever you add new features to your code, the MINOR number increments. Whenever you fix bugs in your code, the PATCH number increments.

There are a few more rules. When the MAJOR number is 0, it indicates initial development. Anything can still change in the code. However, when the MAJOR number shifts to 1, it tells the world the code is stable. From this point onward, its code may be extended by others and therefore, any change needs to be backwards compatible, unless the MAJOR changes again. The first public release has version 1.0.0, while any version below that is still in a development stage.

Any of the numbers can be higher than 9. A version like 0.45.293 is possible. Of course, having too many increments will confuse other developers. A `PATCH` number 293 will also indicate there have been at least 293 bug fixes, which likely indicates your testing is off as well.

When you shift from version 0.9.1 to 1.0.0, there may be some features that are still unstable, while the complete package is already incompatible with the older 0.9 branch. In this case, it is best to package the new version as a pre-release by appending a keyword to the version. For example 1.0.0-alpha or 1.0.0-beta.

15.3 Packaging your plugin

Installing a plugin in Joomla is possible through various methods – e.g. install from web, install from folder, discovering the extension files. All methods - except for the discover method - will make Joomla copy the required files from one place to another. For this copying to be successful, the XML manifest file (covered in chapter 3) is used. Usually, the installation involves unzipping an archive (either a `zip` or `tar.gz` archive) with a structure that matches the XML manifest.

Let's take an example. We are creating a System Plugin called `example`. When unzipped, our package contains the following files and folders:

```
example.php
example.xml
index.html
en-GB.plg_system_example.ini
en-GB.plg_system_example.sys.ini
LICENSE.txt
images/
css/
js/
```

These files are installed by the following XML sections:

```
<files>
    <filename plugin="example">example.php</filename>
    <filename>index.html</filename>
</files>

<languages>
    <language tag="en-GB">en-GB.plg_system_example.ini</language>
    <language tag="en-GB">en-GB.plg_system_example.sys.ini</language>
</languages>
```

```
<media destination="plg_system_example">
    <folder>images</folder>
    <folder>css</folder>
    <folder>js</folder>
</media>
```

Note that the LICENSE.txt file is not installed – it is only included in the package.

Any of the main tags <files>, <media> and <languages> can also contain a folder attribute that allows for a different source folder than the root of the package. For instance, we may change the package files and folder into the following structure:

```
example.php
example.xml
index.html
languages/
media/
```

Accordingly, we change the <languages> tag and the <media> tags like this:

```
<languages folder="languages">
<media folder="media" destination="plg_system_example">
```

You can even follow the Joomla filesystem standard, when packaging your extension:

```
plugins/system/example/
administrator/languages/
media/
```

This would require the following tags:

```
<files folder="plugins/system/example">
<languages folder="administrator/languages">
<media folder="media" destination="plg_system_example">
```

Which folder structure you choose for your plugin, is less important. It depends on your own build process – how you gather the source files and create the extension package. Few people will be bothered if you use a non-standard folder structure here.

Naming your package

When you are packaging up your plugin into an installable Joomla extension, the name of that package is important. If you are creating a **System Plugin** called example, letting your users download a ZIP file called example.zip will be confusing. The filename does not uniquely identify your plugin in their filesystem, once it is downloaded. Good practice is to be as descriptive as possible in your file naming.

Here are some options:

```
plg_system_example.zip
plg_system_example_0.0.1.zip
plg_system_example_0.0.1_j3.zip
plgSystemExample.zip
```

Not including the plugin group in your filename might lead to conflicts when there is both a System Plugin and a Content Plugin named `example`. Including the plugin version and/or the Joomla version in your file name can be seen as optional.

zip or tgz

One of the choices you have to make is whether you want to offer your packages as ZIP file, as TGZ (ending with `tar.gz` or `tgz`) or both. From my own experience, offering only ZIP packages is good enough. ZIP support seems to be present in most hosting environments. Offering TGZ files, besides ZIP files, could confuse some users. In the past, there have been cases where TGZ packages were not properly extracted – mostly in Windows environments. I recommend you stick to ZIP packages.

Share your plugin

Once the plugin packages are created, you may want to share them with the rest of the world. Creating a download directory on your site is one option. Sharing it through GitHub is another. When sharing sources on GitHub, it is good practice to separate the packages from the source files. Also make sure to include a `README.md` (formatted in Markdown) with a basic description of what your GitHub repository is all about. Do not forget to add the GPL in a file `LICENSE.txt` as well.

```
README.md
LICENSE.txt
packages/plg_system_example.zip
source/plugins/system/example.php
source/plugins/system/example.xml
```

15.4 **Phing**

When preparing a new release for your plugin, there is a whole bunch of steps you need to take. You need to copy files from your development environment into a packaging folder. The ZIP package needs to be created from that packaging folder. The ZIP package needs to be copied to your website and/or Git repository.

To automate all these steps, you can write your own shell script or you can use Phing. Phing is a PHP based building system, similar to GNU make or Ant. The fact that it is PHP based, is not something you will notice in the beginning though: All tasks are defined in XML. PHP is only dealt with once you start developing your own Phing tasks.

To start with Phing, you can create an XML file `build.xml` with the following contents:

```
<project name="my_plugin" default="build">
    <target name="build">
        <echo>Building plugin</echo>
    </target>
</project>
```

Next, you run the `phing` command, which will look for the `build.xml` file and run the default target named `build`. It will output some lines including the **Building plugin** statement:

```
$ phing
```

To make the script more useful, let's copy some files from the Joomla folder `/var/www/html` to a temporary folder `/tmp/build`. This is all placed within our existing `<target>` element. We first define these folders as properties and create the temporary folder if it does not exist. We are also adding a destination folder `/var/www/packages`, which will contain our packages.

```
<echo>Building plugin</echo>
<property name="source" value="/var/www/html" />
<property name="builddir" value="/tmp/plg_system_example" />
<property name="packages" value="/var/www/packages" />
<exec command="mkdir -p ${builddir}" />
```

Next, we are copying the Joomla plugin files from this source folder to our build folder. This is done through the `<copy>` task element, which contains one or more `<fileset>` elements, defining which files should be picked up from where.

```
<copy todir="${builddir}" overwrite="true">
    <fileset dir="${source}/plugins/system/example">
        <include name="**" />
    </fileset>
    <fileset dir="${source}/administrator/language/en-GB">
        <include name="en-GB.plg_system_example.ini" />
        <include name="en-GB.plg_system_example.sys.ini" />
    </fileset>
</copy>
```

Any Joomla extension should be GPL licensed and for any GPL licensed software package, it is recommended to also include a copy of the GPL license in the form of a file named LICENSE.txt or COPYING.txt. We add a separate <copy> task for this purpose:

```
<copy todir="${builddir}" overwrite="true">
    <fileset dir="${packages}/">
        <include name="LICENSE.txt" />
    </fileset>
</copy>
```

Next, we want to add all files in the $builddir folder to both a ZIP archive and a TGZ archive. For this we use the tasks <zip> and <tar>, which are almost the same as the <copy> task:

```
<property name="zipfile" value="plg_system_example.zip" />
<property name="tgzfile" value="plg_system_example.tgz" />
<zip destfile="${packages}/$zipfile">
    <fileset dir="${builddir}">
        <include name="**/**" />
    </fileset>
</zip>
<tar destfile="${packages}/$tgzfile" compression="gzip">
    <fileset dir="${builddir}">
        <include name="**/**" />
    </fileset>
</tar>
```

That is it. Every time we run the phing command now, it will automatically create package archives for us, including all required files plus a license file. To automate things even more, we can use the <exec> task to upload the files from our local environment to the website:

```
<exec command="scp ${packages}/${zipfile} mywebsite:~/www/" />
<exec command="scp ${packages}/${tgzfile} mywebsite:~/www/" />
```

When you are using git, you can also use run git commands to commit the changes and push these commits automatically to your remote repository (for instance GitHub):

```
<exec dir="$packages" command="git add *.zip">
<exec dir="$packages" command="git commit -m phingbuild .">
<exec dir="$packages" command="git push origin master">
```

This is just the start. You can use the <phingcall> element to call from one <target> to another <target>. When you have multiple extensions to maintain, this allows for one target to define the properties of a specific plugin, which then calls upon a second target.

This offers a generic way to build a Joomla plugin based upon the properties of the first task. Phing allows you to make your life as a developer a lot easier. It may just take some time to get used to it.

15.5 Documentation and support

When you share your plugin with others, it is good practice to document its features. What does your plugin do? If it has any plugin parameters, how should these parameters be applied? Are there any best practices or tips when using your plugin? To make sure your users do not need to wait for an answer and to save you time answering them, having some kind of documentation in place is definitely a benefit. If you are offering the plugin for download on your own site, make sure to include installation instructions, a FAQ and perhaps even some tutorials.

Having documentation in place when you are releasing an extension, has several benefits. There are obviously benefits for your users. Your plugin becomes easier to use, because instructions are readily available. It will also gain trust, because you have thought of all of this documentation. Some potential users might scan your site for instructions to see whether the plugin fits their needs. When there are no instructions, there will not be that many downloads either.

Having good documentation in place also has benefits for you. You will get less support requests, because your documentation already covers the most common issues. You may even discover the need for new features, simply by looking at your plugin from a different angle.

Do not forget about support either. You could setup a contact form, a support forum or even a complete ticketing system. You could install a third party extension in your Joomla site, use GitHub tickets, or use applications like Kayako and ZenDesk. In any case, guiding your users to the right support flow will help you to give that support efficiently.

Releasing software does not only include writing code. It also requires caring for your users. Providing good documentation and good support will definitely give your plugin a higher score.

15.6 **Summary**

This final chapter gave you advice on how to properly release a plugin. With that, the chapter rounds up this book. Within its 15 chapters, we have learned how to write a plugin, by discussing the different plugin types that are available in the Joomla core. We have looked at the Joomla architecture to give you a broader context and finally, we have gathered neat tips and tricks to help you get the most out of your plugin.

On a personal note, I hope you found the book useful and I hope you benefit from it. Make sure to check the appendices at the end of this book as well. There are flow charts and listings that give you some further details on what is discussed throughout the chapters.

The appendices

Appendix ① Flow chart of System Plugin events

JAuthentication::STATUS_CANCEL
JAuthentication::STATUS_FAILURE
JAuthentication::STATUS_EXPIRED
JAuthentication::STATUS_DENIED
JAuthentication::STATUS_UNKNOWN

JAuthentication::STATUS_SUCCESS

⚙ onUserAuthenticate

❓ Any plugin returns true?

Yes — No

⚙ onUserAuthorisation

⚙ onUserLoginFailure

JAuthentication:: STATUS_EXPIRED
JAuthentication:: STATUS_DENIED

❓ Any plugin sets state EXPIRED or DENIED?

Yes →

⚙ onUserAuthorisation Failure

No

⚙ onUserLogin

⚙ onUserLogout

❓ All plugins return true?

❓ All plugins return true?

Yes

Yes

No

⚙ onUserAfterLogin

⚙ onUserAfterLogout

⚙ onUserLogoutFailure

Appendix ② Flow chart of the login process

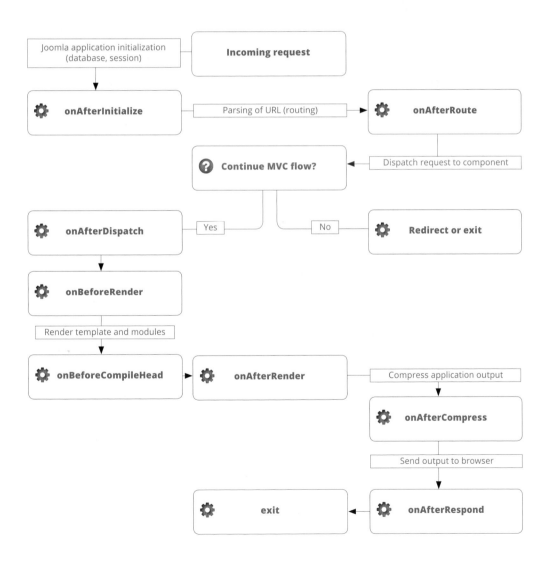

Appendix ③ Listing of code examples

Chapter	Plugin name	Events
02	plg_content_ch02test01	onContentBeforeDisplay
03	plg_content_ch03test01	onContentBeforeDisplay
05	plg_content_ch05test01	onContentPrepareForm onContentAfterSave onContentAfterDelete onContentBeforeDisplay
05	plg_content_ch05test02	onContentPrepareForm onContentAfterSave onContentAfterDelete onContentBeforeDisplay onContentBeforeSave
06	plg_system_ch06test04	onAfterInitialise
06	plg_system_emailcloak	onAfterRender
06	plg_system_ch06test02	onAfterRoute
06	plg_system_ch06test01	onAfterRender
06	plg_system_customscripts	onBeforeCompileHead
06	plg_system_ch06test03	onAfterInitialise
06	plg_system_articletext	onAfterRender
07	plg_system_ch07test02	onAfterRoute onUserAuthenticate
07	plg_authentication_imap	onUserAuthenticate

The listing below gives an overview of the plugin examples per chapter and the events they implement. You can use this listing to look up a certain event and find out in which code example in which chapter deals with it. Note that some event methods of the example plugins are not discussed in the book. Their code can be found online in the book's GitHub repository.

Chapter	Plugin name	Events
08	plg_system_usergroupdescription	onAfterInitialise onContentPrepareForm onContentPrepareData onUserAfterSaveGroup onUserAfterDeleteGroup
08	plg_user_ch08test01	onUserAfterSave
08	plg_authentication_blocker	onUserAuthenticate onUserLoginFailure
08	plg_user_firstlast	onContentPrepareForm onContentPrepareData onUserAfterSave onUserAfterDelete onUserLoad
09	plg_search_music	onContentSearch onContentSearchAreas
09	plg_finder_song	onFinderChangeState onFinderCategoryChangeState onFinderAfterDelete onFinderAfterSave onFinderBeforeSave
09	plg_search_sphinx	onContentSearchAreas onContentSearch
10	plg_captcha_example	onInit onDisplay onCheckAnswer
11	plg_extension_custom	onExtensionBeforeSave onExtensionAfterSave

Appendix ④ Alphabetical Index

So Long,

And I Hope You Enjoyed the Fish